·CONTENTS·

Wisdom in this book is heard in the feminine voice.

TO THE FEMININE VOICES IN MY LIFE:

To my mother who bore me, Ermagene Virginia Hicks.
You gave me life and a belief,
you taught me "I can do it," if I just believe,
you have always been there, what a relief,
thanks for putting up with all my grief.

To the wife of my youth, Cynthia Bliss (Cinny).
You seem to get younger, while I get older,
but if I were younger, I would marry you all over,
so here we are at mid-life, maybe a little wiser,
still together, ready for our next departure.

To my firstborn, Charis, my White Sox fan.
Your wisdom has blossomed, round Jason, your man,
with Christ as center, your vows will withstand,
know for certain, your father is your biggest fan.

To Ashley, my special daughter you will always be.
Now that you're gone, an empty hole is left in me,
a dad is never so proud as when he can see
his daughter all grown up, and seizing opportunity.

In memory of C. N. Hicks
1910–1994

·ACKNOWLEDGMENTS·

Those who have journeyed with me on this search for wisdom need to be acknowledged.

I would like to give credit again to Steve Webb, my senior editor at NavPress, for working with me on this project and being very gracious about extending the deadline. I do worry about that term though. Why do we call these things "dead" lines? That's scary! After three books (and a fourth in progress), I genuinely give credit to you, Steve, and your staff, for your professional and personal support of me. It is a pleasure working with you.

To my lover-of-books friend, Steve Griffith, you are far more than a literary agent. You do pull off some fine "win-win" deals, but even more than that, you are a true bibliophile. You love and appreciate books as carefully sculptured products of the human spirit. I always feel refreshed, stretched, and inspired because of my time with you. You always get my literary juices flowing, introduce me to some new literary friend, and then plan the next couple of years for me! You are "a brave and honest man who has stuck to this writer through times of bitter stress and doubt, and would not let me give in to my own despair." Only you, Griffith, know from whose pen this comes.

Doing a popular approach to a book of the Bible is always difficult. I try to be faithful to the Hebrew text of Proverbs, but I do not consider myself a Hebrew scholar. But, while risking the criticism from my learned professors, I do want to thank the men who taught me this wonderful language. Drs. Bruce Waltke, Don Glenn, and Allen Ross had an all-too-serious (for this pastoral theologian) contribution to my life and mind. Even though this work will never measure up to your standards of Hebrew scholarship, I want you to know how much I appreciate your role in imparting to me a love for the Hebrew language. At least I'm still using it!

As I think through these acknowledgments, another name comes to mind. My friend, fellow colleague, and brother-in-arms, Barry Leventhal. When I think of the wisdom literature, for some reason I think of you. I'm sure it is because of the hours we have spent thinking about this material together, sharing helpful books back and forth, and teaching together. I have always appreciated your wisdom on the wisdom literature and, as well, all the lunches we have shared in exotic places. Remember the Blue Nile?

I'm not sure how many times a writer can thank his own family. I guess the answer is "never enough." So, to you, the most precious gifts a man can have, goes my deepest appreciation. Cinny, you told me for years to do this book. Thanks for your diligence to keep asking me, "When are you going to do the 'People of Proverbs' book?" So here it is.

Graham, my only arrow left in the nest, I know how you probably get tired of seeing your dad at the word processor. Thanks for just being who you are, a great son.

I must also thank Bob and Pam Synder for the use of their lovely Pocono Mountain house. It provided the perfect place I needed to put the finishing touches on the book. I was disappointed though, because I didn't see the bear!

Wisdom is one of those perplexing human qualities. In the writing of this book, I learned much about wisdom, but I am not sure I am any wiser for the trip. All I usually see are my dumb mistakes and the inappropriate uses of my mouth. But perhaps the search is what is important. Maybe, there is a certain wisdom in knowing one is not wise. Perhaps, going on the search for wisdom is wisdom itself. I hope you enjoy reading about the search!

· O N E ·

The Search for Wisdom

So it is necessary to be a prince to know thoroughly the nature of the people, and one of the populace to know the nature of princes.
NICCOLO MACHIAVELLI
THE PRINCE

▼

Rightly favored is the person who finds wisdom.
PROVERBS 3:13[1]

People! Some of them we just can't stand. They really get to us. A few we really "click" with, but they are the rare, special gifts. People make up most of our lives. Experience says we have problems living with them or living without them. Even those who try to live alone still need people to deliver their food and mail and help with minimal care for them. Remember the reclusive Howard Hughes, who died a long-haired hermit, suspicious of everyone in this life except a few trusted servants? It even takes other people to bury us!

Yes, there are all kinds of people. Some we like, many we don't care for. But they are there just the same. We have to deal with people every day. People in traffic, salespeople, people on the phone, people at work, people we worship with, people we just hang out with, and of course, the people we call our own family and relatives. Our wives, husbands, and children are people too! Whether we like them or not, they are the ones most involved in our lives and the ones to whom we must learn to relate. So it is with everyone who comes across our path.

It's nearing the Christmas season and I'm sequestered off in the high country of the North Carolina mountains working on this book. I met a couple of friends for lunch in Boone. Amidst our busy conversation, it finally dawned on us that we had no spoons or napkins. I got up to look for some, but my pursuit failed. They were not in sight. Finally I asked the bus-boy where I could get some. I must admit I was truly hoping he would take it upon himself to go and get us the needed utensils. However, instead he muttered, "Ask your waitress," and quickly walked off. That was precisely the problem, we hadn't seen a waitress for twenty minutes! Finally my friend (unnoticed by me) went to the manager and complained. After that we were "bothered" every few minutes. I thought to myself, *What causes people not really to care about doing a good job in their work?*

On the way home I stopped to buy a Christmas tree. (My job is to get everything decorated before the family arrives.) Even before I got out of the car a strapping man emerged from a small trailer located on the lot, walking with a distinctive limp and aided by an aluminum crutch. As I walked toward him, he noticed my Air Force flight jacket and right away wanted to know where I had served. We talked for about fifteen minutes about each other's military career. He was an RF-4 (reconnaissance-fighter) crew chief before a Vietcong mortar round took away his leg. By the time I paid for the tree, we had covered everything from what's happened to the current military organization to where General Westmoreland is now living (nearby).

As I drove back to Blowing Rock, I compared the two inci-dents. Both had involved people, but radically different kinds of people. The first had dealt with people who were either too busy (the gracious perspective) or too unmindful of doing a good job to give us adequate service. The second event reflected deep caring. Here was a patriot still serving his coun-try and his fellow disabled vets by selling Christmas trees so that the profits could go directly to those worse off. Both were the sorts of people who come across my path on an otherwise reg-ular day. People I had to deal with, interact with, make decisions with, and make financial expenditures with. Is your life any different? These people were very much like us—the people we are and meet every day.

THE QUEST FOR UNDERSTANDING PERSONALITY TYPES

Studying and classifying types of people has become quite a science, if not a lucrative business, these days. "Personality inventories" abound. Once used only by psychologists to classify aberrant behavioral types (like the MMPI, Minnesota Multiphasic Personality Inventory), they are now regularly used in the military, business, education, and marriage and family counseling. Tools like Performax, the Taylor-Johnson Temperament Analysis, and the Myers-Briggs Type Indicator attempt to describe various temperaments, personalities, and work styles commonly recognized in the general population. They are based on the assumption that there is an important value in understanding the kind of persons we are. It's also important that we understand how we relate to other types of people. As we better understand the people we are married to, work with, or interact with daily, we will be in a better position to have satisfactory relationships.

I don't deny these premises. In fact, I agree with them. I have found most of these inventories helpful, even when they have been forced upon me. (Try refusing one sometime and see what happens!) My very first job out of college required me to take the Taylor-Johnson. When I applied to graduate school, the MMPI was required to see if I was "crazy" or not. I guess I passed, even though I believe graduate school makes most sane people a little crazy! When I went through an Air Force school for officers, they required me to take the Myers-Briggs. (I'm an INTJ, in case you wanted to know.)[2] When Cinny and I married we were analyzed on the basis of Tim Lahaye's four spirit-controlled temperament classifications, which go back to the standard Greek classifications. Cinny was identified as a classic Sanguine, while I was either a Melancholic with a touch of Choleric, or a Choleric with a dash of Melancholic. I just reached for the dictionary to reacquaint myself with these words. Since *choleric* means "hot-tempered," I guess at this stage of life I am a little more Choleric than Melancholic, being more ill-tempered than prone to depression!

At any rate, my experiences show how deeply rooted the concept of personality evaluation is in our culture, even in the culture of the ministry and Christendom. As mentioned above, I don't debate the value of "knowing yourself," as Socrates encouraged. After all, we can never quite get rid of ourselves. I found out long ago that wherever I go, whoever it is that I am also shows up. I can't get rid of myself!

Likewise, I usually cannot get rid of the people around me. Cinny is my wife by an oath I made before God and witnesses years ago, and I endeavor to honor this oath no matter what. The kids in my life are the children God gave me, and I will never renounce them. The men and women I work with have been hired by others, and whether I like them or not, they are the ones I have to work with. Therefore, it is very helpful to realize how we differ from others and to learn to appreciate the differences and tolerate the quirks. (Hopefully they will learn to accept and tolerate ours.) So understanding different types of people is a helpful exercise.

The crucial questions, however, are: Who gets to decide what the standard personality types are? Who decides what the "normative" personality should look like? And what is behind the classification models, driving the various assumptions? (Assumptions, by the way, will also drive the conclusions!)

Behind the popular Myers-Briggs inventory stands, unashamedly, the psychological theory of Carl Jung. As helpful as that test is, few recognize that Jungian psychology is loaded with unproven assumptions about human personality. If I answer yes to the questions on the MMPI about whether I believe "God speaks to me," I can be labeled "crazy" (paranoid) rather than sane. A Christian psychologist friend of mine doesn't even look at these scores for people who believe in God. The point is, there's a lot riding on these so-called value-neutral personality inventories.

All this is to illustrate that the human desire to classify behavior and personality types is a very important aspect of understanding our social relations. But this desire is not original with the Western-American scientific age. The desire to understand people has dominated some of the greatest minds of the past. Most ancient societies have produced wisdom literature that focuses on the practical realities of dealing with a broad range of people and their behavior. In this sense, the current "people-oriented" management style, which attempts to discover differing work styles among employees (like using the DISC, a simplified, management-oriented Myers-Briggs), merely stands in the long historical tradition of the Persians, Egyptians, Greeks, and Hebrews.

WHAT EVER HAPPENED TO CHARACTER DEVELOPMENT?

Mixed with this emphasis on finding personality types is a current resurgence about giving "moral education" in, of all places, the public school system.[3] It does not take a genius to recognize that something has been fundamentally wrong for some time regarding ethics and morality. The violent, senseless crimes in our cities and the more subtle, "smart" (white-collar) crimes in the suburbs prompt us to ask whether we are a society totally adrift in a self-created moral vacuum.

As a father of three children—all of whom survived (I hope) the public system of education—it often amazed me that a system that prided itself in being "valueless" and gave no serious discussion to moral issues could turn around and kick kids out of school for cheating or stealing! Today, it seems some educators are finally realizing that no school or society can exist without some core of universal moral values. Some of the attempts to rediscover universal ethical values like honesty, responsibility, and cooperation are certainly encouraging, even though I fear these efforts will ultimately be found wanting for the lack of any authoritative source. But recognizing that "character formation" must be a part of the educational system is a start.

After almost a century of "progressive education," which has emphasized either teaching a predetermined body of knowledge or pragmatic career skills, the issue of character development has faded away. The sophisticated debates between content-centered or child-centered curriculum still largely ignore the issue of character formation.[4] Anything that focuses on character is usually accused of being too WASPy or taking public education back to the McGuffey reader!

It seems the popular educational question addressed to the child during this time was, "What do you want to do when you grow up?" However, the kids—being kids—were asking a more basic question. Suburban kids asked: "How do I get through this course and still keep my 3.5 so I can get into a good college, so I can get into a good grad program, so I can get a good job, so I can get a good income, so I can get an attractive spouse, so I can . . . get fired, downsized, merged out, or 'vocationally enhanced,' and then divorced?" Inner-city kids simply asked, "How can I get out of the ghetto alive?" Now many suburban kids are asking the same question. Even my own kids have told me about "heat"–packing classmates in our own "safe" suburban schools!

All this illustrates both the longstanding neglect to do character education in our society and the glaring need to take a more serious look at how character is formed. More importantly, education must help our younger generation ask another crucial question: "What kind of person do I want to be?" I must admit as a parent that I have been so brainwashed by our upper-middle-class, white, suburban, corporate-executive-driven society that I am more concerned about what my kids are going to do with their lives than what kind of adults they will be. That's why I like the book of Proverbs. Let's take a closer look.

• T W O •

The Wisdom of the Proverbs

Wisdom walks in muddied shoes.
THOMAS FULLER[1]

▼

Wisdom shouts in the streets.
PROVERBS 1:20

The unique collection of biblical sayings that is the Proverbs strikes a unique cord within me. These pithy, packed-with-wisdom maxims move me away from my suburban "ghetto" mentality. They force me to think about character—not only my own, but that of others. They make me see people—like the people I deal with daily and even myself—in a different light and put me on a search for wisdom. The book makes me, even as an adult, ask the questions, What kind of a person am I, and what kind of person do I want to be?

Admittedly, Proverbs is not any easy book to understand. Many read it devotionally with the Psalms, taking a psalm and perhaps a chapter of Proverbs a day. However, the proverbs are collections of learned material that function as a body of "studied reflection"[2] for a younger generation of learners. In this sense, the wisdom literature, including Proverbs, may have been used in the Hebrew community as a curriculum for a school of wisdom.[3] The young were trained for national service and affairs of state. Wolfe says,

The people who listen to them are therefore not only
pupils who "hear" and learn the right answers morning
by morning (Isa 50:4); they are also kings (II Sam.
14:2ff.), the sons of kings (II Sam. 16:15ff), royal officials
(II Sam 20:16) and all kinds of people needing advice
(II Sam. 20:22).[4]

The wisdom literature is in the spirit of Machiavelli's classic
admonitions to the Italian Medici princes. They must learn to
rule well and be wise kings.[5]

In a democratic republic where each of us has his own
little sphere of rule, perhaps we too are in the business of educating future princes to rule as kings! More likely, as one commentator suggests, the material was designed to "educate
young people in the ways of good and wise living."[6] It was written for a group of young people (and older ones) in search of
wisdom. Therefore, the book held both a very important
parental function in the home and an educational function in
the larger society. In short, the book's purpose was to facilitate
moral responsibility by teaching young people how to live.
This purpose is seen very clearly in the first chapter.

Solomon, the acknowledged collector,[7] opens the book by
saying:

> The proverbs of Solomon the son of David, king of
>   Israel:
> To know wisdom and instruction,
> To discern the sayings of understanding,
> To receive instruction in wise behavior,
> Righteousness, justice and equity;
> To give prudence to the naive,
> To the youth knowledge and discretion, . . .
> To understand a proverb and a figure,
> The words of the wise and their riddles. (1:1-4,6)

Ross alludes to the twofold purpose of these proverbs: to
impart moral skillfulness and mental discernment.[8] The idea

of skill is rooted in an understanding of the word *hokma*, translated "wisdom." This wisdom is seen in the "skill" of technical work in making garments for the high priest (Exodus 28:3), craftsmanship in metal work (Exodus 31:3,6), as well as the execution of battle tactics (Isaiah 10:13).[9] In other words, wisdom has to do with having the skill and desire necessary to do a good job, which the employees at the Boone restaurant had lacked. It has to do with the successful mastery of something. In Proverbs, it relates more to the successful mastery of life.[10] A person is considered wise only when the whole of his life has been shaped by the insights of wisdom.[11] Interestingly, one philosopher who has specialized in psychology has taken his field to task for its over-reliance on "introspection" and the trustworthiness of the "self-report." In its place, C. Stephen Evans argues for another crucial personal quality:

> The crucial personal quality is one I shall designate by the traditional term *wisdom*.
>
> What is needed to understand meanings is more like recollection than introspection. It requires critical reflection on one's life and the lives of others one has encountered, a critical reflection in which the relationships of various possibilities are sorted out.
>
> What is crucial is an attempt to see things together, to view life as a whole. This kind of understanding of human life is essentially equivalent to what is often called wisdom. We all know people who have a great deal of knowledge, even a great deal of psychological knowledge, who are not wise. Conversely, we all know people who seem very wise who are not up to date on the latest empirical findings. It seems plausible then that wisdom is not to be identified with an accumulation of knowledge or facts.[12]

My understanding of what this professor is arguing for is precisely what the book of Proverbs is trying to accomplish in the lives of its readers. Its goal is to set out both the positive and negative realities of people's lives and ask the question, "Which kind of life do you want?" It puts the learner on a search for wisdom in all its complex, life-oriented realities. It asks the reader to make a choice between two ways of life: the way of wisdom and the foolish way. In this sense, Proverbs forces us to view our worship of God as not in the temple or the church, but in the marketplace and the home.[13] The interaction with such questions builds moral skill and, in the long term, character.

Moral skillfulness is also picked up by a prominent word in Proverbs, translated "instruction" (Hebrew, *musar*). One scholar says this word means "learning from the experiences of those older and wiser than we."[14] Hence, this instruction is a component of wisdom that comes through the multigenerational and environmental influences that life throws at us. When the lesson is finally learned (usually through trial and error), it becomes incorporated and internalized into the young person's life as the disciplining of temper, tongue, passions, and appetites! We don't need any more evidence of violence, sexual assaults, and eating disorders to demonstrate that wisdom is a rare commodity today. Tempers and appetites are very much out of control. A person cannot master life in all its complexity and unpredictability until there is at least some simple mastery over one's own passions.

The wise person in Proverbs is also wise in his relations with others, actively involved in upholding the standards of righteousness, justice, and equity. These are interpersonal, relational values that assume the importance and commitment of doing what is right, just, and fair to those God brings across our paths. Apparently, moral skillfulness is not just a private affair of individual character alone, but also delves into the dirty mess of social responsibility.

A second purpose of Proverbs focuses on the development of mental discernment. Two other prominent Hebrew terms in Proverbs are translated "understanding" (*bin*) and "prudence" (*'ormah*) and convey the idea that having the ability to make critical distinctions between right and wrong is paramount to successful (wise) living. The Hebrew word *bin* carries the unpopular idea that we must make careful distinctions between good and evil (1 Kings 3:9). It means to be *very* discriminating about moral issues. In an AIDS-infested world, I think no one can seriously continue to believe that making the wrong moral decision could not cost him his very life.

The usage in Proverbs 1:6 also alludes to the idea that one needs the critical facility of moral discernment in order to see through all the riddles, perplexities, and nonsense that life contains. I meet people every day, young and old, who have believed various advertising or marketing claims, or have bought into "foolproof" investment opportunities, only to find later that the salesperson and their money are long gone. Today, it takes a healthy dose of personal discernment to live in our society without being ripped off. With all the sophisticated lying going on, carefully concealed as smartly packaged marketing, it's no wonder most Americans are so deep in debt.

In summary, what Proverbs is trying to do is make us all a little street smart. To live righteously from the perspective of the wisdom literature is not to be a monk, isolated in a cave somewhere. It is to be where the action is, in the mess and stench of life, engaging and enhancing the lives of others, because that's what godly living in a fallen world means. What Proverbs gives us is not high-minded abstract principles of life, which was the Greek way, but life experiences of real people. Dyrness explains,

> The goal was an intuitive insight into life, its dangers and joys. The process was typical for the Hebrew way of thinking. He did not begin with abstract principles but with the experience of foolish sons or foolish women. He moves in the area of concrete life that everyone knows about and, with shrewd judgment, intuitively sees what is at issue.[15]

Listen to the feminine guide who calls us to this search of wisdom. Look at where she has stationed herself:

Wisdom shouts *in* the street,
She lifts her voice *in* the square;
At the head of the *noisy streets* she cries out;
At the entrance of the gates *in* the city, she utters her
      sayings. (1:20-21, emphasis added)

Sister Wisdom is a realist. She knows the names of the streets where we fail. We can be very honorable and moral at church (sometimes), but where we fail is in our interaction with the world, and the world that is in us. Consequently, she goes to where we are, in the streets, at the corners of where we live, at our parties, in our homes, in the ghettos, country clubs, unions, and in the private places of our hearts. She stations herself at these life intersections and cries, "Come to me, and learn wisdom."

The message she packages is filled with good news about the cultivation of moral character, even in a sick society. Perhaps this message is the curriculum we need in order to do moral education in our schools, or at least in our homes and churches. Even Harvard professor David Maybury-Lewis alludes to the benefits of moral education done in the family context. The three "wisdoms" he believes have been lost in Western society are a clear sense of family; the right and wrong that is learned there; and the skill learned in families of balancing the needs of one with the needs of the many. Apparently these "wisdoms" work even in minority cultures like Harlem, when a wise child looks around at the drug culture and chooses to listen to the wisdom of his own church and family values. The kind of moral character that results is the kind spoken of in the life of former Chairman of the Joint Chiefs of Staff Colin Powell.[16]

From the book of Proverbs we learn some very important things about this kind of moral character.

WHAT PROVERBS HAS TO SAY
ABOUT MORAL CHARACTER

First, moral character *is* possible, and changing existing character *is* possible. The assumption of Wisdom crying in the streets is that change is possible. This goes against some personality theorists who view character as fixed and unchangeable.

My view of the person is that temperaments (the innate aspects of our personhood we are born with) are unchangeable. Extroverts don't become recluses, nor do introverts become back-slapping Mr. Personality types. Even the "changes" we see in such New Testament characters as Peter and Paul are more changes of direction, motivation, and affections than changes of inborn temperament. Peter was the outspoken extrovert in the gospels, and it is no wonder that it is he who speaks first at Pentecost![17]

However, character is different from temperament. Character refers to each person's developmental and environmental history. It refers to events, situations, circumstances, trials, illnesses, and traumas of life—all the "stuff" that happens to us to shape us and make us the kinds of people we are. It also refers to how I think about my temperament and how I have chosen to respond to all that life has thrown at me. Character I believe is changeable.

Personality is the composite of both of the above. My "persona" or how I am seen by others is the composite of all I am, both innate temperament and character. So I believe very firmly that moral character can be changed. I have seen it in my own life and in the lives of many others. I have seen it go in both directions—sinners who become saints, and saints who return to a sinful life!

The second thing we learn is that moral change is only possible for a few. Many of the people we will study in Proverbs never change. They stay the way they are, because fundamentally they like the way they are. That's why Wisdom says to the naive, the scoffer, and the fool, "How long will you love the way you are?" (1:22). The reality is, many whom we observe as proud, stubborn, or "not open to change" just have no real reason to change. In other words, they like being who they are. This is perhaps a downside of the "healthy self-esteem" issue— a downside few counselors have addressed. However, we will see in this book that most people don't change because it simply costs too much. The pain is too great.

A third reality found in Proverbs is that when change does take place it is driven by very personal choices. Every time I teach about the issue of choice in moral development, it raises some eyebrows and some hands. I call these responses the "you don't really mean it" questions. They usually come from those who sincerely believe moral development is a top-down, externally conditioned affair. Some pastors, teachers, school systems, and parents believe that they can carefully prescribe a certain code of behavior and ask the parishioners, students, and children to abide by that code. Then by enforcing that code they believe they are successfully cultivating a moral personality. However, this view has been severely challenged by both biblical scholars (theologians and students of the Scriptures) and Christian thinkers who study how moral development takes place. One evangelical writer records,

> Cognitive psychologists view morality as developmental in nature and are interested in changes that occur as a person progresses from lower to higher levels of moral maturity. A concept basic to the cognitive position is that *moral development occurs within the individual.* Morality cannot be produced or generated by an outside source. By its very definition, morality must be rooted within the personality. People are not moral simply because they engage in moral acts; they are moral as they understand moral concepts and their subsequent behavior reflects a more mature level of cognitive organization. Although the environment may encourage morality or may produce conditions that impede it, the dynamic remains within the organism.[18]

This means that, until a child, student, or adult begins to internalize and personalize his own moral commitments, he is not really a moral person but just a person "keeping the rules." We often confuse compliance and conformity to rules with morality. On this point, Proverbs is quite contemporary. Solomon, as teacher, father, and perhaps head of a school of wisdom, exhorts,

> My son, *if* you will receive my sayings,
> And treasure my commandments within you,
> Make your ear attentive to wisdom,
> Incline your heart to understanding;
> For *if* you cry for discernment,
> Lift your voice for understanding;
> *If* you seek her as silver,
> And search for her as for hidden treasures;
> *Then* you will discern the fear of the LORD,
> And discover the knowledge of God,
> For the LORD gives wisdom. (2:1-6, emphasis added)

When I teach this concept to my students, I ask a grammatical question: "What does an if-then clause imply?" There's usually silence. Then I ask it another way, "What do we call an if-then clause?" Finally, some student wades back through her college and high school experiences and remembers some diligent grammar teacher who drilled such things into the memory bank. Having rediscovered the term, she blurts out, "A conditional clause!" I come unglued with excitement and ask another question, "What does a conditional clause mean?" Am I a terrible teacher because I don't give students answers? Even when they come up with an answer, I turn around and question their answers! Finally, some student who has been dozing off wakes up and realizes he knows the answer. He responds, "It means it's conditional." Brilliant! A conditional clause means the sentence is conditional! But in this case, the sleepy student is absolutely on target. If-then clauses mean the outcomes are conditional, not assured. And the choice is the student's. In other words, the choice as to what kind of life this "son" wants to have lies in the power of his own choices, not his father's or teacher's. That's insightful. Solomon, as a wise father, knows all he can do is encourage a certain moral direction, but the choice ultimately is the child's. It always is!

The last observation about Proverbs is that the character change encouraged throughout this book is facilitated by contrast, conflict, and comparison. As the young or old learner looks at these various people types, it brings to his awareness the question again and again as to what kind of person he wants to be. Do I want to be a fool, a sluggard, an angry man, a contentious wife, or a strong wife? Do I want to be righteous or wicked, a fool or wise, a scoffer or a healer? Again, the apparent choice is the reader's. No one will make you into anything else. The choice and pursuit must be embraced by the individual.

CHARACTER TYPES OF A DIFFERENT SORT

As we discover this broad range of "character types," we face a confrontation with ourselves. The people of Proverbs are like us. In this pursuit of wisdom, the people we encounter are people like you and me. Every day I see a little of the sluggard in me, some days I am the fool. On some of my more melancholic days, I'm your classic scoffer. In many of my decisions I see the wicked man within me, filled with selfishly cruel motives. I have also been ripped off enough to know that I am still very naive. But my hope is that somehow, by God's grace, there exists within the fabric of my soul a certain amount of wisdom, righteousness, and discernment.

The goal of *In Search of Wisdom* is to place before the reader a different kind of personality inventory. I openly admit the need to understand myself better and the people around me. But I'm cautious about many of the common tools used for determining personality types because they are not derived directly from the revealed Scriptures. They are largely from other sources. Some make attempts to "find" their proofs for such in the Bible. They make David into a manic-depressive, or Peter into a Sanguine, or Paul into a "High I," or Jesus into the perfect balance of whatever personality theory is being promoted.

My own assessment about Jesus is that—by contemporary standards—He was not very "well-adjusted" at all. In any culture, to be "well-adjusted" is not necessarily the *sine qua non* of mental health. After all, to be well-adjusted to a sick society is in my estimation real sickness! In this light, Jesus was not well-adjusted. He took on His teachers, He disagreed with the authoritative rabbinic opinion, and He created the most disruptive political-economic disturbance one could create in His time by throwing out the moneychangers from the Temple compound. In terms of economic impact, that act is comparable to walking into the stock exchange on Wall Street and pulling the plugs on all the computer financial networks, thereby plunging the entire world into economic chaos! It's no wonder the authorities finally came to the conclusion that this "mentally deranged" person had to go (Mark 11:15-18).

My hope is that the people studied in this book will become types and antitypes for the people we meet every day. We will meet the positive kinds of wise characters we hopefully will seek to emulate as well as the kinds of characters we will try to avoid. Hopefully in seeing the demerits of foolishness and the merits of wisdom, as illustrated in these people, we will choose wisdom. Perhaps, years from now, instead of asking people whether their temperament is melancholic or saying, "What can you expect from a type A?" the comment will be, "He's a real sluggard" or "She's a contentious woman" or "I am a fool." Then we will have moved away from making Freud, Jung, the Greeks, or the APA (American Psychiatric Association) the standards for defining personality types. Perhaps such a paradigm shift will put us more in the mainstream of how the ancient sages viewed human behavior.

I mentioned earlier that I believe the current attempts to reinstill a moral curriculum into public school systems will ultimately fail for the lack of an authority base. It is for this very problem that Solomon also counsels his young son that "the fear of the LORD is the beginning of knowledge [and wisdom]" (1:7). The Hebrew word for "beginning" (*re'shit*) carries the connotation of "a first phase, step or element in the course of events" (see Isaiah 46:10).[19]

Therefore, the place to begin this search for wisdom and make the initial steps in becoming a more moral person (wise) is not by studying moral dilemmas (Kohlberg) or by getting in touch with how the moral values we do have were socially conditioned (Harmin and Simon—*Values Clarification*). (I do believe that there is some value in these exercises, though not to the extent that Kohlberg or Harmin would.) Rather, the clear authoritative beginning point for becoming a moral person is by submitting to the authority of God over our lives. This is the ultimate and most important "power" issue every human being must face. And it is both conveniently and intentionally left out of most moral discussion. The moment God or "religious issues" are brought into the debate, these "values" are viewed as either outdated, irrelevant, or biased. The issue of whether they may be true or not is suppressed.

Proverbs says the "fear of the LORD" is the source, the surrounding, and the first step in becoming a wise person. To me, the "fear of the LORD" means both a healthy and hearty recognition of His presence over my life, combined with a personal sense of my returning to and being loyal to Him. My understanding of this concept grows out of the vast theological import of "Yahweh," the most important Hebrew term used for God.[20]

This Yahweh is a God who speaks out, breaks in, and binds Himself to us in blood. As a God who speaks out, He is a God of ethics. He loves us enough to tell us how to live. That's what the revealed Law of God is all about (see Exodus 20:1-17; Deuteronomy 4:1-13,37; and 6:24). Moral character, then, begins with Him. He is also a God who breaks in. Throughout the Testaments, He breaks into the affairs of men, He intervenes in history on behalf of His people. He hears the cries of His people Israel and *does* something about it (Exodus 3:7). As such, He is the God of history and the mover of history. History indeed was His story, and still is! But He is also a God who binds Himself to His people . . . through blood. He made a covenant with Israel pledging His loyal love to them through a blood oath (Genesis 15:9-18). He did the same in the New Testament, whereby the messianic Son predicted by the prophets would likewise secure a new covenant in blood (Isaiah 9:6, 53:1-12; Matthew 26:27-28).

To fear this Yahweh also means that I must do something in return. In response to what He has done as a speaking-out, breaking-in, and binding-Himself-to-me kind of God, I return to Him my own pledge of loyalty. In other words, I seek to submit to His authority over my life. Without this first step, I will be like many of the people in Proverbs who refuse to change because they have refused this first step.

Our country today must rediscover this most important of steps. Our founding fathers were never confused about this point. They may have debated about how the government was to be organized and led, and each of the states wrestled with whether or not it would have one dominant church. But all the founders were agreed on the importance of the fear of God to building a successful nation. Noah Webster, educator, signer of the Declaration, and the first to call for a constitutional convention, and who later established Amherst College, wrote the leading text on American history covering the period. In this standard text, used for generations, he wrote,

> When you become entitled to exercise the right of voting for public officers, let it be impressed on your mind that God commands you to choose for rulers "just men who will rule in the fear of God." The preservation of our government depends on the faithful discharge of this duty; if the citizens neglect their duty and place unprincipled men in office, the government will soon be corrupted; laws will be made, not for the public good so much as for selfish or local purposes; corrupt or incompetent men will be appointed to execute the laws; the public revenues will be squandered on unworthy men; and the rights of the citizens will be violated or disregarded.[21]

Webster was an educator, not a prophet, but his warning is now front-page news in almost every American newspaper. We have rebelled against the authority of God in our lives and have paid dearly for it. We need to return to the search for wisdom that begins with God, in order to bring about this kind of change. The need is for wisdom in the individual, in the home, and in the larger communities.

Fortunately, one who is open to change is the naive. Sister Wisdom offers her counsel first to the one called naive or simple. If you have ever been taken advantage of, or have trusted in the wrong kind of people, or are just too gullible, then the next chapter is for you. The naive is a person like you or me, one desperately in need of wisdom.

But before we look at the naive, I must clarify how I intend to use gender in my writing style. I hate trying to be consistent in using gender-neutral language. It seems so impersonal to always use "wise person" instead of "wise man." Further, being consistent about pronouns can also be cumbersome. Having to say "whatever he or she decides to do" over and over again not only drives me crazy when I write it but also when I read it. Therefore, rest assured when I use the word *man* or *wise* or *naive* or *sluggard*, etc., I do not have any particular gender in mind. Fools are fairly equally distributed across both genders. Sin is never gender-specific. When I have to go one way or the other, I prefer the masculine. But remember, the feminine voice in this book gets the best position. Wisdom is personified as a woman, not a man. Sorry, men! So with this little aside finished we can now look at a group of people we all know: naive people, lazy people, wicked folks, the wealthy, and the poor.

· T H R E E ·

The Naive

There is a smile of deceit.
WILLIAM BLAKE
BARTLETT'S FAMILIAR QUOTATIONS

▼

The naive believes everything.
PROVERBS 14:15

I have always been fascinated by sports cars. It started in high school. I remember when the richest girl in our junior class got the classic red Mustang convertible. College friends in my fraternity had Corvettes. But I have always been the kind of guy who likes what others don't have. Therefore, I've always been attracted to the "true" sports cars, which are British. There's nothing like a TR-3, 4, or 6 on a fall afternoon. You put on your wool cap, driving gloves, and sunglasses, and off you go. TRs sound like a sports car ought to sound, not like the tinny Japanese kind or the overpriced German models. They smell right too! But everyone knows their electronics are terrible, and they are made for wealthy Oxford dons who love tinkering and adjusting their carburetors every time they drive them. But I still love them.

I finally bought one. A TR-6, British blue, with the Britannic flag on the side. I loved it. I remember seeing it advertised in the paper. I told Cinny about it and we both went to look at it. I thought I asked all the right questions. The price seemed to be fair. The man selling it was an attorney whose other car was a Jaguar, so I figured the car had been well cared for. As one final confirmation, I called the man and said I wanted to take it to my mechanic and have it put up on a lift so I could look underneath. Suddenly this friendly man got a little irate. He questioned my character for distrusting his. So I backed down. I bought the car.

The first thing to go wrong was that the driver-side door quit working. It wouldn't open at all. Also, for some reason the car went through tires. While driving one day I had a blowout. I put on the spare, and no sooner had I got the spare on than it blew as well. Now, I was stranded. Finally, I got a tow and got it to a garage. When we put it up on a lift, the entire underside of the frame was rusting! When I asked the mechanic how much it would cost to get it fixed, he just laughed. It was totaled!

The entire incident was a costly lesson in being too trusting. It was a tale of one gullible traveler! By the way, even though this incident is still a sore spot in our marriage (and one of those "I told you so" decisions), I would still like to have another one! But next time, I'll put it up on a lift.

My experience with this Triumph sports car (which was no triumph) reveals the first thing we learn about the character of the simple: He is too trusting.

WHAT THE CHARACTER OF THE SIMPLE IS LIKE
Just as I was too trusting and too "open" to this attorney who wanted to dump his problem car on me, so is the character of this first person to be studied. The simple (1:20) in Hebrew carries the idea of "open-mindedness, or inexperience," and thus is open to deception. Cohen calls the simple "a person of undecided views and thus susceptible to either good and bad influence."[1] The Hebrew verbal root has the idea of "being spacious, wide or open."[2] You see, I was too spacious, giving too much freedom to this man. Proverbs 14:15 states it very clearly,

The naive believes everything,
But the prudent man considers his steps.

I hadn't adequately considered my steps, and consequently I got ripped off.

He Is Too Trusting

Trust is certainly a positive character trait. But the naive or simple is too trusting because he literally believes whatever is said
to him or her (these are not gender-specific traits). The naive
is then the perfect target for salespeople and get-rich-quick
scammers. One life-insurance man told me that the easiest
people to sell insurance to were college students, because they
were, as a class, so naive. They would believe anything. What
a commentary on higher education! What further persuasion
do we need that educating the mind does not necessarily
touch the moral framework of one's being?

I used this college-student illustration at a men's retreat
once, and after I finished speaking a man came up to me and
said, "I can top that one." He was a pharmaceutical salesman,
and after selling pharmaceuticals to physicians for over twenty
years, he had concluded that *they* were the most gullible of
people. They would buy anything.

Recently I attended a dinner party and told the above
story, upon the completion of which one couple at the table
told me professional athletes were the most naive of people.
Their ministry was to this group, and after watching the lives
of so many of these rich and famous, they concluded most
were not really smart when it came to money. After all, they
make their living with their bodies and not their brains!

So, it seems, many are competing for the top slot. In one
sense, we are all born naive. Children naturally trust their parents, neighbors, teachers, etc. That's why child abuse and child
theft are so easy. It usually takes being ripped off to finally realize not all people are trustworthy!

Sometimes as Christians we can be the worst in this
regard. We call ourselves "believers" and we "trust" in God. But

perhaps our trust of God spills over into our trust of people. How many Jim Jones massacres will it take before we realize people are not God? Jesus said very clearly, "No one is good except God alone" (Mark 10:18). Perhaps we ought to be more like the Berean believers, who were a little skeptical about "traveling preachers" until they had checked out everything they said in the Scriptures (Acts 17:11).

But the naive has another fault.

He Loves the Way He Is

It's bad enough to be naive, but the penetrating cry of Wisdom asks, "How long . . . will you love simplicity?" (1:22). It's a Hebrew play on words. The word for naive and the word for simplicity are the same. Hence, Wisdom is essentially confronting the naive for loving his own condition. This is an extremely necessary confrontation, because until one faces this "self-love" rationale one will have no desire for change. The reality is, the naive is very settled into his own character. She likes the way she is. The simple love their condition. For the naive, this seems a little strange. How could someone pride himself in being ripped off or taken advantage of?

The answer probably lies not so much in the results of behavior as in the condition. In fact, the naive gives little thought to the results of behavior. Apparently, this kind of character type enjoys being "open-minded" or keeping options open, because to be otherwise would mean making decisions and value judgments.

I romantically long for the era when handshakes could seal any agreement. It's a nice thought to believe that an individual's word can be trusted, even in the church. However, as the popularity and number of attorneys illustrate, we must realize that what someone says or commits himself to today can change tomorrow. Therefore, we live in the age of contracts. The naive doesn't get it in writing. One scholar has observed that the problem of the naive lies in his having never learned to think for himself. Aiken notes, "To let others do our thinking for us is always easier and much less troublesome than doing our own thinking and it is especially tempting when we hear what we want to hear. But we do it at our peril and often the peril of others."[3]

This willingness to let others do our thinking for us illustrates the third characteristic of the simple.

He Lacks Moral Sense

I define adulthood as follows: having the freedom to make one's own decisions but also being willing to accept the consequences of those decisions. In adolescence, the desire to make one's own decisions becomes extravagated. However, it's amazing how often teens still want the parent to "bail" them out of their failures. It's a characteristic of the times. Being adult means accepting the reality of both sides of the definition. The naive does not have enough moral fortitude to look behind the pleasant appearances of life and see the consequences. Therefore, lacking this moral sense, his own life and the lives of others become injured. This is clearly illustrated in an extended Wisdom metaphor, where Lady Wisdom observes the behavior of this young naive:

For at the window of my house
I looked out through my lattice,
And I saw among the naive,
I discerned among the youths,
A young man lacking sense,
Passing through the street near her corner;
And he takes the way to her house,
In the twilight, in the evening,
In the middle of the night and in the darkness.
And behold, a woman comes to meet him,
Dressed as a harlot and cunning of heart.
She is boisterous and rebellious;
Her feet do not remain at home;
She is now in the streets, now in the squares,
And lurks by every corner.
So she seizes him and kisses him,

And with a brazen face she says to him:
"I was due to offer peace offerings;
Today I have paid my vows.
Therefore, I have come out to meet you,
To seek your presence earnestly, and I have found you.
I have spread my couch with coverings,
With colored linens of Egypt.
I have sprinkled my bed
With myrrh, aloes and cinnamon.
Come, let us drink our fill of love until morning;
Let us delight ourselves with caresses.
For the man is not at home,
He has gone on a long journey;
He has taken a bag of money with him,
At full moon he will come home."
With her many persuasions she entices him;
With her flattering lips she seduces him.
Suddenly he follows her,
As an ox goes to the slaughter
Or as one in fetters to the discipline of a fool,
Until an arrow pierces through his liver;
As a bird hastens to the snare,
So he does not know that it will cost him his life. (7:6-23)

The naive, because he has not listened to the voice of wisdom, is a poor judge of character, courts evil, is finally persuaded by it, and is ultimately deceived by it to his own destruction. This downward slide begins because the naive is not a good judge of people. This idea is so graphically portrayed in the above text because the woman is in reality a harlot, but she is cunning enough to not reveal what she really is. One Hebrew scholar notes, "She is of a hidden mind, of a concealed nature; for she feigns fidelity to her husband and flatters her paramours as her only beloved, while in truth she loves none, and each of them are but means to the indulgence of her sensual desires."[4]

Whether male or female, we are a nation of the naive. The

great American pastime of shopping and trying to get the best deal only sets us up for the trickery and bait-and-switch deals that are so easily thrust upon us in the marketplaces. Whether we are shopping for some sensuous experience, a romantic interlude, a makeup that will do wonders for our skin, or the ultimate lawn tool, we are naive believers in sales presentations and promises. Our deception illustrates our lack of true moral sense. The truly moral person questions the promise, looks for the concealed nature, and sees through the flattery for the sake of a buck!

In an interesting twist, naive people also like and seek out others like them. In other words, they not only like being naive themselves, they also like being around other naive.

He Hangs Around the Naive
Several years ago when the famous NBA star Wilt Chamberlain published his autobiography, the American public was stunned by his open admission that he had thousands of one-night stands during his NBA career. Feminists used his admission to condemn the irresponsible sexual natures of most men, and even men I know who have very little to do with moral values were put out with his rampant infidelity. But I can't remember one columnist, critic, or talk-show host even asking about the other side of the one-night stands. After watching one talk show on the subject, I commented to my wife that it was almost the biblical woman-caught-in-adultery story in reverse. Someone is missing in the crime! "What kind of woman sits around hotel lobbies and bars waiting for NBA stars to come back from games so that they can have one-night stands with them?" I asked. "They certainly aren't women looking for a relationship, a commitment, and from Wilt's own admission, they weren't prostitutes." Cinny just shook her head and answered, "I can't imagine."

The answer may lie in the shorter version of Wisdom's call to the naive:

The woman of folly is boisterous,
She is *naive* and knows nothing.

And she sits at the doorway of her house,
On a seat by the high places of the city [hotel
    penthouses or bars]
Calling to those who pass by,
Who are making their paths straight:
"Whoever is *naive*, let him turn in here,"
And to him who lacks understanding she says,
"Stolen water is sweet;
And bread eaten in secret is pleasant."
But he does not know that the dead are there,
That her guests are in the depths of Sheol. (9:13-18,
    emphasis added)

Notice the connection between the two naive in the passage: One naive is taken advantage of by another. In the proverbial account, no one escapes the spotlight of moral scrutiny. There are no innocent victims here, only two naive people forging an unholy alliance for the sake of some secret, stolen pleasure. Whether it is the afternoon romantic affair, a maxed-out credit card from shopping sprees, or the pleasure derived from bingeing on junk food and then purging, each illustrates the character of a very naive person. Ultimately, the pleasure turns sour, what is stolen is revealed, and the principle of death that was hidden in the pleasurable moment takes another dear soul to Sheol, the final gathering place for the naive. The reality the naive has difficulty grasping is that evil is usually hidden and therefore largely unrecognizable.

He Cannot Recognize Evil
My father worked in the aviation industry and was a pilot himself. He had a little V-tailed Beech Bonanza for business and personal use. As a young kid I spent a lot of time flying with my dad (often to my mother's deepest fears).

I remember flying cross-country once and, as usual, he let me take the controls for a while. I was cruising along enjoying the beauty and serenity of the clouded sky when all of a sudden my father grabbed the controls away from me, banked the plane sharply to the left, and put the nose down to descend under some clouds. As a very large cloud passed by on my above right (one o'clock high), I asked my dad, "What's wrong?"

He responded, "I didn't like the way that cloud looked. That's a big, dark cloud, and this is a small, fragile plane. It might tear our wings off if there was much turbulence in there."

I looked back at the cloud, now behind and above us, and couldn't see anything! I was young and inexperienced. I was naive about weather, turbulence, and the capabilities of the airplane. As my dad said on many occasions, "There are old pilots, and there are bold pilots, but there are no old, bold pilots." What a lesson for a young man to learn. I did not see the potential evil lurking inside what appeared to me a very beautiful puff in the sky. The experienced and wise quickly considered the potential, sorted out the options, and in an instant made the decision to divert the plane's path.

This is exactly what Proverbs says the naive lacks:

The prudent sees the evil and hides himself,
But the naive go on, and are punished for it.
    (22:3; see also 27:12)

The naive does not see what the prudent sees, and therefore does not do what the prudent does. As we have learned from psychiatrist M. Scott Peck, the evil in people's lives is rarely apparent on the surface. Evil people appear so normal. As he writes, "My own experience, however, is that evil human beings are quite common and usually appear quite ordinary to the superficial observer."[5] To a naive people, this means we are easily seduced both to tolerate and cooperate with evil. Prudence, or wisdom, is the only way we can free ourselves from our naive natures.

As would be expected, the course of the naive personality's life differs greatly from the one who has been on the search for wisdom.

WHAT WILL CHARACTERIZE
THE COURSE OF HIS LIFE?

In college I had a fraternity brother who worked at a pizza shop. When he first got the job, all the brothers were excited in the hopes of obtaining free pizzas. Sure enough, almost every night he worked he would bring home all the pizza that was still lying around at closing. By the end of one month, our entire fraternity house was sick of pizza, and my friend never wanted to eat a pizza again!

Satisfaction That Leads to Destruction

This illustrates that what often appears free and unlimited can lead very quickly to an extreme loathing. In other words, within the very character of the naive are the seeds for his own destruction. Notice what the writer of Proverbs says about the naive and his eventual outcome:

> So they shall eat of the fruit of their own way,
> And be satiated with their own devices.
> For the waywardness of the naive shall kill them,
> And the complacency of fools shall destroy them.
> But he who listens to me shall live securely,
> And shall be at ease from the dread of evil. (1:31-33)

Given enough time, the continual turning away from wisdom and the knowledge of God[6] forms the very seeds for the naive's destruction. The naive wants to do his own thing and ends up being literally satiated with it. One commentator calls this eating too much of what they wanted: "The 'reaction' is compared to that of an overloaded digestive system. Just as over-eating produces surfeit and loathing, so the pleasure which men get out of the cleverness by which they secure their advantage at the expense of their fellows will eventually turn to disgust."[7]

In the end, the naive's openness comes back to haunt him. Because he did not seek wisdom and choose the fear of the Lord, but did his own thing, he must face the consequences of his freedom. We are certainly free beings made in God's image, but we are not free from the consequences of our freedom. Our current epidemic of AIDS should send a wake-up call to a generation of the naive who once believed that sex was free and that there were no consequences to what one did with one's sexual appetites. Even if sexuality is defined as preference, preferences are not immune to consequences. But there is a second element to the naive's eventual outcome.

He Will Inherit More of the Same
Listen to Sister Wisdom:

> The naive inherit folly,
> But the prudent are crowned with knowledge. (14:18)

The only reward the simple gets for his life and activities is more irrational conduct. He does not improve himself or learn from the consequences of his actions. Over the course of his life he only illustrates more fully what he really is—a naive fool! The contrast with the prudent is striking. What comes to the prudent is having his head surrounded with more knowledge.[8] The individual who goes on the search for wisdom and finds her has his head graced or wrapped with more wisdom and knowledge!

If, at this point, you are saying to yourself, "Wow, there is no hope for this guy or gal," hang on. Apparently, the Lord has a certain special sympathy toward these ones who are so open to the temptations of life.

He Is Protected by the Lord
Whether it is the result of inherited tendencies or behavioral upbringing, the naive gets himself into trouble because of his openness to the influences of life. What is interesting to me is that the Scriptures don't ever deal with how we got to be the way we are. They just address us as we are. Thus, when the psalmist begins to think about his own deliverance and

salvation, he acknowledges God's loving superintendence over his life before he was saved. The psalmist recites,

> The LORD preserves [guards] the simple;
> I was brought low, and He saved me. (Psalm 116:6)

This passage strikes me as an illustration of biblical irony: Since no one can do anything about the naive tendencies of the human soul, God Himself has to! The point is clear. God in His grace looks with some regard toward the naive and guards their way and saves them from themselves. The prophet Ezekiel demonstrates that a special atoning sacrifice should be made for the naive (Ezekiel 45:20). This may be in light of the category of unintentional sins mentioned in Numbers 15:27-28 and Leviticus 4:2. Perhaps God looks upon this group of people called the naive with special grace. He knows they do many wrong things simply because they are naive and without moral instruction, and therefore require a special atonement. Apparently, God also places a unique watchful care over the naive. He guards their way.

As I reflect upon my own life, I have certainly seen this care. I was not raised in a home where the Scriptures were openly taught. When I went to college I got involved in many things that I now consider wrong. But as I look back on this period of my life from a distance of nearly thirty years, I can honestly say God protected me. I would like to believe that in some strange way God honors our ignorance and simplicity, and out of His own graciousness toward us protects us in order that we might ultimately come to know Him who has protected us from a distance.

But can the naive change? The answer is a mix of good news and bad news.

Can the Naive Ever Change?

The good news is that he can! The bad news is that it is through very painful processes! The writer of Proverbs says, "Strike a scoffer and the naive may become shrewd" (19:25), and "When the scoffer is punished, the naive becomes wise" (21:11). One benefit of the naive's openness is that he is so influenced by the behavior of others when they are punished or fall, he can learn from their mistakes. Apparently, the naive can change, but it is at the expense of others who have to suffer extreme forms of punishment. In fact, as noted in the above passages, the punishment does nothing for the scoffer, but the scoffer needs to be disciplined for the sake of the young and naive who can learn from it. In other words, the naive needs some graphic visual aid to bring him to the point of repentance and a change of life. Being a creature of the moment, he needs something in the moment to jar his thinking enough to bring about change.

I still remember being quite sobered when one of the most popular girls in my high school was killed in a car accident. Most high school students are naive when it comes to death and dying, but in one afternoon an entire high school was confronted with its naive view of an invulnerable world. I and most of my friends quickly realized that if it could happen to her, it could happen to us. At least for a while, we grew up a little, our attitude about life matured, and perhaps we became a little wiser. The naive can learn from the hard realities of life. They can also learn and change in ways that are less abrupt and serious.

The Word of God Changes the Naive
The naive is most characterized by his lack of moral sense and his openness to believe anything. His life is truly a tale of Gullible's Travels! In other words, what the naive lacks is a sufficient moral base from which he can evaluate life and its circumstances. The Word of God can become the anchor for his soul and the very means of delivering him from the consequences of his nature. The psalmist again writes,

> The law of the Lord is perfect, restoring the soul;
> The testimony of the Lord is sure, making wise the
>   simple [naive]. (Psalm 19:7)

In another place, the psalmist says,

> The unfolding of Thy words gives light;
> It gives understanding to the simple [naive].
>   (Psalm 119:130)

It is the law of the Lord as found in the Holy Scriptures that brings moral and ethical integrity to a person. It is the revealed insight of Scripture that brings healing, restoration, direction, and guidance to the open-minded and vulnerable.

In the final analysis, it is God who must speak to the naive in order to bring about change. The naive *can* learn from the hard realities of life, but any knowledge so gained may be short-lived. From the understanding of God's Word, the naive is enlightened about the course of his life.[9] The condition of the naive's heart is revealed by the Word of God. The Word of God becomes the chief change-agent in the naive's life and brings a stability that takes away the naive's susceptibility to the whims, fashions, and enticements of human living.

I have a pastor friend who has gone through the painful "dark nights of soul." After his wife died of a long illness, he began to reevaluate his life and career. He realized that he had placed most of his trust, not in God, but in institutions, people, and boards. As a disillusioned mid-lifer and widower, he began to go directly to the Scripture again, in an attempt to reexamine his life. He admitted to me, "Studying the Scripture, I began to see I had expected the church, church boards, and people to care for me, in ways that only God can." My friend concluded that he had been too naive about who was really responsible for his life. He subsequently left church ministry and now has an extensive ministry with men, but on his own terms. He told me, "I've never been more fulfilled. I feel grown-up for the first time. I wish I had the understanding I now have when I was twenty."

In many ways this man illustrates how the naive can begin to change. For my friend, it took the realization of a displaced trust mixed with a lot of disillusionment. His return to the

Scriptures provided the necessary key to growth. Without this return, he might not be in ministry today or even walking with Christ. But in the painful process of recognizing that "the naive believes too much," he went back to Scripture to find his moral and spiritual anchor.

We all begin life trusting in others. We are born naive. But as we emerge from adolescence into adulthood, perhaps we haven't finished our growing up yet. We carry our childlike belief systems into adulthood. Then when people rip us off or don't fulfill our expectations or break promises, when churches blow apart or our kids don't turn out as we thought, a little bit of the naive is eroded. We can see this as painfully losing something or as becoming a little wiser, a little more grown-up. In our search for wisdom we need to identify those naive places in our spirits. When we find them, Lady Wisdom calls us to bring them to her. The light of her scrutiny imparts understanding and wisdom that can carry us the rest of our lives. I will never buy another Triumph without checking underneath first! Of course, the next time it could be the engine!

One reason I sometimes don't do what I ought to do is because I'm just a little sluggardly. In our search for wisdom, this is the next personality type in the book of Proverbs.

The Sluggard

There's very little difference among men,
but it's the little difference that makes a big difference.
UNKNOWN

▼

Slothfulness casteth into a deep sleep;
and the idle soul shall suffer hunger.
PROVERBS 19:15[1]

I once had a secretary who on occasion made me want to change careers and become an ax-murderer. Actually, this plain, gentle volunteer was as sweet, sincere, and dedicated as a church secretary could be. The problem was, she was just so incredibly slow. I could give her a short, simple letter to type and with a smile on her face she would set about the task of hunting and pecking. Hours later she would return, looking so proud of her accomplishment. I would look over the letter and usually find several typos or strikeovers (no self-correcting typewriters or word processors in those days). Somewhat less radiant, she would go back to her desk and set about retyping it. By the time she had an acceptable letter, it was time to go home.

I really enjoyed the lady, but her slowness in typing drove me crazy. This, of course, is one of the problems with church volunteers—they are difficult to fire! What drove me to sharpening my ax was the amount of time it took her to do the simplest of tasks. In our continuing search for wisdom, we will now look at one of the most colorful portraits . . . the sluggard.

44

PERSONAL CHARACTERISTICS OF THE SLUGGARD

The proverbial character called sluggard translates from the Hebrew word *'atzal*, which means "to be slow, hesitant or sluggish."[2] One writer describes this character as "a figure of tragic comedy with his sheer animal laziness."[3] When all the material in Proverbs about this personality is taken together, a certain psychology emerges. In other words, we can look into the brain of this being and see what is going on inside his head. We can begin to see what makes him tick, and as a result perhaps better understand him. We might also see a little of the sluggard in our own life!

First, a word about translations. Some translations use the word *slothful*, others *sluggard*, others just plain *slow*. But they all translate the same Hebrew term, *'atzal*.

Now, on to the inner psychology of this person.

He Is Not a Self-Starter

I have come to realize on my journey of life so far that there are two types of organizations, committees, or groups that don't work well. One is made up of all chiefs with no Indians. The other, all Indians and no chiefs. It seems for things to work well there always needs to be the balance of leadership mixed with someone to do the work. The sluggard is definitely an Indian and not a chief. He lacks internal motivation. Therefore, he must be given specific instructions and constantly checked on to make sure a job is done. In a somewhat humorous tone, the sluggard is presented as one who even lacks the necessary motivation to get food to his mouth.

> The sluggard buries his hand in the dish,
> And will not even bring it back to his mouth. (19:24;
>   see also 26:1,5)

Whether he lacks energy or is just waiting to be told what to do is not clear. But the reality is the same. Even the basic functions of living become a problem for this person.[4] The writer of Proverbs asks,

How long will you lie down, O sluggard?
When will you arise from your sleep? (6:9)

Apparently, the sluggard lacks the necessary internal motivation to get out of bed in the morning. I can identify with this point. My wife and I handle stress radically different (like most husbands and wives!). When Cinny gets stressed out she goes into a massive housecleaning frenzy. I go to bed! When it comes to stressful situations, I feel so worn out I have to go to bed to recover. The phone can ring, my kids can come in and out of the bedroom, but I don't move. I have for the moment become a sluggard. I have often said the difference between me and other dysfunctionals is that I choose to be dysfunctional at times. I choose to be the sluggard for awhile. Obviously, if both Cinny and I are under stress at the same time, this relationship doesn't work very well. She wants to work (and wants everyone else who happens to be in the house to do the same), while I want to sleep.

The sluggard is told to take a course on "antology" in order to gain insight into his own slothful nature.

Go to the ant, O sluggard,
Observe her ways and be wise,
Which, having no chief,
Officer or ruler,
Prepares her food in the summer,
And gathers her provision in the harvest. (6:6-8)

I took this literally one afternoon. Spying some tidbits from lunch that had been left on the kitchen counter, I noticed a little trail of ants journeying from the counter up to a crack in the wall. I took several moments just to watch. Ant after ant came, somehow positioned a huge bread crumb on its head, and then carried it in orderly fashion across the counter, up the wall, and into the crack. Out from the same crack came other ants on the return trip. The proverb rang true to what I was observing. I saw no union bosses on this project, no coffee breaks, no sit-down times, no ants on the side with a club or whip making sure ants didn't sneak off in another direction. Apparently, there was something going on internally within the ant that made it want to prepare its colony or household for the oncoming winter. The sluggard is told to go to the ant to learn this necessary reality about life, because he lacks this crucial sense of preparation.

He Lacks a Sense of Preparation

As the ant has an innate instinct toward preparing for the future, the sluggard lacks this sense, ultimately to his own ruin. The reason he doesn't prepare is because he has developed over the years the acute strategies of rationalization and procrastination. In the extended "antology" account, we can see what is going on in the sluggard's head while he lies on his bed. He says,

> "A little sleep, a little slumber,
> A little folding of the hands to rest"—
> And *your* poverty will come in like a vagabond,
> And your need like an armed man. (6:10-11, emphasis
>   added)

The sluggard has his own unique form of rationalization. He says to himself, "Sleep is a necessity of life, sleep is good; therefore, what's wrong with a little sleep? After all, a little sleep never hurt anyone, right?!" Wrong. What the sluggard does not realize is that a lot of nothing amounts to a lot of something over time. What's a little cholesterol, nicotine, or alcohol? What's a little affair, or a little fooling around, or a little dishonesty? Right! The writer of Proverbs answers, "So shall *your* poverty come."

But the sluggard not only rationalizes his behavior, he also procrastinates about doing what he believes he needs to do. Here lies the subtlety of the sluggard's psychology. He knows what he needs to do, wants to do it, even desires the results of doing it, but procrastinates about moving in a direction to accomplish it. In another humorous quip, we see that . . .

The sluggard does not plow after the autumn,
So he begs during the harvest and has nothing. (20:4)

Having been raised in the wheat country of Kansas, I have seen this important agricultural reality. In my college fraternity, I had many friends who left school in October to help on the harvest. The harvest is what paid their college tuition. If they didn't get home to help on the farm, they couldn't stay in school. When the harvest was finished there were always several days of celebration, perhaps longer if it was an exceptionally good harvest.

The tendency at this time of the year is to think, since we have just finished the difficult time of hard labor and the harvest is in for another year, "Let's just enjoy the fruit of our labor for a while." Why go back to work so soon? But God has built in some hard realities about the seasonal nature of life. If one does not immediately prepare the soil for next year, there will be no harvest. Therefore, as soon as the harvest is in, one must get back on the tractor and begin turning over the soil to prepare it for the new seeds to be planted.

The sluggard procrastinates. As a farmer he knows he needs to and probably wants to have a harvest next year, but he just doesn't plow. "What's a few more days, a little more time off, a little more time to party with my friends?" he reasons. Then winter sets in, snow covers the ground, and he can't plow. By the time winter is over, others are watching the first sprouts emerge from the ground. The sluggard then realizes the agricultural cycle cannot be reversed. Consequently, when others are eating, the sluggard has to beg. Haven't we sort of become a society of sluggards, wanting others to feed us while we maintain our own rationalizations and procrastinations about why we can't or shouldn't work?

I recently learned this lesson the hard way. Having just finished my taxes, I came to the hard realization that I had grossly underpaid my prepayment. As an author with several books in print, I cannot predict with much accuracy how well books are going to sell. Therefore, trying to accurately prepay taxes on expected royalty income is impossible. However, every time I got a royalty check during the year I knew I needed to put a certain percentage aside for taxes. I didn't. Of course, I had my reasons. Car repairs, college tuition, debt repayment, plus a few new techno-gadgets seemed to take all the royalties. Then judgment day came—APRIL 15. Ouch! I owe that much?! Why did I so procrastinate? Why didn't I better prepare myself financially this year? I asked myself these questions several times. I asked my wife, also! The answer was simple. I was a sluggard when it came to taxes last year. I hope to do better this next year.

He Lives with Unsatisfied Desires

Some people I know don't have any real desires. They are "low-maintenance" sort of people who either don't demand much or don't need much attention. But the sluggard is not one of them! The sluggard desires greatly, but he never acts on any of his desires. Proverbs states,

> The desire of the sluggard puts him to death,
> For his hands refuse to work. (21:25)

The word translated "desire," *'avah*, seems to imply the full range of human desires covering everything from the physical appetites and desiring of good things to lust and covetousness.[5] Sluggards, like many other men and women, are driven by their normal human desires. But unlike humans of wiser cut, sluggards will not lift their hands in order to try to satisfy their desires.

One of the increasingly new trends in our adult population is called the "Whine of the Times." In a recent *USA Today* article, Cathy Grossman writes, "Whining is the anthem of the '90's." As a part of the X Generation (children of baby boomers), Grossman notes, "Outraged entitlement and affronted privilege are premier whine cellar selections. Also: over-dramatization and a stylish hopelessness in harmony with one's heritage." Her explanation for this phenomenon? "If you expect everything to come to you and it doesn't, you're going to be grumpy. You're going to whine. What you see with the X-ers is the transformation of the 'Me' generation to the 'Grimme Generation.'"[6]

The sluggard desires but doesn't obtain, and it eventually leads to his own downfall. Perhaps this generation of whiners are just sluggards in disguise. They view themselves as entitled, but their yearnings are never satisfied because they haven't learned the hard lessons of industry. They haven't labored as an ant. Puritan pastor Thomas Brooks wrote, "Oh, then, be ashamed, Christians, that worldlings are more studious, and industrious to make sure of pebbles, than you are to make sure of pearls." Isn't this often the case? Men and women who have nothing to do with spiritual realities work harder for nothing than Christians do for the Ultimate Someone. Feeling we are entitled to things without being willing to do the necessary labor to obtain them makes us a society of sluggards.[7]

He Is Irrationally Fearful

I know a man who studied the stock market for years. He had elaborate charts tracing the market from its inception. When computers came into vogue, he transferred all the data to a home computer. One room in his house was filled with charts, printouts, books, and piles of stock-related information.

I asked my friend, "With all this technical information on the market, I bet you have made a mint over the years."

He looked a little surprised by my question. "Oh, no, I have never invested a dime on the market; it's just my hobby."

Later, his wife told me he was too fearful to put any money into the stock market! Some might think this wise (especially in October of 1988), but in light of this man's knowledge, it might be better to presume his fear of losing money overrode his somewhat expert knowledge. Others might believe his fears were irrational.

Proverbs gives us another primary motivator in the sluggard's life, that of irrational fear. The sluggard may give the appearance of being slow, lazy, and not willing to work, but his primary motivation is fear. Our life observer writes,

> The sluggard says, "There is a lion outside;
> I shall be slain in the streets!" (22:13)

In a parallel passage, he adds,

> The sluggard says, "There is a lion in the road!
> A lion is in the open square!" (26:13)

What keeps this individual from attempting things he wants to do, or feels he needs to do, is irrational fear. He stays cloistered inside his house for fear that there might be some danger outside. Apparently, wherever this character looks, he sees lions. Lions in the streets, in the square, on the roads.

Now, where I live (in the northeastern United States) this may seem like a reasonable precaution, but in biblical times, it would seem strange for wild lions to be roaming the city streets. It is more realistic to assume that these lions are imagined in the mind of the sluggard. They become another way of justifying his being sluggardly. He lives in a world of subjective fear, paralyzed to move outside his comfort zone and do something constructive with his life.

I wonder how many well-intentioned people see lions in their life at every turn. Their ultimate concern is clearly evident; "I will be slain," the sluggard says. The sluggard's imagined fear rests solidly in his own self-concern and self-preservation. Sister Wisdom would encourage the sluggard to take some risks, to give up self-concern and move beyond the irrational fears that keep him locked safely in the protective homes of his own making.

I must differentiate at this point what I believe to be irrational fears from rational fears. To drive in some parts of my city (Philadelphia, the City of Brotherly Love) at 1:00 a.m. should evoke rational fears for most sane people.[8] However, to conceive daylight dangers when locked in one's own home with supportive "at-home" neighbors on each side is irrational. The sluggard lives with irrational fears as an excuse for the way he is. To see lions where lambs are is to be one sick puppy!

He Is Defeated by Obstacles

I counsel many people who have an utterly faulty view of God's will. Somewhere in their faith journey they have picked up the teaching that life ought to be easy and problem-free. If an obstacle is placed before them, then their direction is obviously not in the will of God. In spite of being clearly unbiblical (think of Job, Jesus, the apostles, and Paul; see 2 Corinthians 4:8-9, 11:23-28), Proverbs says,

> The way of the sluggard is as a hedge of thorns,
> But the path of the upright is a highway. (15:19)

In other words, the lifestyle of the sluggard is characterized by his attitude toward obstacles. When he looks at life, all he sees is a hedge of thorns surrounding him.[9] We have all known people like this. They may complain about their circumstances, express their discontent, and vent their pain. But when one starts to offer solutions or alternatives, all they see is a hedge of thorns. To make any moves to remedy their situation would cause them pain, as it would one moving through a hedge of thorns.

We used to live in Hawaii. Someone had to go and do that job! In a tropical climate one almost has to employ a gardener just to keep the jungle out of one's yard. We lived on the windward side of Oahu, and we had a bougainvillaea shrub almost completely covering our driveway. I sometimes wondered if the previous owners moved out because they could no longer get into their garage. At any rate, I put off cutting the plant back. It was so large and had so many prickly thorns, I knew it was going to be one of those all-weekend jobs once I finally submitted to tackling it. Every time I looked at the shrub, I just saw one large, painful job. The perceived amount of effort and pain overwhelmed me, and made me not even want to attempt the job. I finally talked one of my friends into coming over and tackling the job with me. With machetes in hand, I was surprised to see how fast the job went. We were finished in about one hour! This realization made me really feel like a sluggard.

The sluggard sees a hedge of thorns in almost every area of his life. When obstacles present themselves on the sluggard's path, he backs off, sits down, or goes back. The contrast in the proverb is striking. The righteous apparently raises up a highway over the obstacles.[10] Obstacles are the same for both, but the righteous is willing to break a sweat, have his hands get bloodied from the thorns, and build a highway over and around the rough areas. The sluggard quits at the first prick of pain.

I don't necessarily consider myself a successful writer. But I have been writing in some way ever since high school when I took a journalism class and became the sports editor for our school paper. I have written for years, but it has only been in the past four years that I have done it more seriously. What changed? When I am asked during radio and television interviews why I wrote a particular book, I usually humorously answer, "My kids are in college." But there is a certain truthfulness to my answer. I really wasn't willing to suffer the rejection notices that every writer has hidden somewhere in his life until I was desperate to send my children to college. All I saw in trying to get published was a hedge of thorns. I saw myself without a machete and didn't want my spirit to be crushed or my own blood shed through the rejection process. Maybe, having five books in print, I have raised up a mound of dirt over my fears of rejection. Maybe I am not as sluggardly as I once was!

He Is Stuck in His Own Self-Deceit

One final commentary on the sluggard:

> As the door turns on its hinges,
> So does the sluggard on his bed. . . .
> The sluggard is wiser in his own eyes
> Than seven men who can give a discreet answer.
> (26:14,16)

While the industrious pass to and fro through the active doors of life, the sluggard is glued or stuck to his bed, stationary, suffering from the disease of "initial inertia." However, verse 16 reveals his inner deceit. The sluggard actually thinks himself wiser than other men because he isn't caught up in their busy, mundane affairs. He believes he is smarter for avoiding pain and trying to enjoy life and not doing anything too difficult. As the sluggard evaluates his own life in contrast to others, there is apparently no regret or sense of failure within him. What is worse, he feels his way of life is superior! At its extreme, this attitude contributes to the criminal mind. Why work eight to fourteen hours a day when one can get much more money merely robbing, cheating, or embezzling? Most criminals feel they are smarter than the law-abiding citizens who work hard, pay taxes, and barely have any left over for themselves.

INTERPERSONAL REALITIES OF THE SLUGGARD
Even though the sluggard is happy within himself, glorying in his own self-pride, for those who have to work and be around him it's a different story. What this kind of person does to others is entirely negative.

He Is an Irritation to His Employers
Like my secretary sweetly volunteering her time and almost driving me to the funny farm, in another way the sluggard irritates those for whom he works. Proverbs states,

> Like vinegar to the teeth and smoke to the eyes,
> So is the lazy one [sluggard] to those who send him.
> (10:26)

Just as the acidic nature of vinegar or the first glass of fruit juice in the morning has a certain irritating "bite" to the teeth, so is the sluggard to the one who gives him a job to do. Apparently, when you give a sluggard a job, he carries it out so slowly that it "eats away" on your nerves.

The other metaphor suggests his interpersonal abilities cause temporary blindness. As the wind blows smoke up in your face when you're charbroiling a hamburger, so is the effect of the sluggard on the one who sends him on an errand. One commentator observes, "They who send a sluggard, i.e, who make him their agent, do it to their own sorrow; his slothfulness is for them, and for that which they have in view, of dull, i.e. slow and restrained, of biting, i.e. sensibly injurious operation."[11]

A word of wisdom here for any employment personnel officers. Even though this is terribly discriminating on the basis of character types, Sister Wisdom would encourage *not* hiring such a person. He will only do harm to the company and those who have to work with him. He literally does not handle responsibility well, or at least in the time frame that most work must be accomplished. But in addition, there is a second dynamic in his interpersonal relations.

He Becomes Dependent on Others
As noted earlier, because the sluggard lacks the sense to prepare for the future, he creates his own need to have others help him. "He begs during the harvest and has nothing" (20:4). Because of his stubborn refusal to work, mixed with his own rationalizations and procrastinations, he has nothing when others are rejoicing at the plentiful harvest. He, therefore, becomes dependent on the generosity of others.

In Israel, care for the poor was commanded (Deuteronomy 15:7-11), and after every harvest the leftovers that accumulated in the corners of the field were to be left for those who lacked food. It's always interesting to me how our God never asks how these widows, sojourners, fatherless, and poor came to their condition; He just commands their care to others. But Proverbs deals with the realities of life: The sluggard is the kind of person who becomes overly dependent on others.

Let's move this dependency outside the realm of money and food. We may have other areas of our lives where our dependency needs are being unjustifiably met by others. Even the Apostle Paul had to tell one church they were unjustifiably caring for some and needed to encourage more responsible independence upon them (2 Thessalonians 3:7-12). In my counseling, I have seen wives sometimes use the "My husband is the head and umbrella over my life" teaching as a cloak for their own irresponsibility before God. Could it be they are just sluggards, not willing to take responsibility for their own spiritual lives? I have also seen men who are so dependent upon their work that they have no real identity apart from a job. Are they sluggards in the area of personal identity, not willing to have their identity stretched and broadened?

All of us have areas where we perhaps have become a little sluggardly. When we look at these areas, it is only proper to ask, "What is the long-term effect of our sluggardness?" Proverbs answers with two discouraging words.

What Is the Outcome of a Sluggard's Life?

Our sage advises us to look at the end result in the sluggard's life:

> "A little sleep, a little slumber," . . .
> Then your *poverty* will come as a robber,
> And your want like an armed man. (24:33-34)

The first outcome envisioned for the sluggard is poverty. This state is likened to what happens when one is robbed completely of his possessions. Despite the sluggard's philosophy that "a little" is not a lot, the logical and eventual conclusion of this view is one of complete poverty. As complete and final as if someone robbed him of everything he has. The results are the same: standing in need, without the most minimal of possessions.

Whatever the sluggardly areas of my life are, this proverb should help me envision the long-term results of my sluggardness. My little laziness, my little lack of doing what needs to be done, my little lack of preparation for the future—all can result in irreparable harm and loss for me.

I have a particular concern for many independent church pastors. When I was in my twenties, pension funds and such were of "little" concern to me. Now that I am almost fifty, I realize that my spiritual commitment to "serve the Lord" and not worry or prepare for my later years was nothing but a well-motivated sluggardness on my behalf. For my first seventeen years in the work force I worked for institutions that provided no pension programs, and I had none of my own. From my perspective now, I can't believe I never even thought about it. I can't believe the institutions I worked for also never made it an important part of their employee packages. Now, when I talk to independent pastors and their boards, I try to encourage them to take this area of life a "little" more seriously.

The second long-term result for the sluggard is outright death. Again, the proverb noted previously says,

The desire of the sluggard puts him to death,
For his hands refuse to work. (21:25)

The literal reality is clearly true enough. Given enough time, mixed with the refusal to work, the sluggard will die of starvation, as perhaps some of our homeless do today.

However, I also think the passage can be taken more figuratively. Whatever areas of sluggardness we have in our lives, our refusal to deal with them ultimately brings about some kind of death within us. Whether it be in my marriage, my stewardship, my parenting, or my vocation, whatever I am putting off dealing with can die a certain death while I procrastinate or rationalize. Obstacles and problems never go away, they just give birth to more of the same. I'm terrible about dealing with problem people or making difficult phone calls. I put off seeing the people or making the calls. I try to get others (like my wife or secretary) to do my dirty work for me. Anything but deal with the issues directly. I have had too many times in my life when, had I dealt with the problems sooner, they would have been much easier to resolve. At least now, my sluggardness is more recognizable and conscious than it used to be!

Well, I'm sure you're already asking the question we raised with reference to the naive. Can the sluggard change, can he learn enough to become wise? Again, I respond by offering a wholehearted "Yes, there is hope for this individual."

How the Sluggard Becomes Wise

Apparently, Solomon, in giving fatherly wisdom to his sons, believes that change is possible. He tells his son (who has an obvious proclivity toward sluggardness), "Go to the ant, O sluggard, observe her ways and be wise." All a father or any other mentor can do is encourage a certain direction for change. But also, in the admonition is a presupposition that change is possible. That's the good news. The sluggard can learn and change.

The New Testament also gives us helpful insight into a "cure" for the sluggardly areas of our lives. In the familiar post-Resurrection narrative, Jesus reveals Himself to two disciples on the road to Emmaus. He calls them "foolish" and "slow of heart" (Luke 24:25). I believe all our hearts are somewhat foolish and slow, especially slow to believe what the Scriptures have to tell us about the Messiah and life. On this occasion, Jesus explains to them all the prophets had to say about Himself. From this realization, their lives begin to change. In addition, the Apostle Paul tells us more directly, it is through the encouragement of the Scriptures that we have hope (Romans 15:4).

What the sluggard needs in his life is, first of all, a personal exposure to the living Christ, rooted in the objective reality of the Scriptures. The experience with Christ can provide a new motivation in the life of the sluggard; the Scriptures provide the important element of knowing what to do once the sluggard has a new motivation for change. But the real change-agent is the Holy Spirit of God.

All of us are so entrenched in our sins, personalities, and character disorders that it takes an extraneous Spirit to move our stubborn, sluggish human spirits. The sluggard lives in constant fear, which immobilizes him. The discipline he needs to accomplish anything worthwhile in life is severely lacking. This is precisely what the Holy Spirit of God deals with. The apostle writes, "For God has not given us a spirit of *timidity* [fear], but of power and love and *discipline*" (2 Timothy 1:7, emphasis added). The Holy Spirit can work within the fabric of the human spirit to bring about the needed discipline in the sluggard. The Spirit also begins to replace the irrational fears of the sluggard with feelings of power! Literally, the Spirit can empower the sluggard to get moving in his life, accomplish things, make preparation for the future, and deal with his fears.

I have seen this in my own life. When I graduated from college I was tired of school. I was not an honor student, but merely did well enough to stay eligible for football. Languages I especially hated and never did well in. But my last year of college I came to know the Savior. From day one of my conversion, I felt a new motivation in my life. I loved to read. I would read a book in one sitting, which I had never done before in my life. I also became fascinated with studying Greek, in order to be able to read the Greek New Testament. Five years later when I went to seminary, I went with fear and trembling, especially about formally studying Greek and Hebrew! To my surprise, I did well. In some courses I received A's. Even though I don't remember ever saying to myself, "I need more discipline or I will be disciplined," I can remember many nights when I was so engrossed in my studies that I barely moved from my seat all night. In retrospect, my only explanation is that God, through His Spirit, changed my motivation, took away my fear of failure (especially about Hebrew), and gave me the discipline I needed to get through graduate school. My sluggardly approach to studies was transformed by coming to know Christ and having the Spirit of God come upon my life in power. Now, years later, as I have had the opportunity to meet men and women from all over the world, I have come to the same conclusion uttered by someone in my past: "There's very little difference among men, but it's the little difference that makes a big difference."

The Wicked

I cannot do all I want, but I can undo all things.
SAM
IN *THE TRIAL OF GOD*[1]

▼

The mouth of the wicked conceals violence.
PROVERBS 10:6

The scene is Shamgorod, a small village lost in oblivion after
Jewish pogroms removed such places from the face of the
earth. In a large room of an inn, candles in empty bottles are
placed upon tables to signal the beginning of the Jewish festi-
val of Purim. Three itinerant actors show up to perform a
Purim play. To their horror, only two Jews have survived—the
innkeeper and his crazy daughter. All agree that instead of
doing their "Purimshpiel" they will stage a mock trial of God,
indicting Him for allowing His Jews to be slaughtered. But who
will be God's defense attorney? A stranger who looks oddly
familiar shows up and offers to take the role. Charges against
God are made between the serving of drinks, various distur-
bances, and the stranger's shadowy conversation. As the hour
comes for the pogrom to continue once again, Mendel, one of
the minstrels, says to God's defender, Sam:

MENDEL: Just? How can anyone proclaim Him just—
now? With the end so near? Look at us, look at

Hanna, search your own memory; between Jews
who suffer and die, and God who does not—how
can you choose God?

SAM: I must. I'm His servant. He created the world and
me without asking for my opinion; He may do with
both whatever He wishes. Our task is to glorify
Him, to praise Him, to love Him—in spite of
ourselves.

MENDEL: But how can you?

SAM: It's simple. Faith in God must be as boundless as
God Himself. If it exists at the expense of man, too
bad. God is eternal, man is not.

MENDEL: Who are you, Stranger?

SAM: I told you. I am God's defender.

MENDEL: Who are you when you are not performing?
When you are not defending Him?

SAM: Why do you want to know?

MENDEL: Because I envy you. Your love of God: I wish I
had one measure of it. Your piety: I wish it were
mine. Your faith: mine is less profound, less intact
than yours. Who are you?

SAM: I am not allowed to reveal myself to you. And what
if I told you that I am God's emissary? I visit His creation and bring stories back to Him. I see all things, I
watch all men. I cannot do all I want, but I can undo
all things. Have I said enough?

MARIA (a servant girl): You're crazy, you're all crazy . . .

MENDEL: You are a tzaddik, a Just, a Rabbi, a Master—
you are endowed with mystical powers; you are a
holy man. Do something to revoke the decree (of
death upon the village). If you cannot, who could?
You are God's only defender, you have rights and
privileges: use them! For heaven's sake, use them!
Oh holy man, we beg you to save God's children
from further shame and suffering!

(Sam, smiling reassuringly, walks toward Mendel and stops
before him.)

YANKEL (ANOTHER MINSTREL): It's Purim. Let's wear
   our masks!
(Sam pulls his out of his pocket and raises it to his face.
   All shout in fear, and *Satan* speaks to them, laughing.)
SAM: So—you took me for a saint, a Just? Me? How
   could you be that blind? How could you be that stu-
   pid? If you only knew, if you only knew . . .
(Curtain)[2]

When Hannah Arendt covered the Nuremberg trials, the
thing she said so disturbed her was how "normal and sane"
Adolf Eichmann looked. Such is the often banal appearance of
evil and evil men. It is this false appearance that makes them
so difficult to recognize—and this study so imperative.

It is sometimes the very defenders of God who are the most
insidiously disguised emissaries of the Devil. In this chapter we
consider the one who is seen as the furthest removed from wisdom. This evil person is referred to over fifty times in Proverbs
alone, thus making him one of the major players in the book.

The two Hebrew words that are translated "wicked,"
rasha', and "evil," *ra'*, show a range of activity from "the utter
rejection of God, to idolatry, abuse of people and property and
harsh slavery"[3] to "those guilty of violation of social rights, violent, oppressive, greedy, engaged in plotting against and trap-
ping poor people and who are quite willing to murder to gain
their ends."[4] In short, they seriously threaten a community
because they are boldly immoral and oppose the things that
are honorable and right. They are God's chief adversaries, even
though they may, like Sam (Satan) in the Purim play, give the
appearance of being holy and religious.

In this chapter we will look at three aspects of the wicked
person: his *inner soul*, his *pathology*, and his *relations to the
righteous*.

THE WICKED'S INNER SOUL

It should not surprise us that the evil person does not necessarily appear with horns and forked tails. Our Lord has told us

that the essence of evil lies in its deceptive nature. Satan appears as an angel of light (2 Corinthians 11:14), and his own nature is such that he is incapable of standing in the truth because there is no truth in him. He is a liar and the father of all lies (John 8:44). Marguerite Shuster writes,

> The key point is that Satan and his hordes conceal themselves in the structures of the world and human life, making the world and humankind instruments and bearers of their power. In that sense the cosmos is indeed possessed, so that energy and structures meant for good, meant to serve God, are turned against him and his purposes.[5]

Therefore, the first thing we learn about the wicked person is that he can be very attractive in many ways.

His Appearance Is Attractive Yet Deceiving

We recently received a letter from an old friend explaining how she had recently remarried and then after only one month divorced. Her words grabbed me: "He changed almost within hours after the wedding." Such deception, I believe, has only one source, and clearly shows the evil nature of the person. Proverbs agrees: "A wicked man shows a bold face" (21:29). This one shows one kind of face, a positively appealing, bold one, while being inwardly something far different. Commentator C. H. Toy says this man "deports himself toward facts and persons, unblushingly maintains what suits him, without regard to truth."[6]

One of the major problems the media has created are the Hollywood images that promote pride and arrogance as virtues. These deceive us into thinking that men with big ideas and visions are virtuous creatures. Proverbs says otherwise:

> Haughty eyes and a proud heart,
> The lamp of the wicked is sin. (21:4)

I have known so many women in counseling who have believed the big lies about who a man was or what he was going to do with his life, only to be terribly disappointed and some-times abused by the deception. The wicked can come across as very bold, assertive, and confident (and they probably are). The only problem is, they are that way in every area of their life. Eventually, the power moves break down and don't work any-more. The wicked and those aligned with them tumble down-ward also.

The next verse shows that the wicked can also be all things to all people. He can come across very seductively (or sensi-tively, for nineties' men) in speech. Wisdom says,

> Blessings are on the head of the righteous,
> But the mouth of the wicked conceals violence. (10:6)

The wicked is smart enough to conceal the violence in his heart. Behind the polite speech of wicked men is a deep-seated aggressiveness and hostility.[7]

Although violence in this politically correct society has become a gender-specific issue (the perception is this: men are violent; women are victims of male violence), Proverbs does not hold to this oversimplification. After all, both Wisdom and the Whore are feminine! Apparently, the adulterous woman does as much "violence" to men as men to women. Her lips are smooth, speaking lies and painting romantic portraits for her lover (7:10-18). She takes a man's hard-earned goods, eats his flesh, and brings him to utter ruin (5:1-14). One British writer observes, "Others [women] preferring power to pleasure, use their sexuality as a means of asserting dominance. Although her male victims often become emotional casualties, the femme fatale is not unknown in psychiatric practice."[8]

Wickedness seems to be equally distributed between the sexes. Both keep their wickedness carefully disguised with sin-cerity and an appealing countenance. But their hearts are the same, using and abusing others to achieve their own violent purposes. In fact, M. Scott Peck believes the evil person is so narcissistic he is incapable of genuinely caring about another human being. He writes,

We all of us tend to be more or less self-centered in our dealings with others. We usually view any given situation first and foremost from the standpoint of how it affects us personally, and only as an afterthought do we bother to consider how the same situation might affect someone else involved. Nonetheless, particularly, if we care for the other person, we usually can and eventually do think about his or her viewpoint, which may well be different from ours.

Not so those who are evil. Theirs is a brand of narcissism so total that they seem to lack, in whole and in part, this capacity for empathy.[9]

What else could be expected from one who lacks moral sensitivity?

He Lacks Any Sense of Moral Values

The portrait painted here would be humorous if it weren't so wickedly serious. The evil man, when compared to the righteous in terms of valuable metals, doesn't even have a heart that ranks on the scale.

> The tongue of the righteous is as choice silver,
> The heart of the wicked is worth little. (10:20)

What he is able to earn, he earns in two ways: first by deception, second by plunder. "The wicked earns deceptive wages" (11:18), and "The wicked desires the booty of evil men" (12:12). In other words, he feeds on his own. As other wicked men fall by the side, having succumbed to the error of their ways, instead of taking their downfall to heart, the wicked rejoices because he can prosper from their downfall.

This strikes me as precisely what has happened in the present American business climate. I have a friend who, as a former CEO of a large corporation, said he would never work for another public company. His reward for turning the company around and making it profitable was to create a feeding frenzy for the cash of the company by its competitors. When men, in the guise of company interest and survival, begin feeding on other companies' pension funds, laying off thousands, while lining their own pockets before they chop up the company, they only illustrate what they are—evil men. They feed on the carnage of the dismantled and the unemployed!

In the final analysis, the soul of the wicked is driven by his utter contempt for the upright (29:27) and his openness to receive bribes and pervert justice (17:23). His "way" is in stark contrast to that of the righteous man, who makes careful decisions about friendships. The wicked's way takes him down a road completely free of absolute moral values. He will do anything to become profitable and use anyone to get there. He would sell his own mother if the price was right. "A righteous man is cautious in friendship, but the way of the wicked leads them astray" (12:26).[10]

What motivates this person is not complex. We can see his greed, his willingness to take bribes and use people. But underneath, what motivates the inner psychology is fear.

He Is Dominated by Fear

In the psychological literature there seems to be a running debate as to which is the more powerful motivator, love or fear. I won't answer the question because I haven't a clue about how to prove such things. But I do know both of these human emotions are very powerful motivators. A simplistic explanation might see the righteous as being motivated by the love of wisdom, whereas the wicked is motivated by his own fears. We find that

> The wicked flee when no one is pursuing,
> But the righteous are bold as a lion. (28:1)

The reality of the wicked's worst fear is confirmed by psychiatrist M. Scott Peck. In his illuminating book *People of the Lie*, he observes about these people, "Forever fleeing the light of self-exposure and the voice of their own conscience, they are the most frightened of human beings. They live their lives in sheer terror. They need not be consigned to any hell; they are already in it."[11] He goes on to say he believes these people have a specific form of mental illness and should be the subjects of more research.

The righteous can sleep at night and has a lionlike, strong assurance in God. But the wicked's fears are not unfounded. He has every reason to be fearful, because his fears are eventually borne out: "What the wicked fears will come upon him" (10:24). In the inner life of the wicked is a certain self-fulfilling prophecy of doom. What he dreads, happens. Whether it is full disclosure of who he really is, or how he "really" built his business, or fear of going to jail, or whatever, the gnawing, anticipated downfall eventually comes to pass on his life. Then he becomes prey for the other wicked who have been circling nearby waiting for his misfortune. Living with this kind of impending doom, one would think the wicked would change his ways immediately. But this apparently never enters his mind. He is very much stuck in his wicked behavior.

He Is a Slave to His Behavior

I heard the story of a pastor who was speaking at a particular "spiritual life" conference. For years he had been fighting his bondage to pornographic material. When he went off to do conferences he would take two briefcases with him, one with his conference material and the other with his magazines for late-night enjoyment. During one morning session the pastor got up to the lectern and realized he had forgotten his notes. He asked a man in the front row to open his briefcase and retrieve his notes. You guessed it! The pastor had brought the wrong briefcase. The oversight cost him not only his reputation but also eventually his job.

Proverbs instructs us that the wicked ends up being completely caught in his bondage:

His own iniquities will capture the wicked,
And he will be held with the cords of his sin. (5:22)

This verse implies that even though the wicked might want to break out of his manner of life, he can't. He has lost the ability to break free from the snares in his soul. Cohen, quoting Schechter, reveals, "As man throws out a net whereby he catches fish of the sea, so the sins of man become the means of entangling and catching the sinner."[12]

I have just watched the funeral service for President Richard M. Nixon. Personally I liked the man and do feel he accomplished far more after his disgraceful exit from public life than while in office. But with all the Watergate events replayed for a week on TV, I was again reminded how stupid the burglary was. Apparently, no one yet knows what the "plumbers" were looking for (except Gordon Liddy, and he still won't talk). A stupid break-in cost Nixon the presidency. Was it really worth trying to find out whatever was in the Democratic headquarters? Nixon was caught by his own self-authorized tape players, installed at his own request. The "smoking gun" tapes provided evidence of obstruction of justice by the highest official in the country and secured his downfall. He set his own trap!

The wicked's entrapment is also likened to trying to get around in the dark:

> The way of the wicked is like darkness;
> They do not know over what they stumble. (4:19)

Again, this somewhat humorous picture reveals the wicked as living in a dark existence. He has so adjusted to the darkness of his life that he doesn't know what the light looks like. But unlike the scoffer and the fool, he gets introspective about his condition. Apparently, he wonders why he keeps bumping into things in the dark. The wicked know something is wrong but can't connect the pain to their lives. They can't identify what it is they stumble over. They are so enslaved to the way they are, they do not know they stumble over themselves in the darkness of their own lives. Their future is bleak.

His Future Is Bleak

Having contempt for moral principles, using and abusing people, deceiving people, and maliciously destroying others are serious crimes. Proverbs affirms throughout that God has ordained life in accordance with moral principles. Therefore, those who ignore them ultimately pay the penalty for their rebellion.

The broad strokes painted for the future of the wicked are not good. How could it be otherwise, and God be who He is? Sister Wisdom informs us that "the years of the wicked will be shortened" (10:27); "When a wicked man dies, his hope perishes; all he expected from his power comes to nothing" (11:7);[13] and "The wicked is thrust down by his wrongdoing, but the righteous has a refuge when he dies" (14:32).

The contrast made in these verses is between the righteous, who lives longer and dies well (with a refuge, an Old Testament forerunner to the developed New Testament concept of eternal life; see 1 Peter 1:3-5), and the wicked, who dies young as a result of his calamitous life and has no expectation beyond the grave.

When I think about this pathological portrait of the wicked, I can't help but think of two groups of people. One is very close to where I live, the Mafia. Everyone knows Mafia families are very generous to certain causes, both church and civic. But the reality stands: They make their living off greed, high-interest loans, drugs, protection, illegal disposal of garbage! These are the wicked who walk in darkness but don't know it.

The second group I must be more careful about. I realize there are many AIDS-infected people who fit the category of the naive better. Some were husbands and wives and young kids experimenting with sexual activity who thought "a little" sex is not much. These are not wicked people but naive innocents. Others are tragic victims of incompetence in hospitals (infected needles or transfusions).

But there is another group who have secretly denied the alarming failure rates of condoms and the frightening changing composition of the AIDS virus.[14] These are the ones who believe "safe sex" is found in synthetic rubber that only works part of the time, and by commonly known standards has holes that are larger than the AIDS virus. These are wicked people who promote the deaths of millions by their own rebellion and unwillingness to submit to the simple precepts of wisdom:

> Hear, my son, and accept my sayings,
> And the years of your life will be many. (4:10)

Many are dying because they refused to hear the wisdom of God as found in the Holy Scriptures. This pathological denial is deep and needs to be examined.

THE WICKED'S PATHOLOGY IN SOCIETY
We have come to an interesting point in American history. The privatization of values has produced an atmosphere, if not a rampant belief, that what one does in one's private life doesn't really matter. My neighbor can be having an affair with someone's wife, the principal of my kid's school can be using drugs both before and after school, and my local state representative can be working out real estate deals under the table as a private citizen. When any of these issues are questioned as unethical, the individuals quickly retreat to the sanctity of the division of the public and private sectors. "What I do in my private life doesn't affect my policies for the public good," is the common reply.

This is very far from what our founding fathers envisioned. A text on George Washington, heavily relied upon by Abraham Lincoln, said, "Public character . . . is not evidence of true greatness, for a public character is often an artificial one."[15] The work cited General Benedict Arnold as an example of this point. In his public life he was an early war hero at the battle of Saratoga and an outstanding general in Washington's army. Yet, at the same time he was privately embezzling supplies destined for the starving at Valley Forge to his own profitable pockets. Ultimately, he betrayed West Point to the enemy. Students over a hundred years ago were asked, "Which was more indicative of his true character, what he did in public or what he did in private?"[16] Then, it was obvious. Today, the issue is the economy, dummy!

Proverbs stands firmly in the tradition that private and public righteousness are connected. As well, private wickedness compounded only results in public wickedness. "When the wicked increase, transgression increases" (29:16). When the numbers of individual wicked people increase, corporate (public) transgressions[17] grow proportionately. The whole social order and public group is affected by the individual wickedness done by men. A nation's appropriate response to this reality should be on two levels: the leadership stratum and the local community level.

Leaders Should Not Allow Wickedness in Their Administrations

A leader who truly desires his administration be wise and righteous must take the winnowing wheel to his appointments and the laws of his country. Wisdom says,

> A wise king winnows the wicked,
> And drives the threshing wheel over them. (20:26)

The metaphor implies that the king has enough moral discernment to know what wickedness looks like and enough moral courage to set up processes whereby the wicked will be purged from his rule.

Two other proverbs address the same concept:

> Take away the wicked from before the king,
> And his throne will be established in righteousness. (25:5)

> If a ruler pays attention to falsehood,
> All his ministers become wicked. (29:12)

Government politics never change. There are always those around the king (president) who desire his favor and therefore become political animals telling their leader falsehoods, or at least not all the truth, in order to enhance their own positions. Toy notes the lesson here, "falsity in civil administration and political relations, whereby, the courtiers adjust themselves to the prince"[18] is created by a ruler who pays attention to untrustworthy aides. Who a leader surrounds himself with and listens to is probably the most important single issue of any administration. A wise leader will scrutinize his advisors and ask them not only to live righteously but to tell him the truth. He will demand it, no matter how bad it might be.

Our recent political climate is anything but this ideal. The climate has been created by the lack of principled men in all three branches of government. The indictments and allegations against senators, congressmen, and even our highest executive and his wife are evidence of how these most fundamental of moral principles have not been followed. Watergate, Whitewatergate, and Nannygate all illustrate how wickedness has moved from the private to public sector without much restraint.

But our leaders are not the only ones to blame. So are the people.

The People Should Not Tolerate Wickedness in Their Leaders

The first words of the preamble to the Constitution say, "We the people." Our nation is unique among the nations of the world because of this insightful concept. We have no divine right of kings, no ruling family, no royal bloodlines to trace our descendence as a people to. We are a nation of the people, governed by the people and for the people. But leaders, being what they can become when power is bestowed upon them, need the constant accountability by the people. Therefore, it is imperative for the people to make sure righteous men and women are put in government in order to ensure the benefits of liberty and the public good.

Proverbs makes this very clear with reference to the wicked:

When the righteous increase, the people rejoice,
But when a wicked man rules, people groan. (29:2;
    see also 11:10-11)

This proverb illustrates a simple fact. A nation's populace has a more enjoyable life when the government is crowded with righteous leaders.[19] Imagine our capital, Washington, D.C., and our state capitals crowded with men and women who not only desire to live godly, righteous lives, but pass laws that reflect their own character. Imagine the opposite. What is the result? People groan. The word for groan, *'anah*, in this passage is used of the people of God groaning in bondage under Pharaoh (Exodus 2:23), and of the people of Jerusalem scrounging for daily necessities after the destruction of their city by the Babylonians (Lamentations 1:11).[20]

Which do we hear today, groaning or rejoicing? The answer explains which kind of leaders we have. And in our constitutional republic, who elected them? We groan about our taxes, immoral leaders, and unjust laws simply because we have allowed wicked men to rule. Noah Webster affirms, "If our government fails to secure public prosperity and happiness, it must be because the citizens neglect the divine commands, and elect bad men to make and administer the laws."[21]

We cannot study the wicked in Proverbs without also learning much about the righteous. Because of the close association in the parallel thought of Proverbs, we must also consider how the righteous should respond to the wicked.

THE WICKED IN RELATION TO THE RIGHTEOUS
By nature this has been a very negative chapter. But Proverbs reveals some encouraging words about the righteous in relation to the wicked among them.

The Righteous Are Not to Fear the Wicked
My spine shivers at the thought of the wicked. To think that I might be dealing with an evil man causes me to start packing for the mountains. This once happened at a counseling center

where I was working. I was the director of the center, and one of my counselors told me she was counseling a woman whose murdered husband had been involved with the Mafia. I listened to the counselor and sort of just wrote off the information as part of another supervision session. Then, when listening to my telephone messages, there was a threat on my life if the counselor did not stop seeing (counseling) this woman! For a few days I felt a little panic. I informed the police of the threats and thought about carrying a gun. Fear gripped me, until I was reminded that God is in charge of my spirit. I'm not going home any sooner than He allows!

The righteous are not to allow the wicked to get to them. The Lord promises to protect the righteous against the wicked:

> Do not be afraid of sudden fear,
> Nor of the onslaught of the wicked when it comes;
> For the LORD will be your confidence,
> And will keep your foot from being caught. (3:25-26)

Even though the righteous may fall on occasion, they get up again; the wicked stumble severely when calamity strikes.

> A righteous man falls seven times, and rises again,
> But the wicked stumble in time of calamity. (24:16)

The righteous are survivors, while the wicked, not having God on their side, will ultimately fall through their misfortune. This is good news to the righteous when we see the wicked prospering and in power in high places.

Proverbs also envisions the wicked bowing down to the righteous:

> The evil will bow down before the good,
> And the wicked at the gates of the righteous. (14:19)

Whether in this life or the next, the wicked will bow down to the righteous. This promise is helpful when the righteous are tempted to follow the ways of the wicked.

The Righteous Don't Consider Following the Ways of the Wicked

When I worked as a bank teller during graduate school, we were so poor I was often tempted by the money I exchanged daily. Especially on the Friday late shift. I worked as an outside teller in a Dallas bank. We would balance our windows on Friday afternoons at three o'clock. After that we would reopen the window, but any funds exchanged thereafter would be counted on Monday's business day. From 3:00 to 6:00 p.m. on Friday was one of the busiest times of the week. Large amounts of cash would come in and go out.

Often as I balanced my window at the end of the shift, I would look at the twenty thousand dollars or so in my cash box. It was all Monday's money already on Monday's business day, but here I was with no more than a few dollars in my own pocket and a wife and kids at home who barely had enough to eat over a weekend. Who would know if I took even one ten-dollar bill over the weekend as long as I could get it back by Monday at 3:00 p.m.? Or better, just write it off as a discrepancy. In those moments of temptation, a lot goes through one's mind. What if somehow I got caught, or what if this would lead to larger crimes, or what would this really do to me as a person, or does God really see such things? What was worse, I knew others who occasionally did such things, and they never got caught.

The temptation for the righteous to envy and copy the behavior of the wicked is great. But Proverbs makes it very clear:

> Do not enter the path of the wicked,
> And do not proceed in the way of evil men.
> Avoid it, do not pass by it;
> Turn away from it and pass on. (4:14-15)

> The righteous one considers the house of the wicked,
> Turning the wicked to ruin. (21:12)

It wasn't too long after working at the teller job that the FBI came in and gave lie-detector tests to all the employees. Shortly after that, one of our employees "disappeared" rather suddenly. Our manager figured the employee had embezzled close to fifty thousand dollars over a five-year period! I was glad I had wrestled within myself over entering the evil way and had won over the temptation. But I was still tempted to envy the one who got away!

The Righteous Are Not to Envy the Wicked
The reality Proverbs paints is that the wicked has no real future, so why should the righteous envy his life? Wisdom warns,

> Do not fret because of evildoers,
> Or be envious of the wicked;
> For there will be no future for the evil man;
> The lamp of the wicked will be put out. (24:19-20)

We usually don't have the opportunity to see the people we envy die. We see them when they are on top, in the public eye, on "Lives of the Rich and Famous." But we are not there in the hospital room when they are dying of AIDS, or cancer, or loneliness. We are not there in their drug rehab, or when they just crashed their two-hundred-thousand-dollar Ferrari and are paralyzed for life. No, we don't see their end, their later days. We are envious of what we see in the present, not the future. The more the righteous reflects, the freer he becomes of envy of the wicked.

In fact, the righteous is called to far more than just becoming free of envy toward the wicked. He is to become politically active and stand in his way.

The Righteous Are to Stand In the Way of the Wicked
Somewhere between the 1920s and 1976 the evangelical church went crazy.[22] We thought we could separate massively from the larger society, build our own Christian institutions, keep our kids in the fold of Christendom, and

ensure a godly heritage for the next generation. But, it seems to me, something was forgotten: We overlooked the serious ill effects the wicked could have on society over time, when Christians removed themselves from the public sector. In leaving the significant public, "secular" realms, we left education, politics, science, and the media to those having no real moral consensus of values. Proverbs chides this kind of thinking:

Like a trampled spring and a polluted well
Is a righteous man who gives way before the wicked.
　(25:26)

But to those who rebuke the wicked will be delight,
And a good blessing will come upon them. (24:25)

The clear teaching of these passages is that the righteous have a moral imperative to stand in the way of the wicked. Otherwise, the wickedness of men will muddy the pure waters of righteousness to the blame of the righteous for not standing up to them and blocking their way to the streams. The wicked need to be rebuked and rebuked by those of moral integrity, the righteous!

Today our nation is as polluted as the waters of the Hudson, the Delaware, and the Mississippi. The only way to stop the pollution is to prevent the dumping! Perhaps the righteous need to gather together and form an MEPA, a Moral Environment Protection Agency! But the ultimate question is not what the righteous will do about the wicked, but how God views them.

THE HOPE FOR THE WICKED

The news is not really good for the wicked person. Only one passage, Proverbs 16:6, gives a little hope for this person:

By lovingkindness and truth iniquity is atoned for,
And by the fear of the LORD one keeps away from evil.

The verse positions two concepts before the reader: atonement (*kaphar*) and avoidance (*sur*). The twin attributes of lovingkindness (*hesed*) and truth form the ground of God's relation to all men. Apparently, as God looks down on sinful humanity, His covenant love for His human creation and His commitment to truth are resolved in the concept of blood atonement. The portrait I have of how our righteous God looks upon us is what Job does for his own kids. Being a righteous man, but concerned about even the potential sins his children might commit, he offers a burnt offering for them. Just in case! (Job 1:5). We also know that God put a unique provision in Israel's sacrificial system. Each Israelite (male) was to bring his own sacrifice, but once a year on the Day of Atonement the high priest confessed the sins of all Israelites upon the head of a live goat. This first and only true scapegoat was then led into the wilderness and released (Leviticus 16:20-22). The picture is clear. There existed a provision for even those who weren't yet in a condition to acknowledge their own sin.

Today, the wicked has a provision in the Lamb who died, was raised, and returned to Heaven. The hope for the wicked is that they turn to the Savior, saying, "Be merciful to me, a sinner." In doing this, they are turning to God and learning to fear Him, which is the key to turning away from evil (16:6). The writer of Proverbs affirms,

> The LORD has made everything for its own purpose,
> Even the wicked for the day of the evil. (16:4)

God uses even the evil of men to praise Him. It may be the evil that evil men have done that brings them to both the need and knowledge of a redeemer!

▪ S I X ▪
The Wealthy

If I were rich man, I would . . .
TEVEYA
FIDDLER ON THE ROOF

▼

The rich man's wealth is his strong city.
PROVERBS 10:15, KJV

B eing raised in a midwestern, middle class family in the U.S., I was not really knowledgeable of the classifications of rich and poor. I guess that's one of the benefits of the great American middle class. You are sandwiched between people who have more and others who have less. Therefore, the categories of rich and poor become somewhat arbitrary and meaningless. I had friends who lived in smaller houses and friends who lived in much larger ones. Some had swimming pools in their back yards (a big deal then), while others had railroad tracks. Personally, I thought the railroad tracks were more fun than the swimming pools! But I didn't think much about it. It wasn't until I graduated from college and got exposed to a much larger slice of the world that I realized the words *rich* and *poor* truly applied to some people.

My first year out of college I spent touring the eastern United States with a Christian singing group. We gave concerts on university campuses, where we would perform a segment of popular songs and then in the second half give our Christian testimonies. Even though our audiences were college students,

79

our benefactors and supporters were largely the wealthy and those with discretionary incomes. As a result, sometimes we were invited to the homes of heavy contributors to both our cause and our organization. It was the first time in my life I remember being in homes of people I would definitely call wealthy. Estates, complete with maids, servants, governesses for children, and such, were the commonplace elements of their lives. They were the rich.

Many years later I found myself teaching in the country of Bolivia, the poorest country in the southern hemisphere of the Americas. I remember the day I got my shoes shined in the Cochabamba square. At the time, the American dollar was equivalent to three thousand Bolivian pesos. The average Bolivian income was around the equivalent of two hundred American dollars a year. Having finished shining my shoes, the little Bolivian boy looked up at me. I asked, *"Quantos qesta?"* (How much?)

He answered, *"Centos"* (One hundred).

I quickly figured in my head how much that was in American money and was shocked. Less than one cent! I then realized how poor this country was. I have never gotten over the feeling. One Bolivian friend felt my embarrassment when he asked me how much my camera cost. When he realized it was over half the Bolivian annual income, he said, "Don't worry, anyone who can get here, or who has a ticket out of here, is wealthy." It was the first time in my life I was viewed (correctly) as being wealthy. It was a very uncomfortable feeling for me. In the U.S., I had "felt" poor many times, but never rich. In Bolivia, I was rich.

The conditions of wealth and poverty are both very real conditions. We can play very pious games about being "poor in spirit" or "rich in Christ," but we all live in a material world where we must pay our bills, taxes, and living expenses in real, material dollars—even though they are terribly inflated! Some people *are* rich and some *are* poor.

It is this fact of life that Proverbs addresses. To be wise about life, we must have a clear understanding of how money influences our life. We must understand the realities the rich face and develop sympathy and sensitivity toward the poor. To develop the skill of living our lives rightly before both God and man, we must understand the wealthy.

What we find here are the simple facts of life. As one writer suggests, "Some folk are rich and others poor. Some can afford all the luxuries of life; others have to struggle to make ends meet; while many are destitute. That is a fact of life. Israel's sages accepted the fact; they did not try to change it. They were neither political economists or social reformers."[1] Even though Proverbs has much to say about the poor and being compassionate toward them, the main focus in Proverbs is on wealth and its advantages and realities. But before getting into what Proverbs has to say to us about the wealthy, I should define some terms.

In the book of Proverbs, two main words get translated "wealth" or "riches." The first one, *'ashar*, is translated "be or become rich" and is related to the Arabic idea of "abundance of herbage, and goods."[2] Hence, in biblical times, wealth was measured in agricultural terms. He who had the most and biggest crops and the biggest house had the most toys! The other term, *hon*, picks up the ideas of "being easy, or gentleness of mind and in the noun form, substance."[3] The genteel life of the gentleman farmer is more in view with this term. One who has money can live a pastoral, stress-free life with gentleness of mind. This word apparently also picks up the aspect of having a lot of stuff (substance), which is the symbol of one's wealth. Societies never change; only the nature and price tags of their stuff and toys change! So what does Proverbs have to teach us about being wise in regard to the wealthy?

It tells us how to obtain wealth, what it can do for us, how the wealthy are characterized by it, and a couple of things that are even better than it. If you are curious to find out such things, read on.

HOW TO OBTAIN WEALTH

Most of us remember the commercial. The closing line was, "Smith-Barney"—remember the punch line?—"we make money the old-fashioned way . . . we earn it." Despite the fact that the old-fashioned way of earning money was inheriting it, this commercial strikes very deep into the American psyche. Legitimate money is earned money. To have legitimate wealth, it must have been earned in good old hard but honest work.

Wealth Obtained by Hard Work

I would not call my father wealthy. But all he had was earned by working hard and moving up the corporate ladder. He took extra jobs and was willing to work in another town with an inconvenient commute in order to support his family better. He was usually at work an hour before the employees he managed arrived, and he stayed at least an hour or two after the closing whistle.

I inherited far more than wealth from my father. I inherited a model of a father who worked hard for the sake of his family. Proverbs affirms this work ethic:

Poor is he who works with a negligent hand,
But the hand of the diligent makes rich. (10:4)

This is the old-fashioned way of becoming wealthy. The palm of slackness (literal translation) produces nothing but an empty hand, while the active, daily, diligent palm produces a hand that is filled with good things. The Jewish (and Protestant) ethic has always exalted the dignity of work and its essential place in the scheme of life.[4] Certainly God's instruction in the Ten Commandments to work six days and rest one has set the pattern for the dignity and value of industry throughout most of the Western world (Exodus 20:9-10). Saint Paul also chided one of his missionary congregations for tolerating those who refused to work with their hands as the apostles did (2 Thessalonians 3:10-11).

Work is an activity that not only has inherent meaning and dignity for the support of one's life, it is also the first and probably foremost way of becoming wealthy. However, just because one happens to be wealthy does not mean one has obtained the wealth by hard work. There is another way wealth can be obtained.

Wealth Obtained Through Inheritance

As mentioned earlier, the true old-fashioned way to wealth was through inheritance. Many today are wealthy, but not through their own ambition and years of hard work. They merely happened to be born into the right family or married a wealthy spouse. Some women have outlived their husbands and have become terribly rich ladies, not through their own hard work, but through good fortune, long life, and luck! Again, Proverbs affirms this second means of appropriating wealth: "House and wealth are an inheritance from fathers" (19:14). My literal translation would be, "A house and lots of stuff is the inheritance of fathers."

Proverbs simply declares this kind of appropriated wealth a reality. It gives no comment as to whether this reality is ethically good or bad; it just is. We all know it just is. Some people happen to have been born into such wealth, others marry into it. It just is. In my opinion, it's a pretty good way to become wealthy, even though it has a downside. But there is another way to become wealthy, one that has a clearer moral value to it.

Wealth Obtained by Oppression of the Poor

From our enlightened twentieth-century perspective, it is hard to imagine Western, educated, Christianized men and women tolerating and promoting the evil of slavery. Taking another human being away from his native country, family, and culture and packing him into a slave ship to go around the world is virtually unthinkable today. What could have motivated these people? The same thing that motivates men and women to become incredibly wealthy today—greed mixed with oppression. Proverbs again notes, "He who oppresses the poor to increase his wealth and he who gives gifts to the rich—both come to poverty" (22:16).[5] Even though the translation is rough and difficult to make parallel, Cohen clarifies: "The first clause declares that it is possible to increase wealth by dishonest gain."[6] Ross agrees: "Oppressing the lowly is gain." Literally, to the one who oppresses the poor there is muchness. Merchants without conscience increased their muchness through the trade of human beings.

Likewise today, in the streets of our major cities, men and women trade on the addictions and pleasures of other human beings, who through drug sales become millionaires in a short time. Proverbs, once and for all, should purge our meritocratic thinking that just because someone is wealthy, that person has earned his money fairly and honestly. It's amazing how we fall into thinking that the very presence of money and power justifies its own existence. But here Proverbs does reveal that an ultimate judgment will fall and the unjust gain will fail. Just as it is a waste of good money to try to bribe the wealthy, so is the process of becoming wealthy off others' misery.

I still remember reading an article written by a Swiss physician who said he had serious ethical problems with his American counterparts. How could American (even Christian) physicians become so wealthy off the ills of humanity? He felt it was not only very unchristian but terribly unethical in principle. In his closing remarks, he likened the profession to nineteenth-century slavery, whereby southern landowners and owners of British and French trading companies lived like kings because of their profit off the pain of others. At least it is something to think about!

In the early 1900s, American industrial capitalists became rich beyond the dream of kings. In 1900, Andrew Carnegie's steel mills brought him $25 million, and that was before inflation and income tax even existed. In 1913, John D. Rockefeller made $900 million. Some have noted that what created the need for labor unions in this country was the rampant unjust working conditions and near slave-labor conditions in these first American companies.

Proverbs tells it like it is. Wealth can be obtained by the overt oppression of the poor. But is this kind of wealth appropriate to being a wise person? Of course not, but the reality and possibility of this kind of wealth are always there wooing us to come and have a try. But there is even another way to become wealthy.

Wealth by Extortion

I live in Philadelphia. We have a lot of Italian Mafia jokes here. But some are not all that funny because they are true. A recent one goes like this: "Did you know that at the Melrose Diner (in South Philly) there are two sections now?" Answer: "No, I didn't know that. What are they?" Punch line: "Shooting and nonshooting."

The reason this is both funny and sobering is because we have been in the middle of a mob power play ever since our leading mobster was indicted and sent to prison. One evening a mob hit took place right in front of the diner, thus creating the typical Philadelphia humor. One of the primary, long-standing means the mob has used in obtaining money is extortion. By threatening to burn down stores, kill relatives, or smear personal reputations, the "family" extorts money in return for protection from themselves. The threat of violence is all that is usually needed to make the exchange happen.

Proverbs faces this reality squarely and again merely acknowledges its existence and profitability. In a somewhat strange parallel we are told,

> A gracious woman attains honor,
> And the violent men attain riches. (11:16)

The violent men here translates the Hebrew term *'orits*, which means "one who puts terror" into someone.[7] It carries the idea of obtaining something by force or threats or some other illegal compulsion. Violent men are those who strike terror into someone in order to achieve their purpose: to become wealthy or achieve other political ends.

In the past couple of decades we have seen terror become somewhat institutionalized as an effective means of gaining political power and recognition. One expert writes, "It could well be, then, that there are now more conditions conducive to terrorism, that more people may see terrorism as the only way to remedy their problems, that more people have access to the means to effect terrorist intentions, and that technological changes have produced circumstances greatly increasing the leverage and power which may be exercised by terrorist methods." In short, "Terrorism is now an export industry."[8] In other words, terror is a very effective way of increasing one's wealth and power. By threats of violence one can accumulate wealth or gain what one wants.

The contrast in the proverb is highly instructive. Power and violence can obtain wealth, but true honor is seen in the gracious spirit of a woman. Again, Proverbs counsels us to be wise about life. We are tempted by the use of power and violence to achieve what we want. But graciousness brings a true and respectable honor. Which do we want? It is our choice about what kind of life we want. But there are some more positive ways of obtaining wealth. One is, believe it or not, through humility.

Humility Can Bring Wealth

I know a man who by all the world's standards is wealthy. Yet to be around this man is to be struck by his utter humility. Over a period of several years, I occasionally had lunch with him. He would always ask me about my life, what was happening in my ministry, how my kids were doing, etc. He was genuinely interested in me, unlike so many other wealthy folks I had known. Now, I'm not sure how, in the economy of God, he actually obtained his wealth. But one thing this experience taught me was that wealth and humility could coexist. Wealth does not have to puff up or put one on a massive power trip. So, by argument, perhaps humility can bring about a certain kind of wealth. Proverbs agrees. Our sage writes,

> The reward of humility and the fear of the LORD
> Are riches, honor and life. (22:4)

Ross observes that the passage contains "two spiritual qualifications (humility and fear) and then three rewards."[9]

The implicit promise is that piety (humility and fear) can produce the triune rewards of wealth, honor, and life. Even
though it is hard to conceive of anyone in our culture today
rewarding piety with money or honors, Wisdom does tell us
these can come to one of such fear and humility.

Related to humility is another source of wealth, wisdom
itself.

Wealth Comes by Wisdom

The feminine sage who has taken us on this search for wisdom
tells us she personally rewards her followers with material
benefits. She says,

> Long life is in her right hand;
> In her left hand are riches and honor. (3:16)

> Riches and honor are with me,
> Enduring wealth and righteousness. (8:18)

> By wisdom a house is built,
> And by understanding it is established;
> And by knowledge the rooms are filled
> With all precious and pleasant riches. (24:3-4)

Put more simply, "The crown of the wise is their riches"
(14:24).

These passages all argue that one of the rewards for being
a wise person is wealth. They might be combined with other
passages about making wise financial decisions and not taking
bribes or pledges, but the principle still stands. Wealth can be
the delightful fruit of wisdom. And unlike wealth obtained by
other means, this wealth apparently endures. Because the person obtaining the riches is wise, he also knows how to use
money wisely once he has it. Therefore, it endures. Wealth
accompanied by wisdom beautifully adorns the person.
Wealth, according to the wisdom literature, is the fitting decor
of the wise. The fool may be rich, but it doesn't fit his character. But the wise can graciously wear the apparel of wealth, a
clothing that fits perfectly.

Wealth attributed to the wise is apparently a wealth not sought, but is a reward for seeking wisdom rather than wealth. It is like Solomon's wealth. When given a blank check from God, Solomon sought, not riches or honors or the lives of his enemies, but the necessary wisdom to lead his people. Because of his "wise" choice God gave him both wisdom and wealth (2 Chronicles 1:10-11). When wisdom is present, the wealth given does not become a pitfall but a springboard for many other wise endeavors.

When I reflect on the differing monetary stations of the many people I have known during my fifty-some years of life, I can draw a couple of conclusions. First, the happiest people I have ever known are those who are wealthy. Second, the unhappiest people I have ever known are those who are wealthy! I can actually take it further. Some of the happiest people I have known are the poorest I have come in contact with (Bolivians). At the same time, some of the unhappiest people I have met are those whose poverty has completely stripped them of all dignity and worth as human beings (the street people of Philadelphia).

What makes the difference? Wisdom. Some have the skill of properly using their wealth to enrich their own lives and the lives of others. The unhappy ones have never learned this skill. They use and abuse their wealth in foolish schemes, scams, and shams. They are not wise about money or the people to whom they entrust it. Consequently, they themselves are the losers in the long run.

But there is still one more way to become wealthy. Through the unique blessing of God!

Wealth as the Unique Blessing of God

Many today have fallen under the spell of the "prosperity gospel." For those who haven't heard of it, these folks believe God has promised to make every believer prosperous and wealthy. Of course, the means of obtaining this blessing is by giving large sums of money to the evangelist's organization, or by signing over the title deed of one's house to the person.

These actions are viewed as the "seeds" that must be sown in order to reap the large harvest at a later date. I know many who are still waiting for their crop of wealth to come in. Meanwhile, the leader's barns are well stocked.

I seriously doubt both the integrity of the person who makes such claims and his ability to understand the totality of biblical teaching on the subject of wealth. From our study in this chapter alone, we should realize that there are many ways to become wealthy. Proverbs serves as a reality check to show us that mere wealth cannot automatically be equated with God's blessing. However, at the same time, from Proverbs we do learn that there is a special, unique blessing from God that makes one wealthy. Our teacher writes,

> It is the blessing of the LORD that makes rich,
> And He adds no sorrow to it. (10:22)

This verse affirms a contrast between the wealth obtained by men, which brings pain and sorrow, and the wealth God provides, which doesn't. Apparently, this second type of wealth can be enjoyed with a peaceful heart and clear conscience. Out of God's goodness, He gives a wealth that is both undeserved and unsought and brings with it enough peace of mind to use and enjoy it to the glory of God. The word translated "sorrow" here picks up the "garden under judgment" language that was placed upon the first couple as a result of sin. The pain and sorrow (*'etzev*) with which man must now labor is said to be removed from this kind of wealth. In other words, psychological pain or fear of possible loss is not found among the people God has blessed with this kind of wealth.

I admit I don't have a clear understanding of this verse. In simpler language, it affirms that there is a blessing that comes from God alone that bestows riches upon a person. There exists no ground for this gift other than the unconditioned and benevolent grace of God. Nothing in the person has earned it or deserved it. It is a sheer gift of grace, like salvation. This may be the thought on Paul's mind when he tells Timothy to "instruct those who are rich in this present world not to be conceited or to fix their hope on the uncertainty of riches, but on God, who richly supplies us with all things to enjoy" (1 Timothy 6:17). The gift of riches that God gives can be enjoyed simply because the wise person does not trust in it or is not conceited about it. He merely accepts it for what it is, the unique blessing of God!

This is obviously the kind of wealth we would all desire. To have God supernaturally bless us with winning the lottery or the *Reader's Digest* Sweepstakes would be the greatest of blessings, right? Wrong! If we truly desire wisdom, we must be attuned to what wisdom suggests. Wisdom says, don't wait around hoping to win the lottery; be responsible, work hard; don't give in to the hand of slackness. No one knows what will or will not happen in the future. Therefore, be wise, seek wisdom, and if wealth comes, then it is the gift of God to be enjoyed and shared. If it doesn't, then you will have other rewards of wisdom. Perhaps honors, or life itself. Just being wise is a unique reward by itself.

We all have plans for that lottery money (if we win, of course): Buy a bigger home, pay off our existing one, send the kids to college, buy a new car. However, the realism Proverbs presents about wealth is not so much aimed at the toys we can buy when we have money but the deeper psycho-spiritual issues that wealth represents. Wealth can do much more than empower us to collect more stuff!

· S E V E N ·

The Wealthy and the Poor

Wealth wants not for worship.
JOHN CLARK[1]

▼

A good name is to be more desirable than riches.
PROVERBS 22:1

We moved to Philadelphia's Main Line area from Texas. In the South we became accustomed to southern hospitality. When we had moved into our home in Dallas, our move became a community effort. We got to know our neighbors and we enjoyed the warm, open, and helpful friendships that emerged.

But the Northeast is different. As one southerner put it, "The people in the East are not mad because they are cold (emotionally). They are cold because they are cold"! Well put. But I must defend to a certain extent where I live. The climate is tougher, and the people move and talk much faster, but underneath there are some unusual touches of caring.

Having said that, let me return to when we arrived. The only house we could afford was on the bottom of a buyer's market. We made an offer on the house before it was even listed and wrapped up the deal the day we first saw it! But the price tag was low for a reason. If you have ever seen the movie *The Money Pit*, you know what I am talking about. Every time we pulled off wallpaper or old paneling, we found not only another surprise but another big bill. With few friends, I would ask advice from my neighbors and the few acquaintances we had made. I even asked total strangers in our church for help on our house. I learned quickly that help on the Main Line was spelled differently than in the South. Help in the South means people coming over and helping me put a drain around the house so water won't come in under the walls (which it did). On Philly's Main Line, help means giving out the carefully protected name (and telephone number) of the best lawnscape and drainage man. By the end of our first month, I had plenty of names, but our home was still a wreck. The reason was simple. I was a pastor on a very limited income, with no savings or reserve. To those who have such things, life is easy or, I should say, easier. Even though the wealthy do develop their negative whines—"Oh, my goodness, do you know it took me a whole month to get Bruce out to do my window treatments!"—it's tough to work up too much sympathy. And the fact that Bruce charged her ten thousand dollars to do the job is beside the point. Life is rough when one has to wait so long. The point of this extended whine is that one of the things wealth can do for you is to give you a sense of financial power or security.

Wealth Brings Security

Several of the Proverbs affirm this reality:

> The rich man's wealth is his fortress,
> The ruin of the poor is their poverty. (10:15)

> A rich man's wealth is his strong city. (18:11)

When one does not have a large trust fund, savings account, or other liquid resources that can be converted to cash for the unexpected emergencies, one learns the reality of this proverb quickly. The trust fund, or growth account, is his fortress and the walls of his protected city. Money protects the rich man from being taken down by the normal misfortunes of life. Wealth affords a reserve and a source of quick help.

The poor do not have this benefit, therefore they are wiped out by even small misfortunes. It wasn't too long ago in our own home that the repair bill for a broken-down car took two weeks' worth of food. The options were few. Either fix the car (our only source of transportation) and eat peanut-butter sandwiches for two weeks; or not fix the car, eat normally, but have no way to get to work!

The reality is that the wealthy have more options. They have a strong city, a high, thick wall that fends off normal attacks. But this protection is not as secure as they may think. The whole of 18:11 says,

> A rich man's wealth is his strong city,
> And like a high wall in his own imagination.

Here our sage lets us in on a secret: The rich only imagine they are secure. Their security is in their heads. Ross comments, "Wealthy people often assume that their wealth brings security . . . any protection wealth may bring is limited."[2] Another proverb is even more frontal about this misperception: "He who trusts in his riches will fall" (11:28).

Again, Proverbs states the reality: The wealthy trust in their riches, but this trust is displaced. It is not a secure trust. Psalm 49 makes this very clear. How quickly we have seen millionaires go broke when a prosperous economy peaks out. I am told there is even an "ex-millionaires fellowship" in Texas, a sort of well-heeled (or well-healed) support group of Christian ex-millionaires who are trying to reach out to other ex-millionaires for the cause of Christ. For many of them, the dream of wealth both came and ended quickly.

In addition to providing a certain delusional security, wealth also buys friends.

Wealth Buys Friends

As repeated in the Proverbs, money does buy friends. The lives of the rich and famous attract us all. We want to see how they live, where they dine, and where they take their fantasy getaway vacations. We live vicariously through their wealth.

Proverbs affirms this reality without much ethical comment:

> The poor is hated even by his neighbor [friend],
> But those who love the rich are many. (14:20)

The Talmud records, "At the door of misery there are no brothers and no friends."[3] The irony of our inner cities is expressed in this proverb. When one looks at the misery of our large cities, one does not see brother helping brother, but friend turning on friend, and brother *killing* brother! Poverty breeds hatred for the poor, while wealth attracts those who just want to be around the rich.

Unfortunately, even the ministry falls into this trap. Pastors and presidents of Christian organizations can so cultivate the deep pockets of the wealthy that they unwittingly compromise the ethics of Christ and the admonition of Saint James. I don't think I have ever heard a message on James 5:1-3—"Come now, you rich, weep and howl for your miseries [of being rich!] which are coming upon you. Your riches have rotted and your garments have become moth-eaten. Your gold and your silver have rusted; and their rust will be witness against you and will consume your flesh like fire." Heavy stuff.

Proverbs gives us the reality and tendencies of our own hearts. I would much rather be with the wealthy than the poor. I am far more attracted to up-and-outers than to down-and-outers. Both need ministry. But Proverbs shows me the rank reality that money does buy friends.

For the rich, their money also buys them something else. Their money makes them excellent targets for ransom.

Wealth Ransoms One's Life
Proverbs states the reality of the wealthy in very pointed terms:

> The ransom of a man's life is his riches,
> But the poor hears no rebuke. (13:8)

Ross notes, "The rich person is exposed to legal and powerful assaults and uses his wealth as ransom. The poor is free from blackmail and so ignores the attack and endures the consequences of difficulties."[4]

This is again a good news–bad news reality. The good news is that the rich have the means to pay a ransom. The bad news is that, because they have money, they are the targets of ransom. No one, in my fifty years, has asked me for a ransom yet! The poor do not have that worry. It is the rich who must carry insurance, simply because their assets are targets.

This raises an even more pointed question. Are the wealthy protected by their wealth and insurance and other perks? Another proverb says no.

> Riches do not profit in the day of wrath,
> But righteousness delivers from death. (11:4)

Wealth may buy off a man's prosecutor, kidnaper, or opposer, but what about when total economic collapse occurs? Scripture is clear. Wealth will not save one from the day of God's total economic judgment on a land. The prophet Ezekiel, speaking for the Lord, envisions the reality of what this looks like:

> "They [the rich] shall fling their silver into the streets, and their gold shall become an abhorrent thing; their silver and their gold shall not be able to deliver them in the day of the wrath of the Lord. They cannot satisfy their appetite, nor can they fill their stomachs, for their iniquity has become an occasion of stumbling." (Ezekiel 7:19)

Some remember the total economic collapse of 1929. My mother and father remember having money and going to the bank, but not being able to get it out. The men and women who lived during the Great Depression remember what money essentially is—nothing. It is only useful as long as it is honored and recognized, but you can't eat it. In the Depression, at least farmers were in some ways better off than city folk. They could eat off the land! Most people my age and younger don't believe this could ever happen again. Others believe there is another major economic collapse coming. I don't know. I'm no prophet. But I do know that all money and wealth is a fragile commodity. With most money being nothing more than mathematical images on a computer screen, our entire monetary system is even more precarious than in 1929.

Money and wealth may provide a ransom for one's life from those who want what the wealthy have. But money does not provide a safe refuge when God's judgment falls. The ones who find safety in the middle of God's judgment are those who have cultivated a righteous life. Even though the proverb does not explain how the righteous are delivered, it does say they are literally "plucked" or "snatched" from the upheaval.[5]

I have friends who have emigrated to Israel. Being Jewish Christians, their life in Israel is not always secure. Fellow Jews hate them for being Christians, and many of the Arab Christians hate them for being Jewish. But during the Gulf War, they saw how their lives (along with many others) could be protected in the middle of potential disaster. One night when incoming Scud missiles were landing in northern Tel Aviv, they donned their gas masks and took cover. The next morning, upon looking down into the playground across the street from their apartment building, they noticed an undetonated Scud missile lying on its side. It looked as if someone had carefully and softly laid it there. The bomb experts defused it and confirmed that it was very much live. But how did it get there, and why hadn't it gone off? The bomb experts didn't know. My friends knew. God had protected them. Angels had caught the Scud in flight and laid it gently in the field. The Gulf War, money, wealth, and power do not protect one's home. Apparently more safety was found in a righteous life!

But there is one more reality to the rich man's life. As noted above, money always buys political power.

Money Buys Power

The bumper sticker sums it up, "I owe, I owe, so off to work I go." Cute, humorous, but painfully true. Proverbs says,

> The rich rules over the poor,
> And the borrower becomes the lender's slave. (22:7)

I know the reality of the verse. The debt on our house, car, or credit cards shows me that the borrower ends up being owned by the lender. Hence, money buys power or rule over other people's lives. Again, this verse does not comment on the "oughtness" of the concept. It just places the stark reality before the reader. Taking money from those richer than us, whether it be the government, our employer, bank, or friends, places us in a master-slave relationship. Proverbs does have much more to say on the subject of debt (6:1-6, 22:27), but not here. The money paid back or the work done only increases the wealthy's power over the poor. It is a reality that most of us don't want to think about when we are on the debt side of the ledger. However, to those with the money to lend, it is a way to increase wealth and power. Wisdom must dictate the choices in this regard.

We summarize our discussion on the wealthy with two convenient ways, given by Proverbs, of characterizing those called "rich."

HOW THE WEALTHY ARE CHARACTERIZED

Country clubs are not exactly havens for the cultivation of wisdom. This may be a little sour grapes, as I've never belonged to one, but I have always had friends and relatives who did. That's the cheap way to receive the benefits of such places. But country clubs are places where you can learn much about the wealthy. Whether it is in the nineteenth-hole lounge or the more feminine dining rooms, the posture, appearance, and language of the people are fascinating. The wealthy are characterized by how they talk.

By Their Speech

Our sage informs us about the deportment of the rich:

> The poor man utters supplications,
> But the rich man answers roughly. (18:23)

The rich's tone of voice is peculiar to their income. Apparently, one's social status influences the tone of one's voice. The wealthy can speak harshly (*'azzot*), pointedly, and combatively. Their posture is not one of supplication. They don't ask if they can have something, they just demand it.

This has always amazed my with my own wife. Cinny always asks the waiter if she can have what is already on the menu. She is far more in the entreaty mode than I am. I just say what I want. The places where the rich dine, mingle, and do business are not characterized by politeness and propriety. The rich simply demand what they want. The poor have no other option but to plead for mercy (*tahanunim*) in order to obtain what they need.

Speech is a telltale sign of the wealthy. To the rich man, the poor man's speech is supplicating; to the poor man, the rich man's speech is humiliating. But the rich are also character-ized by their own self-delusion.

By Their Self-Delusion

I believe we are all a little self-deluded. But Proverbs 28:11 informs us that the rich are very deluded about themselves:

> The rich man is wise in his own eyes,
> But the poor who has understanding sees through him.

> There is one who pretends to be rich, but has nothing;
> Another pretends to be poor, but has great wealth. (13:7)

Back to my country-club scene. Listening in on the con-versations of the wealthy and watching them play their golf and do their lunches, I am always struck by the rampant artificiality. It often appears to me that these are the "hollow" people—people who appear well and talk powerfully, but underneath there is no one home.

I once had one of these country-club wives, named Virginia, in counseling. At one point in our conversation I paused and said, "Who is Virginia?" She looked at me with a smile on her face. Then her perfectly contoured body and face-lifted countenance slowly began to change. Finally she looked a little puzzled and said, "I don't know. Who do you want me to be?" A hollow, shallow human, all dressed up, doing lunch and making politically correct conversation, but no one was really at home. Her wealth was in her head.

The man or woman who has wealth without wisdom is wise only in his or her own eyes, but even the poor man can see through it. A literal translation of 28:11 reads, "Wise in his own eyes is a man of wealth, but the poor with understanding sees through it to expose it for what it is."[6] The poor man, aided only by the insight gained through wisdom, can see the wealthy for what they are. Many pretend to be rich while they are poor, but many of the truly rich (those with wisdom) pretend by their humility to be poor. Wisdom apparently is no respecter of social rank. Which raises a question: If wisdom isn't, why are we?

For those who still want to win the lottery and become wealthy, let me remind you of two things that are better than wealth.

THREE THINGS BETTER THAN WEALTH

As good and valuable as wealth may seem, Proverbs puts the material side of life into perspective. Wealth has its upside and its downside. But there are three things that are better than wealth. The first is what is so lacking in our culture today, *integrity*.

Integrity Is Better than Wealth

Some things are better than others. Proverbs does present a hierarchy of values. Even though wealth is presented as a better state than poverty, the wisdom writers apparently wanted to demonstrate that wealth is not the highest of values. One's individual integrity is.

> Better is the poor who walks in his integrity,
> Than he who is crooked though he be rich. (28:6)

> Better is a poor man who walks in his integrity
> Than he who is perverse in speech and is a fool. (19:1)

> Better is a little with righteousness
> Than great income with injustice. (16:8)

> A good name is to be more desired than great riches. (22:1)

These proverbs make it very clear: One's personal integrity in life is what is most important. The Hebrew word for integrity, *tom*, comes from the verbal root meaning "to be complete."[7] Integrity, then, brings up the idea of wholeness or wholeheartedness.[8] Taken together, these proverbs then present integrity as a certain purity in speech (19:1) and action (28:6), which constitutes righteousness (16:8). Even though the man or woman may not have the riches of this world, integrity of heart and purity of life constitute a much greater net worth than money or riches. We can watch the constant parade of wealthy rock stars, politicians, and Hollywood starlets who in some way or another have sold their souls to become famous, rich, and powerful. Most have little integrity. Proverbs stands as a beacon shedding the light of a better way. Wisdom says, "Don't compromise your integrity to gain more power or wealth or status." A good reputation is far better than having the public know your name (22:1)!

There is one more thing that is also better than wealth. Reverence for God.

Reverence for God Is Better than Wealth

I have often wondered how the Levites felt when they were all lined up with their fellow Israelites after crossing the Jordan

River. God had promised His people shares in the Promised Land. When Joshua began parceling out the real estate under God's direction (Joshua 13:7), I'm sure each of the tribes waited with anticipation to see what portion of the land would be theirs. Judah got theirs, Ephraim and Manasseh likewise. Benjamin and Simeon got their sections, along with Zebulun and Issachar. Then came Asher, Naphtali, and Dan. Reuben and Gad even got theirs. The tribe of Levi waited patiently. Finally, the entire list had been called, and they knew they had to be next. At last, their name was called, but instead of giving the boundaries of their piece of real estate, Joshua simply said, "For the tribe of Levi, their inheritance is the Lord" (see Joshua 13:14). "The Lord?!" "What a ripoff!" "Everyone else gets land, but we get the Lord?!" I'm sure there were some upset and jealous Levites, human nature being what it is. But the text is truthful. The tribe of Levi would get the Lord and service in His tabernacle and, later, temple. Their wealth had to be found not in real estate but in the fear and service of the Lord. Though Deuteronomy 8:1-8 makes it clear about the land division, I still conceive some of these Levites as secretly hoping for a more material inheritance. So it is for all of us. Proverbs says,

> Better is a little with the fear of the LORD,
> Than great treasure and turmoil with it. (15:16)

Two realities grow out of this proverb. First, submitting to the Lord and His way of life brings a certain tranquility and peace. In the parallel, turmoil is in contrast with "fear of the LORD." Hence, fear of the Lord brings peace and removes turmoil. Second, it affirms that wealth brings with it its own added anxiety. The more stuff we accumulate, the more we have to insure it against loss, and the more insurance we have, the more we have to pay to buy it, and on and on. Accumulation just adds to mental and physical consternation. But the simple fear of the Lord in one's life (even when wealthy) can be an antidote to this anxiety. In this sense, to fear the Lord is better than wealth.

But wealth has one more somewhat cryptic quality. It's not as good as moderation.

Moderation Is Better than Wealth

One desire (prayer) of Agur was a life with moderation and balance. He asks,

> Two things I asked of Thee,
> Do not refuse me before I die:
> Keep deception and lies far from me,
> Give me neither poverty nor riches;
> Feed me with the food that is my portion,
> Lest I be full and deny Thee and say, "Who is the LORD?"
> Or lest I be in want and steal,
> And profane the name of my God. (30:7-9)

As noted earlier in this book, I was tempted very strongly when I was a bank teller to "borrow" money over a weekend. Why? Because I was broke. The temptation is real. Poverty can drive even the most committed to God to steal and thus deny their Lord.

At the same time, wealth has its own corrupting influence on our lives. It does empower us, but often in ungodly ways. When we are full of ourselves and our wealth, we are prone to becoming self-sufficient and likewise denying the Lord, by forgetting who He is. We may acknowledge Him, even say we trust Him, but we are probably more realistically trusting in our bank account. In many ways, it is harder for the wealthy than the poor to trust in God. The poor have no option. The wealthy do, and besides, no one ever knows what or who he is trusting, except the Lord Himself. I can say I am trusting God with something, but when I have the financial capital to do it without the Lord, who really knows in what I am trusting? So Agur prays for moderation. To have enough to live on, so either self-sufficiency or poverty might not drive him to extremes. Both extremes bring about the same result, which is denial of God and denial of wisdom. One can be wealthy and wise, but it is much harder than being wise with much less.

Throughout this chapter, the focus has been on the wealthy. But in this final section I want to demonstrate that Proverbs also has much to say specifically about the poor. In a nutshell, those called wealthy do have a moral responsibility toward the poor. The wisdom literature, in an attempt to bring about social justice, does mandate care and concern for those less fortunate.

WHAT ABOUT THE POOR?

When I am in center-city Philadelphia the panhandlers are present everywhere. Some just sit on the sidewalk and take the more passive strategy with their tin can or plate clearly visible for your offerings. Some are even developing integrity and just say, "Change for booze." For most of us, these moments are confrontations of culture. As Phil Collins sings in his song, "It's just another day in paradise" until a homeless person stops us.

What do we do? Do we look the other way, or put something in their hand, or take them and buy them breakfast? I usually walk by, but I don't feel good about it. There is something within me that says, "Do something." Especially when I have been told that 80 percent of the homeless men in my city are Vietnam vets. I have high regard for these never-honored men who sacrificed their adolescence, limbs, and lives for something they thought worthy enough to fight for. They need my support and care.

Proverbs is clear that regard or lack of regard for those in this category is not unconnected with my relationship with God.

Insulting the Poor Is an Insult to God

As I write this heading, I feel conviction upon my soul. Proverbs' assessment is radically different from my own natural one. It states:

He who mocks the poor reproaches his Maker. (17:5)
He who oppresses the poor reproaches his Maker,
But he who is gracious to the needy honors Him. (14:31)

Basically, my treatment of the poor illustrates how I treat the Lord. Ross observes, "How people treat the poor displays their faith in the Creator. Here is the doctrine of the Creation in its practical outworking. Anyone who oppresses the poor, shows contempt for his Maker, for that poor person also is the image of God."[9]

Jesus affirmed the same truth. When the hungry are hungry, it is Jesus who is hungry. When someone is sick, it is Jesus who is sick. When one is thirsty, Jesus is thirsty. When one is naked (unclothed), it is Jesus who is naked! (Matthew 25:31-46). It is easy to write off such passages as for an earlier age, but personally, every time I see a homeless person I wonder if Jesus isn't sitting there. The teaching is one of the most consistent in the Scriptures. Most of us just walk on, as the priest did on the old Jericho road after viewing the injured man.

More specifically, care for the poor is commanded in Proverbs.

Care of the Poor Is Commanded

Even though the wisdom literature generally gives us the practical realities of life without entering into ethical issues, on the subject of poverty, the texts are clear. The poor are to be granted honor and cared for. Many proverbs focus this concern:

> He who is generous will be blessed,
> For he gives some of his food to the poor. (22:9)

> He who is gracious to a poor man lends to the LORD,
> And He will repay him for his good deed. (19:17)

> He who shuts his ear to the cry of the poor
> Will also cry himself and not be answered. (21:13)

> He who gives to the poor will never want,
> But he who shuts his eyes will have many curses.
> (28:27)

Apparently, this is serious business to the Lord. Just as our lack of care toward the poor illustrates our lack of commitment to God, so our positive regard toward them brings God's blessing on our lives.

Where once Christians and nonChristians alike held a community spirit that valued philanthropy and mercy hospitals, today all has become institutionalized and put under government agencies. Anyone thinking that the government has made any real dent in helping the truly poor needs to spend some time in our ghettos. Some believe that, rather than helping, the government makes things worse.[10] This means the followers of Christ must return to the old tasks of charity and benevolence. We cannot afford any more to stay huddled in our secure suburbias believing it's "just another day in paradise." God commands and commends us otherwise. The simple reason for this admonition is that God is always concerned about those who lack the power to truly help themselves. Therefore, God commands their care and prohibits their abuse.

The Poor Are Not to Be Oppressed

The reason people are tempted to take candy from children is because it is so easy. (It never was with mine.) The poor, since they have no inherent power to defend themselves with either money or social strength, can easily fall victim to those who wish to use and abuse them for their own profit. Today the poor are used by politicians to solicit votes under the guise that they will genuinely care about their plight. But once elected, their poverty programs and platforms are used more for the political purpose of staying in power than truly helping those who are needy. It must have been equally true in the ancient world. Proverbs says,

> Do not rob the poor because he is poor,
> Or crush the afflicted at the gate. (22:22)

> There is a kind of man whose teeth are like swords,
> And his jaw teeth like knives,

> To devour the afflicted from the earth,
> And the needy from among men. (30:14)

To "crush the afflicted at the gate (22:22) means to deprive them of justice."[11] This is a major theme in the law court of Israel.

Even though it was apparently not followed (the prophet Micah condemns Israel for not following it [Micah 3:2-3]), the law clearly demanded that justice be done to the poor and repeatedly warns against denying them their rights (Exodus 22:22-24, Deuteronomy 10:17-18, Isaiah 1:23). The imagery here is of men with fangs ready to devour what little means the poor have. It seems so senseless to try to make a buck or obtain power by using and abusing the poor, but Scripture makes it clear that this is often the case. God, through Scripture, looks to human beings to have enough revelatory light within themselves that they will defend the poor, the widow, and the orphan. Saint James makes this observance the essence of the spiritual life (1:27).

Humans still fail in the God-ordained task of caring for the poor. As a reminder that God, even without human agency, sees the poor as worthy of care, Proverbs reveals God as the ultimate protector of the poor.

God Defends the Poor
Again, Proverbs does not suggest how God does the defending but merely states the reality of the intervention. Our wisdom collector writes,

> Do not rob the poor because he is poor,
> Or crush the afflicted at the gate;
> For the LORD will plead their case,
> And take the life of those who rob them. (22:22-23)

> The LORD will tear down the house of the proud,
> But He will establish the boundary of the widow.
>   (15:25)

Where humans fail in maintaining justice toward the poor, God still defends their case. Somehow, He defends their boundaries. Aiken notes, "The 'landmarks' (22:28; 23:10; 15:25) were stone pillars or cairns erected to mark out the boundaries between properties and to mark legal ownership. To remove these stones was regarded as a very serious offence (Deut 19:14; 27:17; Job 24:2) since it meant illegally depriving a family of their plot of land."[12]

What these verses acknowledge is the universal watch-care of God over the poor. He sees what happens to them and rewards or curses appropriately. As one of my first teachers said, God keeps the books, and He doesn't miss anything. All of us have the responsibility to do what we can to give the poor a sense of dignity and justice. Even when justice fails, as perhaps in the Holocaust, Somalia, Uganda, Bosnia, Cambodia, and other places where the rivers and extermination camps were red with blood, God sees the injustice. In the final portrait, God Himself defends the innocents (Revelation 20:12), and the guilty are judged.

When all the proverbs are looked at, the only conclusion that can be reached is the one given in Proverbs itself:

The rich and the poor have a common bond,
The LORD is the maker of them all. (22:2)

The rich and poor in God's created world live side by side. Both are realities in every culture of the world. Wealth has certain advantages, but so has poverty. The rich man is sued, while the poor is not. The rich has plenty of friends while the poor doesn't. But in the final analysis, God must be recognized in both lives. Wealth is never condemned, while the care of the poor is enjoined. In short, one can be wise in either poverty or wealth. If wealthy, you are not to oppress the poor but have respect and care for their estate. If poor, you can still have more wisdom than the rich in the country club set!

In short, we are all like Teveya, dreaming about what we

would do if we were rich, while having to be about our mundane, poor responsibilities every day. At least we can be wise about both poverty and our wealth!

The Child

They say, best men are moulded out of faults,
And, for the most, become much more better
For being a little bad.
WILLIAM SHAKESPEARE
MEASURE FOR MEASURE

▼

The father of the righteous will greatly rejoice,
And he who begets a wise son will be glad in him.
PROVERBS 23:24

Before my father passed away (in January '94), I remember telling him how concerned I was about having my sixteen-year-old son start driving a car. My father always had a quick, short-answer wit about him that put complex issues into succinct little tidbits. He just answered, "I was driving a tractor when I was twelve, didn't even have a license till I was about twenty-five." That's all he said.

What struck me immediately was the contrast of my father's world in the 1920s to my world in the 1990s. Implicit within my dad's round-the-barn way of saying "my grandson will be okay" was a tacit analysis of how the agricultural environment of my father's upbringing had been so different from the crazy techno-industrial-informational-MTV-highway world that I was raising my kids in. Think of a society where most skills and trades were learned through apprenticeships; where no one was licensed for anything; where work was just what people did to support themselves, no more, no less; and where there were no books, tapes, radio and television programs informing parents how to be parents. The parent-child connection seemed to be more fundamental than incidental then. Children increased the work force and gave a couple far more value in the community than their own wealth (Psalm 127). But times, as they say, have changed.

As I listened to my father, I wondered, *Have times really changed so much?* Is the nature of my son any different from my dad's nature when he was raised or mine when I was raised? Good question.

It would be tempting to say the wisdom literature is too outdated to relate to modern child-raising. After all, the fields of psychology and child development are barely a century old. What could the Bible contribute to a field that is so heavily influenced by Dr. Spock, Piaget, Freud, Maslow, and even our own Christian brands of family teaching? I believe it has plenty to offer. Proverbs was not only a manual on child-raising, but it also used a device throughout the book that has the Teacher of Wisdom, personified as a woman, addressing the young pupils of Israel. In ancient times, the home was not only the central place of education, but for most young men and women, it was the only place. There were no elementary schools or even secondary schools. Only the young princes and other elites were allowed into the wisdom schools. Hence, "Wisdom for living, like life itself, should start at home."[1] But first, I need to define what I am talking about when I use the term *child*.

In Proverbs' Hebrew text, two main words are used in regard to children. The first is *na'ar*. When the roots for this word are consulted, cognate languages give meanings of "growl, cry, scream, roar, gush and agitate."[2] My own summary of this material sees the child as one who makes loud, unusual noises and moves around a lot! The age of *na'ar* is not specific. The range runs the gamut from the child in the womb (Judges 13:5) to just born (1 Samuel 4:21) to infancy (Exodus 2:6) to adolescence (Genesis 37:2) to marital age (Proverbs 5:18). Therefore, the child in biblical terms covers the entire developmental period from conception to marriage. We are still addressed by Proverbs as "children" no matter how old we are. We still need to come to Wisdom to learn and educate ourselves about the skill of living.

The other term used is the Hebrew word *ben* for "son, child or children." This is the most general of terms and can be used of children of any age, even young animals and members of guilds or prophetic orders.[3]

It is these "sons" and "children" Lady Wisdom attempts to turn toward her advances so that they might love and embrace her (3:15). The entire book of Proverbs is then addressed to children and their parents. As such, the literature becomes a manual on child-training, or putting it another way, it is God's textbook on child psychology. These proverbs give us insight into the nature of the child, the role of discipline, and the rebellious realities that children create. Children can be a parent's greatest joy or deepest grief. But for the most part, our feminine sage calls developing children to be responsible for their own lives and choose wisdom. The choice is theirs. Wisdom and parents call, but the child has to choose. What makes these choices so difficult is the oppositional nature of the child.

THE CHILD IS KNOWN BY HIS NATURE

From the beginning, the field of psychology has wrestled with not only the nature of the child but also the nature of humanness. But the debate over the nature of the child has certainly been hot. Ever since Rousseau wrote his fascinating story about Emily, a sweet, innocent child so eager to learn once the puritanical restraints were taken off her, the psychological community has followed suit. To be childlike is to be viewed as innocent and pure. Certainly there is some truth to this, but children are also selfish, demanding, manipulating, and hateful. Who can forget the downward spiral of the boys in *Lord of the Flies* when left to themselves?

The more commonly accepted psychological assumptions of the innocence of children have achieved profound status in much of current self-help literature. Where once only real children were perceived this way (innocent), now the mysti-cal "child within" is as well. One critic of this movement writes, "Inner children are always good—innocent and pure—like the most sentimentalized Dickens characters, which means that people are essentially good. . . . Even Ted Bundy had a child within. Evil is merely a mask—a dysfunction."[4]

This assumption about the inner child and children in gen-eral is radically different from what we find in the Proverbs. Proverbs states very frontally that the child's heart is full of foolishness.

The Child's Nature Is One of Foolishness

In striking contrast to contemporary society and ill-conceived psychology, Proverbs says,

Foolishness is bound up in the heart of a child;
The rod of discipline will remove it far from him.
    (22:15)

The term *foolishness* in this passage carries the idea of "thickness of fluid." What is bound in the heart of children is not purity and innocence but a stubborn thick-headedness. Proverbs unapologetically affirms that the child is born a stub-born fool. That's what parents get at the beginning of life. Bound around his or her cute, cuddly goo-goos and smiles is a heart wrapped and warped in thick, obdurate stubbornness.

Based on this understanding of human nature, the second line of the proverb follows suit. Only the rod of discipline (*musar*) can distance the foolishness from the child's actions. What I believe this makes clear is that the rod (being either physical or verbal or circumstantial) does not eradicate the nature of the child but only educates the child. Even adults have natures that are still foolish. But hopefully we have learned through trial and error and have disciplined our natures beyond doing foolish things.

I find many Christians are confused over this doctrine. I was too for a while. I felt all I had to do to raise good kids was to be the proper disciplinarian. I guess I thought I could break the will without breaking the spirit. (Faulty anthropology, especially in Hebrew, which never separates will, mind, heart, and spirit, was my problem.) Even my married daughter confessed to me recently that my discipline of her never worked! Discipline cannot eradicate the sin nature, it just educates it.

I should make clear at this point that discipline (*musar*) does not involve only corporal discipline. In fact, most of the usages in Proverbs about discipline have to do with listening to verbal instruction, and not corporal punishment (4:1-9, 29:1; compare "reproof" with Job 13:6, 23:4). Simply, Proverbs outlines three types of discipline: corporal punishment (rod), verbal tongue-lashings or reasoned arguments (reproof), and circumstantial realities (ravens plucking out one's eyes, for example). Aiken places a needed caution on the overuse of corporal punishment:

> For there is no question that some children have been nothing short of brutalized and their lives made a misery by stupid parents and teachers hiding behind the letter, if not the spirit, of these proverbs. Of course, because corporal punishment can be easily abused and can be counter-productive does not mean that there cannot be place for its sensible and proper use; but it ought to give pause for thought.[5]

A child is not only known in Proverbs by the condition of his heart, but also by the condition of his conduct.

The Child's Nature Is Known by His Behavior
Conduct always reveals the character within. Our wisdom writer explains:

> It is by his deeds that a lad distinguishes himself
> If his conduct is pure and right. (Proverbs 20:11)

Even a child makes known (*yitnakker*, is known) what he is in his heart by his deeds. His behavior illustrates whether his heart is properly directed (*yashar*, right) and pure (*zak*, unmixed or pure motives).

Often today, psychologists term poor behavior as "acting-out" behaviors. What they usually mean by this is that the child's conduct is really not his own. The child is acting out problems in the family system. Therefore, the abnormal behavior is not his own, but someone else's (usually the parent's). These "codependent" relationships receive a sharp critique from a leading women's writer and attorney. She writes,

> The therapeutic view of evil as sickness, not sin, is strong in codependency theory—it's not a fire and brimstone theology. "Shaming" children, calling them bad, is considered a primary form of abuse. Both guilt and shame "are not useful as a way of life," Melody Beattie writes earnestly in *Codependent No More*. "Guilt makes everything harder . . . We need to forgive ourselves." Someone should remind Beattie that there's a name for people who lack guilt and shame: sociopaths. We ought to be grateful if guilt makes things like murder and moral corruption "harder."[6]

So, a child should be known by his own behavior, not the behavior or failures of his parents.

In saying this, I am obviously aware that we all are deeply marked and affected by our parents, and in turn we deeply affect our children. The sins of the fathers (and mothers) are visited upon succeeding generations (Exodus 20:5). But the counterpart to this reality is found in Ezekiel where the prophet declares, "The son will not bear the punishment for the father's iniquity, nor will the father bear the punishment for the son's iniquity" (Ezekiel 18:20). In other words, each individual is held accountable by God for his own sins. I can't blame my drunken father (hypothetical illustration) for my drinking problem any more than I can claim getting my kids into Harvard was because I was so brilliant. Codependence and single-cause-and-effect thinking have influenced much of even our "Christian" approaches to child-rearing.

If we start with the wrong premise about the child's nature, then the rest of this discussion does not logically follow. Unless one acknowledges at the front end that the child has an innate, inborn inability to respond favorably to wisdom, then his rebellion and the role of discipline will not make any sense. Unless we see the sinful processes active in the heart of every child who has wrapped foolishness in his heart, then parents will be very troubled when they absolutely do not understand the rebellion in their kids.

THE REALITY OF THE CHILD'S REBELLION

I must admit, I think I was very naive about parenting. I was the third and last child in my family of origin. My sisters tell me I just sort of "grew up" on my own (a polite way of saying I was spoiled). However, when I first became a parent I think I took on the formula approach to child-raising. I must also say there were plenty of fairly simplistic formulas being given out in the evangelical circles I ran in. You know, "the five steps to successful parenting" and "break the will without crushing the spirit" and "understanding your child's temperament." These quick lessons on child psychology were all helpful to me, and I still believe they have their place in the literature (perhaps in the appendixes, which people never read). But they didn't really prepare me for the realities I would face with my own kids. I don't know how many times I have said, "How could I have raised a kid like this? I applied all the formulas, but I got a different product. These kids aren't perfect. What did I do wrong?" Personally, I find Proverbs has a much more realistic approach and theologically correct appraisal of the child. Proverbs basically presents the child as a rebel-in-waiting!

The Assumption of Rebellion

From the opening chapters of Proverbs to the end, the consistent assumption about the behavior of the child is that he won't listen, he will stray, he will be in places where he shouldn't be, and he will be introduced to, if not enticed by, a whole range of foolish behaviors that will only get him in trouble. Wisdom's first call is to those who are already foolish in their behaviors: the naive, the scoffers, the fools (Proverbs 1:20-22). Here, at the beginning of the book, she asks the youth of Israel to turn to her reproof (1:23). The assumption? They are still very much stuck in their rebellion and foolishness (1:26,28-29,32).

Whether it is Sister Wisdom or Solomon himself, when the "sons" are addressed, they are addressed with this same assumption. "My son, if . . ." (2:1). Wisdom is a realist. "Ifs" are conditional. "Ifs" affirm the reality that the child has a proclivity if not an occupation with doing otherwise. "My son, do not forget . . ." (3:1). Assumption? There is a proclivity not to hear and if heard, to forget! "My son, give attention to . . ."(5:1). Assumption? He won't, and he will fall into the seductive traps of the adulteress (5:3-14). "My son, if you have become surety [cosigned] a loan for [someone] . . ." (6:1). Assumption? He will! "My son, keep my words . . ." (7:1). Assumption? He won't! "Therefore, O sons, listen to me" (8:32). Assumption? He probably won't.

The entire assumption of the literature is negative but realistic. It tells us what to expect in our children. It doesn't play games with us about formulas. It presents child-raising as something that is not fixed or assured but very conditional, personal, and without any promises. Reading Proverbs thoroughly makes a parent more frightened than anything else. The only formula is correction and even that may not work! The conclusion to this assumption? Even the best of child-training cannot instill wisdom but only encourage it to be pursued.

In one of the earliest Christian attempts to articulate a philosophy of child nurture, Bushnell wrote,

> The growth of Christian virtue is no vegetable process,
> no mere onward development. It involves a struggle
> with evil, a fall and a rescue. The soul becomes estab-
> lished in holy virtue, as a free exercise, only as it is
> passed round the corner of fall and redemption, ascend-

ing thus unto God through a double experience, in which it learns the bitterness of evil and the worth of good, fighting its way of one, and achieving the other as victory . . . For it is not sin which he (the child) derives from his parents; at least, not sin in any sense which imports blame, but only some prejudice to the perfect harmony of this mold, some kind of depravity or obliquity which inclines him to evil.[7]

This obliquity or departure from the norm is evidenced in Proverbs by a number of illustrations.

Some Examples of Rebellion

In the parent-child matrix, the collector who arranged Proverbs has given us an extensive list of possible things a child might do to his parents. I have listed them in descending order from less painful to most painful for parents. See if any of these rings true with your children. "A scoffer does not listen to his father's rebuke" (13:1); "A fool rejects his father's discipline" (15:5); "The eye that mocks a father, and scorns a mother" (30:17); "There is a kind of man who curses his father, and does not bless his mother" (30:11); "He who assaults his father and drives his mother away" (19:26); "He who robs his father or his mother, and says, 'It is not a transgression'" (28:24).

Do you catch the drift? Again, the assumption behind these examples is that they all could happen. There is no comment about the kind of parents these are, whether they deserve such treatment or not, or whether they are so enmeshed in their own stuff that the child has the right to treat them as he does. Proverbs just gives the stark realities of parenting. Any parent who brings a child into the world must face the possibility that the child can, may, or will do such things to him or her. The parents' reaction to such, I will note in the next chapter.

A further list of rebellious examples include: A son may be too opinionated to learn (13:1), or he may be too lazy ever to learn wisdom (10:5), or he may just choose a life of debauchery

(29:3). He may totally reject his parents' attempts to teach him and have authority over his life (15:20, 20:20, 30:17). What a list like this does is raise a host of questions about "successful parenting."

At the seminary where I teach we have implemented a mentoring program for all of our students. A couple of things we have learned are: All the available research points to the conclusion that "toxic mentors" cannot be changed. We would do better to do more training with our students than with the mentors. Good mentors will stay good with or without our training, but our time would be better spent in training our students how to recognize a good mentor!

I believe we find the same reality in Proverbs concerning children. Toxic parents, no matter how many books or seminars or counseling sessions they ingest, are still toxic simply because they are toxic people. It seems no one today wants to call things the way they are. Proverbs does not focus much on the parents; it doesn't give them seven steps to positive parenting and such. Here the focus is on the children, and on encouraging them to respond to life and their parents' instruction in positive ways.

This seems far more sensible and apparently is more in line with modern research about how kids raised in the same family can be so different. If "successful parenting" is built on the premise of right technique and formulas, then how does one explain the vast differences (in personality, behavior, and life) among the children raised with the same parents and principles? In much of the Christian evangelical literature on child-raising there is a narrow cause-effect mentality that the parent is the singular cause for both healthy and not-so-healthy children. This being the case, it is hard to explain how two children raised by the same parents are so different.

Two researchers at Penn State University write,

One thing is clear: siblings growing up in the same family are very different . . . and this discovery not only suggests what is wrong with our previous approaches (determined solely by the parents) to children's development, it also points clearly to what needs to be done: we need to find out what environmental factors make two children growing up in the same family different from one another.[8]

What are some of these other critical environmental factors that determine personality and character? The researchers list such things as these: differing parent-child relationships with each child; differing interactional experiences between siblings, and observing the sibling relate to parents; the impact of growing up with a sibling very different or similar to oneself; overall influences beyond the family (school, friends, etc.); chance; and what the writers call, using Joyce's term, "epiphanies of the ordinary." They conclude, "The personality and self-esteem of each child is affected by each of these relationships. It is a complex network of influence, and a changing one—complex enough to frighten off all but the most foolhardy of researchers!"[9]

What all this means to this humbled and humiliated parent is that ultimately the child must figure out what he is going to do even with the parents God has given him. Every day there is an array of voices calling him, pushing at him to "go there, do this, be that." The child must make hard choices. Any child worth his salt will make some foolish ones. When he does, it is not necessarily the parents' fault. Chalk it up to the child's own rebellious heart and a host of other influences. Simone de Beauvoir acknowledged, "A life is not the mere growth of the original seed. It runs the continual danger of being halted, broken, damaged or turned aside."[10] Children are rebels by nature. But as parents, what we really need to know is, "What can we do with this rebel?"

TRAINING THE CHILD

The Proverbs are realistic. They present a child who stands in need of training in moral guidance. The short list of what to do with a rebellious child is simply one thing: discipline him.

Discipline Him

Aiken encourages, "A kind but firm hand is called for by the nature of the task of child training . . . it is a difficult, important and serious task."[11] Our sage instructs:

> Foolishness is bound up in the heart of a child;
> The rod of discipline will remove it far from him.
> (22:15)

As noted before, the cure, if there is one, for rebellion is discipline (*musar*). This word denotes "correction which results in education" and "one which involved oral instruction based upon the law of God."[12] This concept fits very nicely with the well-known and well-claimed verse,

> Train up a child in the way he should go,
> Even when he is old he will not depart from it. (22:6)

Do Prevention Training

This training is more prevention than correction, although it might involve punishment at times. The verse has been hotly debated because of differing ways to translate the Hebrew text. Some believe it is encouragement for parents to train or initiate their children in accordance with their own natural bent or abilities.[13] When this is done, because it is a well-learned habit, it will stay with the child the rest of his life.

However, other commentators observe, "The thought that the educational process must be tailored to the requirements of the individual is not at all what is intended. There is only one right way—the way of life—and the educational discipline which directs young men along this way is uniform."[14] More pointedly, as observed above, the natural bent of the child is foolishness (this is not to say a parent should never encourage the development of talents and abilities), and to deal with foolishness takes proper child-training. Some have noted the emphasis here on "early imprinting," so to speak, on the child. The word *train, chanok*, from its Arabic roots meant "to rub the palate of the child's mouth with chewed dates" in order to stimulate a newborn to start sucking. Later, the idea developed into "giving the child an experience of something" and finally it was used of dedicating a new house or building, as in Hannukah.[15]

Certainly, there is value in giving children experiences in the way of wisdom—they will have enough experience in the way of fools. Parents must try to balance these natural bents by offering countering experiences that will build wisdom. I believe this goes way beyond making sure our kids are in Sunday school or belong to the youth group. The "way" talked about here is far more than a "cognitive" way, it is experiential. Sending our kids into the ghettos for summer ministries or to third-world countries as developing junior highers are profoundly enriching and disciplining experiences for our children.

The summer our entire family spent ministering in Australia was, to my mind, one of the greatest things I could have done as a parent to "initiate my kids in the way they should go." We slept on the floor together, with no heat, in the dead of winter (it's un-Australian to turn on the heat). We experienced ministry on the university campuses and in the outback. The preventive-discipline aspect of this is that while they were there, there was no MTV, summer house parties (when parents are away), or jerk friends having an influence on them!

I must also make a second comment on this verse. Many have claimed this verse as a promise. Like all proverbs, these are principles more than promises. These are nuggets of reality packaged into small phrases. They shouldn't be claimed as God's promise to us that our kids will turn out right, if we just take them to church and get them active in the youth groups. I believe this is a misuse of the verse and Proverbs in general. Besides, the proverb does not say what exactly the parent is to do to get the child on the right way. The way is just the way of wisdom and righteousness, but this does not give me a specific set of meetings to attend or activities to do in order to ensure the promise. It just tells me I need to be doing something to initiate my child in the proper way of living.

Second, the verse is often misused by Christian parents

when their kids have not turned out as expected. A little comfort might be found in the phrase "when he is old." Most parents quickly compute this to mean "when grown." However, the word for old here, *zaken*, is not the word for young adults (*gibbor* or *achim*), but for very old men and women. It means too old to get a husband (Ruth 1:12), and to be very advanced in years (Genesis 24:1). It is a time of graying hair (1 Samuel 12:2) and failing sight (Genesis 27:1). Therefore, to parents whose adult children still do not walk in the way of wisdom, I say, "It's not over till it's over." There is still hope. Perhaps something cultivated and imparted in their childhood will still grow and blossom in their later years.

Do the Painful Training

Discipline is painful for both the child and the parent. The old maxim "This hurts me more than it hurts you" is to be commended. Of course, children can't see that it is painful for the parent, but they will when they are parents. The first time I tried that line on one of my daughters, she responded by saying, "Sure, Dad!"

But discipline is painful. Proverbs asserts plainly that it must be done.

> Do not hold back discipline from the child,
> Although you beat him with the rod, he will not die.
> You shall beat him with the rod,
> And deliver his soul from Sheol. (23:13-14)

The proverb first assumes that parents may neglect this important area. The "you" in the second verse is emphatic, apparently placing the "obligatory need" upon the parent.[16]

There are probably several contemporary reasons why parents do not want to discipline their children. The first may be rooted in humanistic psychology. Modern enlightened parents may think, *If I spank my child, I will psychologically harm my child.* Proverbs answers this fear almost before one can raise it: "Your child won't die." In fact, the added punch comes in the last line. Not only will the child not die, if you neglect this discipline you may be allowing your child to continue in the direct path toward death (Sheol, the place of the dead). The portrait of the child in Proverbs is that he starts out his life on a path toward destruction and death. Without responding to the voice of Wisdom and listening to the correction of parents, he stays on the path. Discipline is one of the tools parents can use to turn their children from the destructive path.

A second reason parents neglect discipline is because it is inconvenient. It takes time and energy to do it. Our busy schedules today, with two parents working, mixed with the busy schedules of other older children, create situations where behavior misdemeanors go unpunished. It is easy for small and large infractions to fall between the cracks. To this excuse or reality, Proverbs answers,

> He who spares his rod hates his son,
> But he who loves him disciplines him diligently. (13:24)

The terms *love* and *hate* are Hebrew mirrorism that indicates "accepting or rejecting."[17] The parent who does not discipline is one who is consciously or unconsciously rejecting his child, no matter how much he may think he loves the child. Hatred is equated with neglect, love with disciplining early. The Hebrew word *shicharo*, translated "disciplines him diligently," is probably better translated "early."[18] The word in the noun form means "dawn" and in the verbal form, "doing something at dawn or early."[19] The point is clear. Discipline is not something that one starts later in life. To be effective, it must be done from the dawn of the child's life.

Don't misunderstand the point of the passage, however. This is not encouraging the beating of babies or even very young children. It just establishes the principle of not giving in to the natural tendency within the parent to neglect discipline. He should start it as early as possible.

Perhaps a third reason parents today may not want to

discipline is because so much of our own self-esteem is riding on having our children like us. Deep within us we think, *If I really do some serious discipline, my child won't like me.* Apart from being a serious role reversal, this type of thinking only facilitates the child's path toward self-destruction and ultimately brings shame upon his mother. Proverbs says,

> The rod and reproof give wisdom,
> But a child who gets his own way brings shame to his
>   mother. (29:15)

A mother's "love" can degenerate into indulgence toward her child simply because so much of her self-esteem is riding on the child. Ultimately her little darling becomes a disgrace to his mother. Discipline saves the child from himself (his own innate selfishness and foolishness) and delivers him from the evil path, but there are some other added benefits to discipline.

THE BENEFITS OF CHILD DISCIPLINE

Much of what parents want for their children centers around providing a secure home environment. It is hard for me to imagine trying to raise kids in a war zone like Bosnia or some of our inner cities. Without the minimal protection of basic human safety, children do not grow and develop a sense of security. But the important question is, What gives children an adequate sense of security? Is it a father who has a six-figure income, or a house with six bedrooms, or a mother who wears a size-six dress? Proverbs again answers the question of where security for the child exists.

Security for the Child

Security for the child is spelled simply as "a parent who fears the Lord":

> In the fear of the LORD there is strong confidence,
> And his children will have refuge. (14:26)

The image here is of a secure fortress into which children can run to find refuge and protection. The secure fortress is a parent who trusts in the Lord and places his reverential fear in Him. All the discipline in the world cannot convert the child's soul. The best control factor on a child's life, even though he may not be aware of it, is a parent who drinks deeply at the fountain of respect for God (14:27). When push comes to shove and the prodigal comes home, he comes home because there is a refuge there, a refuge in a father or mother who fears God (Luke 15:11-32).

Peace of Mind for the Parents

I occasionally joke with my wife about what I am going to put on her gravestone. (Of course, in keeping with statistics, she will pre-decease me, and then have this opportunity!) My joke: "Where's Graham?" Yes, our son has given both of us our share of worried moments, sleepless nights, and frightening terror. When he was all of two years old, while Cinny was with him on the beach in Hawaii, he suddenly disappeared. She looked frantically up and down the beach but could not see him. She was ready to give him up, thinking he had been washed out to sea, when she saw his little head peeking above some tall grass nearby. He had been watching and apparently enjoying her emotional terror! So "Where's Graham?" may be an appropriate epitaph for either of us.

This illustration also shows how parents struggle to have peace of mind about their kids. Proverbs again states that parental peace of mind comes from discipline:

Correct your son, and he will give you comfort;
He will also delight your soul. (29:17)

This is a wonderful verse. The word translated "comfort," *yinicheka*, is the Hebrew word for rest. It means "to have a certain quietness of soul, or to be settled or have ease."[20] Isn't this what every parent is looking for in regard to his children? To have a settled feeling about them, to be in a position where his mind is at ease about them.

The word for delight is another wonderful Hebrew word. It means to enjoy a "luxurious delight."[21] Nehemiah notes how the people of God luxuriated in the goodness of what God had provided in giving them the land of Canaan (Nehemiah 9:25). So parents can luxuriate in their children when they have been trained and instructed in godly wisdom and discipline. Children, I must say, are far more delightful when they are under control and well-disciplined.

Since Proverbs is written to be a handbook about children, it is only fitting to close with a summary of what the book says directly to children.

WISDOM'S EXHORTATION TO THE CHILD

Two voices are crying in the streets. They call to our children, our youth who are still undecided and incomplete in their development. These children are so vulnerable yet so valuable. Our next generation is dependent upon them.

One voice is the voice of the adulteress. She looks upon our children as prey and says, "Come unto me" (7:18). She knows exactly what she is doing and what she wants. She wants the very life of our children (7:23). Our sons and daughters look upon her, see her flattery (7:21), and are enticed by her calculating persuasions. Many go her way. Too many.

I know a family who defies logical analysis. The two parents love the Lord and have made Him the center of their lives. Yet their daughter has heard the voice of the adulteress. She has been enticed by older men with money, with the delights of drugs, sex, and alcohol. Her perpetual whoring has broken her parents' hearts, yet they have remained true to the Lord and His faithfulness. I admire their courage, radiance, and faithful commitment to their daughter. They have listened to the other voice.

Wisdom also cries out in the streets (1:20). She screams over the MTV and boom-box messages of the streets. She says, "Listen, for I shall speak noble things" (8:6). She utters truth, not lies; she offers instruction rather than flattery; and her ways lead to life, not death (8:35). To the young, who are thirsty or hungry for adventure and breaking free from the restraints of parents, teachers, and systems, she says,

> "Come, eat of my food,
> And drink of the wine I have mixed." (9:5)

The ones who listen to her are few, for her instruction is costly and her price is worth more than gold (8:10-11).

But every so often a rare youth emerges, like a Daniel or a young David or a young Timothy, who decides he will turn aside from the messages of world adulteresses and seek wisdom from the godly examples around him. These few hear Wisdom's exhortation. They take the time to bend low and hear a father's or teacher's instruction about life.

I guess I have to put myself in that category. I was finishing my last year of college when I first heard this voice. Up to that time I had heard many other voices. The voice of fraternity social life, of dating, drinking, and typical pranks. I wasn't concerned about being wise or even being good. In fact, I was known on the football team as a guy to stay away from. I would ring guys' bells in practice just for the fun of it. But through the instrumentation of a fraternity brother, Steve McIlvain, I heard another voice. The voice brought me to myself, and to Christ, true Wisdom. As I reflect on this memory of almost thirty years ago, I wonder, *Why me?* So many others heard but did not respond. Some heard and responded but are no more. But here I am still hearing and wanting more, though I am still very much that raw, pagan, frat brat of thirty years ago. Now I just have Christ. I have no answer for myself apart from the mysterious grace of God, which allows some to hear and others to remain dull. But the reality still stands. A smart son will begin to listen to the voice of wisdom in his life.

A Wise Child Listens to His Parents

Wisdom exhorts,

> Hear, O sons, the instruction of a father,
> And give attention that you may gain understanding. . . .

"Let your heart hold fast my words;
Keep my commandments and live." (4:1,4)

The smart child takes the time to listen to his parents. The listening here is more than listening; it is heeding. Hearing in biblical theology always implies heeding! The verb *give attention*, *qashab*, carries the idea of "bending low or giving careful attention to something."[22] It has the idea of bending the ear toward the person speaking so that one genuinely understands what is being said. Children are asked by Wisdom to do this. Wisdom calls to the child, through his parents, through his wise companions, through his wise elders, to listen to her when she speaks.

Wisdom says listen to her, listen only to her, don't waste your time on anyone else's words. Listen to her and obey and your life will be happy and blessed. Do what is right and you will feel right (5:7, 7:24, 8:32)! Doing what is right comes down to the old-fashioned maxims of honoring one's parents (Exodus 20:12), not speaking ill of them (Proverbs 20:20, 30:11), and not mistreating them (19:26, 28:24).

This is the inexpensive way of becoming a wise child. I can merely listen to the wisdom of others, accept it, and follow it without debate. However, for most of us, it takes a few hard knocks to get the message.

Learn from Life Experiences

"I'll never do that again!" What a beautiful phrase. This is the statement of a truly educated man, woman, or child. Some of the "nevers" on my list are: I'll never loan money to a friend or relative (I'll give it as a gift, but no loans—too much expectation for return and too much disappointment when it doesn't happen); I'll never buy another TR-6 (see chapter 3 for explanation, although I am still tempted from time to time); I'll never trust an organization to take care of me; I'll never trust a Texan when he says the chili is "a little hot"; I'll never trust a friend who says an investment is a "sure bet."

The reason my "never" list exists is the same reason all

"never" lists have life. We have been burned, let down, done in, let go, and thrown out! In other words, we have learned from our mistakes. We have learned from our life experiences. It is the wise child who harks to the messages self-contained in the negative experiences of life.

Proverbs suggests that one of the keys to learning from negative experiences is to be constantly evaluating the kinds of friends one has. Sister Wisdom proclaims:

He who keeps the law is a discerning son,
But he who is a companion of gluttons humiliates his
    father. (28:7)

A man who loves wisdom makes his father glad,
But he who keeps company with harlots wastes his
    wealth. (29:3)

The friends young people make often are a cause for friction between them and their parents. Bad company does corrupt good morals. And a child who ends up being over-influenced by his peers can see his own relationship with his parents sacrificed to his gluttony and harlotry. The result is a deeply felt humiliation in the parents.

Finally, children fundamentally need to keep the law of God in order to be wise in life.

Live Wisely

Proverbs makes it clear: "He who keeps the law is a discerning son" (28:7). These, indeed, are the rare sons and daughters. The ones who cherish and honor Torah (law) are the children of understanding and discernment. What gives any person the ability to make distinctions between truth and error, between trustworthy statements and lies, is the Word of God. Living wisely is living in accordance to what Scripture says. It doesn't mean being a Jesus freak or a Bible-quoting-and-thumping jerk. It means having a solid foundation from which to make decisions and interact with the world. Living wisely means living biblically. But this is wisdom born in pain. As Shakespeare wrote,

> Best men are moulded out of faults,
> And, for the most, become much more better
> For being a little bad.

When Mark Twain reflected on his own childhood, he saw his own mother in a rather different light. "My mother had a good deal of trouble with me but I think she enjoyed it. She had none at all with my brother Henry, who was two years younger than I, and I think that the unbroken monotony of his goodness and truthfulness and obedience would have been a burden to her but for the relief and variety which I furnished in the other direction."[23]

I resonate with Twain. It gives me hope that "bad" kids can turn out well, and are even "better" for their being bad. This is a hard reality for many parents to face, but it is certainly more in keeping with the nature of the child than the one modern psychology has thrust upon us. But it doesn't make parenting any easier. Proverbs is also very realistic about what happens on the other end of the parent-child connection. A true search for wisdom must also address the parent.

The Parent

*Christians have children so we can become
the kind of people who welcome strangers.*
RODNEY CLAPP
FAMILIES AT THE CROSSROADS

▼

*Be wise, my son, and make my heart glad,
That I may reply to him who reproaches me.*
PROVERBS 27:11

There's a gripping scene in the movie *Parenthood* where Steve Martin watches his son trying to get under a high fly ball during a Little League baseball game. While the fly ball is coming down, in slow motion, Steve envisions his son on top of a high university-type tower with a rifle, randomly firing on passersby. The point of the "flash-ahead" is clear. If his son does not catch the ball to win the game, his whole future life is changed for the worse. He will become a mass murderer, even when the father did all he could to raise him to be a successful, productive human being.

Every parent has felt this anxiety. We have felt the panic of what our children might turn out to be if things don't go right with them. The anxiety we feel for our kids raises some interesting questions. Why do we have such deep-seated desires for our kids' success? What is it within us that needs our kids to be successful in order for us to feel good about ourselves? Why do we need them to be successful in order for us to be successful?

Interesting questions. As author and sociology professor Tony Campolo has said, "The only reason left for having kids is what they can do for us, their parents." At least in agricultural times, children had a more productive function: They nurtured younger siblings and supported the home by performing domestic and field labor. Then the home was adult-centered; children were expected to fit into the adult world. Since the 1950s our homes have become increasingly child-centered. This high priority on the child has produced what in the 1980s was called "the superkid and superparent" generation. Harold Smith writes,

> There was a time when raising the next generation
> was a "seat of the pants" operation—literally and figura-
> tively. . . . These days, however, a mother or father can
> hardly make a move without running headlong into a
> talk show, lecture series, or shelf of books brimming
> with advice on how to ensure a child's place in the up-
> and-coming generation. . . . Professional parents are
> downright driven to cultivate their children's abilities
> and college-bound resumes—superparents raising
> superkids. Armed with expert advice, they view parent-
> ing less as an instinctive process than a quantifiable set
> of do's and don'ts which, if applied properly, can trans-
> form any child into a runner by three, a reader by four,
> a writer by five.[1]

In the 1990s a new term has been coined, "cornucopia kids." These are the children of achieving parents, who have been raised with "the mythical horn of plenty always repre-sented as full to overflowing. The downside is that often chil-dren raised in this cozy suburban habitat leave unprepared for the real world and unable to meet adult responsibilities."[2]

It is into this fearful complexity about parenting that the self-help books have carved their popular and profitable niche. Feeding upon parental fears that their child might not read "on time" or have high enough SATs or be the spiritual-minded child he ought to be or catch the fly ball to win the game, this literature continues to make promises that seem unrealistic. In talking about self-help books about children, Clapp writes,

> Some manuals categorize them and predict their futures. Others advise us about childrearing techniques that will form and shape the kind of process we want our child to be. If any of them "worked" as effectively as they all are touted to work, there wouldn't be so many on the market. So why do we continue to buy such books? I think this vast literature reassures us in face of the strangeness, the alien qualities, of our children. These books say we *can* interpret and understand our children; their wildness *can* be tamed.[3]

I love Clapp's term *alien*. Children are aliens that come from somewhere else, live with us awhile, and then leave to go their own way. The parent's part in the process has become a frightening complex of do's and don'ts and should-have's and would-have's and might-have-beens.

Thrown into this mix, the Proverbs strike us as rather simplistic. They don't give the kind of promises to parents that are found on most book covers. I guess I burned out on book promises (including my own).

I also got burned out with counseling. Having been associated with counseling in various forms for the past twenty years (both pastoral and professional), I woke up one morning realizing that most of the counselors I knew weren't doing any better with their kids than I was with mine. In fact, a very high percentage of counselors today are in the field simply because they have had so many problems and "worked" through them.[4] This is not their fault; I empathize with them. But it does make one question the relevance of their therapy knowledge when it has not worked in their own lives.

The other side of this burnout came from my own counseling. Frankly, despite the many hours I spent with people (in the thousands), I'm not really sure my wisdom and insight ever

"changed anybody." My general, very skeptical, and unprofessional opinion is that the role of counseling is one of facilitating insight into the nature of one's problem, but insight does not necessarily bring about change. Dr. Zilbergeld (a psychologist himself) concludes,

> There is no evidence that psychologists and psychiatrists, who have the longest training and command the highest fees, are more effective than social workers, marriage counselors, and other therapists. Even those who regularly refer to a certain therapist frequently have no idea of what kinds of results are achieved. . . . If you simply want to talk to someone, it probably doesn't make a lot of difference whom you select, as long as you feel comfortable and that he or she is listening.[5]

Besides, when people do change, they change not because of therapy or "help" but because they "mature out"[6] or because of some developmental crisis.[7]

No, Proverbs doesn't make promises. Proverbs simply gives us the straightforward responsibilities and realities all parents face with their kids. Nothing more, nothing less. I like that. It doesn't matter whether we understand our kids or not, whether we like our kids or not, or whether they are successful or not, here is what we are to do and expect if we are parents. As Clapp concludes, "For all our scientific understanding, for all our child psychology, children—even modern children—remain mysterious."[8]

So what are the responsibilities Proverbs lays out for the parent?

THE PARENTAL RESPONSIBILITIES

One of the most frequently asked questions when I do couples' retreats concerns who should lead the family in devotions, Bible reading, and prayer. I also get a similar question from women whose husbands are either not Christians or do not want to be involved spiritually with the family. They ask, since they are not the "head" of the home, whether they should "lead" or "teach" their children spiritually. Proverbs answers both these questions directly by affirming that both mother and father are to be involved in the teaching of their children. They are the primary educators of their children.

A Parent Is an Educator

The home-school movement has certainly "rediscovered" this proverbial reality. However, in Proverbs the parent as educator has much more to do with life and living life well than with working through curricula in order to be able to pass the GED. Solomon writes,

> Hear, my son, your father's instruction,
> And do not forsake your mother's teaching;
> Indeed, they are a graceful wreath to your head,
> And ornaments about your neck. (1:8-9)

The father's instruction (*musar*) and the mother's teaching (*torah*) combine in the parallelism to give the child a well-clothed public face. Clarifying the role of the mother here in teaching, Cohen notes that "in all these passages the mother's claim to consideration is equal with the father's."[9] In a further extended proverb we find the same truth:

> My son, observe the commandment of your father,
> And do not forsake the teaching of your mother;
> Bind them continually on your heart;
> Tie them around your neck.
> When you walk about, they will guide you;
> When you sleep, they will watch over you;
> And when you awake, they will talk to you.
> For the commandment is a lamp, and the teaching
>   is light. (6:20-23)

The imagery here certainly picks up the language found in Deuteronomy, where the child is exposed to the life of his parent from his first rising to his going to sleep at night; the complete, well-integrated teaching of the moral law of God combined with normal daily living (Deuteronomy 6:4-9) is what is being observed.

What the child carries away from this life-orientated teaching from both parents is the light of guidance. I think all parents want to be able to surprise their children with gifts that excite and reflect the love they have for their child. Even Jesus alluded to this common parental desire (Matthew 7:9-11). But Proverbs puts its emphasis on properly adorning the child for public life. What should be seen in public when the child is grown are not the emerald rings or Corvettes that the parents have provided, but wisdom and knowledge about life. These are what should be around the neck and on the head of the adult child. These are the things that make children rise up and call their parents "blessed" (Proverbs 31:28).

We are a compulsive society. It is hard for us to imagine anything getting better on its own and without human agency. For most of us, to do nothing is the height of irresponsibility. But my father had learned something of this contrary principle as a pilot. When we flew together, he always let me take the controls for a while. I still remember the day I was "overcontrolling" the airplane. I would correct one way, then correct the other way. We were going up, down, left, right. Finally, he said, "Take your hands off the stick [steering wheel]." I did and the plane flew perfectly straight. This teaching graced my life at that moment. To know that once an airplane is properly trimmed it will fly itself was sheer enlightenment for a young man.

The applications of his aviation advice to other areas of life are legion. Later when I read about the nature of God's Kingdom, this concept was not difficult for me to understand. "The kingdom of God is like a man who casts seed upon the soil; and goes to bed at night and gets up by day, and the seed sprouts up and grows—how, he himself does not know" (Mark 4:26-27). My father's teaching about life connects with the spiritual reality of the Kingdom. God can do things while I am doing nothing! Things grow while I sleep!

Proverbs also gives parents a brief primer on pedagogy. The outline of this pedagogy involves the goal of education, its method, and ultimate purpose. The immediate goal, we have already looked at: to acquire wisdom and understanding (4:5). "The beginning of wisdom is: Acquire wisdom" (4:7). The word *acquire* means "to buy,"[10] as in buying property or cattle. The goal in educating our children is that they become wise. The message to be communicated to them is "buy it if you have to." We certainly spend fortunes in trying to give our children a college education or a Christian education. But again, the parent must transfer to the child the understanding that wisdom is so important it should cost him something learned in life. The parent can only do so much, then it is up to the child. This wise parent in Proverbs is telling his son, "Buy wisdom instead of spending a hundred dollars on sneakers or twenty dollars on CDs or thousands of dollars on dope and dumb deals."

The method of pedagogy is outlined in two passages:

When I was a son to my father,
Tender and the only son in the sight of my mother,
Then he taught me and said to me. . . . (4:3-4)

I have directed you in the way of wisdom;
I have led you in upright paths. (4:11)

Solomon, in the context of teaching his sons in the school of wisdom, alludes to the process of pedagogy by which he had learned the skills of life. He says, in effect, that this is what his father taught him. Just as the principles of life that Solomon had learned from his father David had been ingrained into his soul, now he imparts them to his sons. What has been reliable in one life is handed down to others. What has been useful in the shaping of one generation is given to the next. In other words, the method of instruction for the parent is through intense personal relationships. This was no cognitive classroom built beside the home. This was total environmental learning.

Every year in one of my classes I have my students fill out a developmental questionnaire. Among many questions, I ask them to name the three most influential people in their childhood and early adulthood. Most list parents, grandparents, a teacher or coach, their spouse. The next question on the list asks, "What was it about that person that so influenced your life?" If the answers to the first question are somewhat vague, the answers to the second are very precise. They all say the same thing. It was a personal relationship. Explanations highlight "their caring"; "time spent with me"; "listening to me"; "involving me in their life"—all the deeply personal stuff. I have never had anyone yet list authors, seminars, books, schools, curricula, or a certain kind of school system. It's always relationships. God's method of instruction was through His Son, in giving the world a personal relationship with Him. A parent's primary teaching method is the same.

I have been asked many times by fathers of young children what they should do to provide them with some kind of spiritual input. The question is usually framed as, "What book would you recommend to read with my kid?" My standard response is, "It doesn't really matter." Particularly with small children (up to age eight, nine, or ten), just getting them on your lap and allowing them to feel the strength in your arms and body and listen to a masculine voice is probably more important to them developmentally than anything else. You can read the entire Bible or Hodge's *Systematic Theology* or the complete works of Shakespeare, but if the child does not feel warm, loved, and cared for, then nothing works. Solomon says his father viewed him as the only one in the world and tenderly taught him.

What is always fascinating to me is how contemporary biblical truth is. By the 1830s in American history, child-raising had become the primary domain of the mother.[11] By the 1950s, Dad was long gone, viewed as irrelevant and incompetent. But more recently, some scientists have been observing who the violent offenders are and what they have in common. Seventy percent of young criminals in state reform institutions have come from fatherless homes.[12] This significant father absence has finally led researchers to look seriously at the role of the father in child development. What has been found is striking. In summarizing the vast amount of research on the subject, a University of Rhode Island professor writes, "The role of the father as a representative of social reality and a judge of sex-appropriate behavior as well as companion and playmate can have far-reaching implications for the child's development."[13] In a nutshell, dads are back. They play a significant role throughout all stages of the child's life. One might think from this research that God had something in mind when He designed procreation involving two people who would become parents to a child. Research confirms this ideal:

> The optimal situation for the child is to have both an involved mother and involved father. The child is then exposed to a wider degree of adaptive characteristics. Children who are both well-mothered and well-fathered are likely to have positive self-concepts and a comfort about their biological sexuality. They feel good about being male or female and have a pride in their basic sex role orientation. They are comfortable with themselves and their sexuality and are able to be relatively flexible in their interests and responsiveness to others. Security in sex role orientation gives the child more of an opportunity to develop in an actualized way. Children who are paternally deprived, however, are more likely either to take a defensive posture of rigid adherence to cultural sex role standards or to avoid expected gender-related behaviors.[14]

The father and mother must develop positive personal relationships with their children in order to have the teaching heard. The personal relationship is the critical facilitating factor in the education of the child. But this relationship is very purposeful.

Solomon also says,

I have directed you in the way of wisdom;
I have led you in upright paths. (4:11)

This father was not the sort to tell his son what to do and where to go and then send him off alone. He walked along with him. The Hebrew word for path here, *ma'gal*, means "the furrow made by a wagon."[15] This father walked along the wagon tracks of life with his son.

I went to college in the flint hills of Kansas. Sometimes in the spring a group of us would drive out into these rolling hills of prairie land to cook hamburgers and drink a few beers. (We usually did it to try to impress coeds!) As the spring grass was sprouting, one could still see the well-worn wagon tracks of a century earlier. The old Santa Fe Trail was still there beckoning travelers young and old to go west!

Parents have to find the wagon tracks of life and then walk along with their children until together they get to their destination. I'm not sure when the journey is over. I'm not sure the journey is ever really over. I know my mother still worries about me. I have two kids out of the nest, but I do not have peace of mind about them. Their pain and struggles are still mine. It's tempting at times to pull away from their lives completely. But we are still on the trail. None of us has arrived yet.

Parents will not be content (if they ever are) until they see the twofold purpose of education fulfilled. The first is *when* wisdom begins to be a part of the daily life of our children:

When you walk about, [Wisdom] will guide you;
When you sleep, [Wisdom] will watch over you;
And *when* you awake, [Wisdom] will talk to you. (6:22, emphasis added)

In other words, when we see that wisdom is incorporated into our children's lives, we can rest a little easier. I have had no greater joy than seeing my adult children make decisions about people or situations that are obviously influenced by a mature wisdom. I pray these times will be many.

The second purpose grows out of the first: "To keep you from the evil woman" (6:24). Here Solomon, in the wisdom-speaking motif, says the purpose of observing his commands and not forsaking his mother's teaching is to keep the child from the evil person. Evil influences abound. Every year that goes by I am more convinced and scared by this reality. I claim the blood of Christ over my kids and over our whole household. Evil is never very far away from our children, and they are so innocent about it. Teenagers think we parents aren't "cool" when we see the evil in something. But with the infusion of male and female hormones in adolescence also comes a massive dose of invulnerability. Evil and bad things will never touch them, they think. Therefore, parents as the primary educators of children must always be a little street smart. They need to be at least one, better yet, two steps ahead of their children. Parenting is not for cowards, as Jim Dobson has said. It's messy. Life puts a parent on the line every day—with cranky teachers; longhaired, scraggly friends; lost bicycles; angry parents of your child's friends; swearing coaches; broken neighbors' windows; petty theft; runaway teenagers; and totaled automobiles. And that's sometimes in the same week!

No, this kind of teaching is not Ivy League. It's more like trying to paint someone's portrait while riding a roller coaster. It is life on the run with all its ups and downs. Through it all, hopefully our heart and soul come through to our kids. Now and then we might see that they actually did learn something from us!

However, if this teaching is difficult, correcting our kids is even more painful.

The Parent As Corrector

I must confess, several years ago I frankly ran out of gas and started getting tired of being and playing the policeman in our home. I have a suspicious mind to start with. I can recall all the things I did as a teenager and college student, and it terrifies me to think my kids might do the same things. I believe the thing I got tired of was having to come home and hear about what one of the kids had done that day, and then having to be the disciplinarian. The old phrase "Wait till your dad gets home" still puts fear in my heart for all the times I heard it as a child. It really made me excited for my father's homecoming! But Proverbs makes it very clear about this second responsibility a parent has. The parent is to be in the correcting business with his child.

Correction has to do with creating, maintaining, and encouraging moral boundaries. I distinguish moral from emotional boundaries at this point. Clarifying emotional boundaries has recently found its way into the Christian literature and has filled a long-empty gap in evangelical self-help. One of the most helpful books (in my opinion) defines what I call an emotional boundary as "a boundary [that] shows me where I end and someone else begins. They define what is me and what is not me."[16] This is a needed clarification.

Emotional boundaries are important and are related to moral boundaries, but in Proverbs what parental correction establishes are the moral boundaries for the child. In time, if the child heeds the moral boundaries placed upon him, he will internalize them and make them his own. It is the fool who has no moral boundaries.

> A fool rejects his father's discipline,
> But he who regards reproof is prudent. (15:5)

> Whoever loves discipline [*musar*] loves knowledge,
> But he who hates reproof is stupid. (12:1)

Again, the Hebrew word *musar* carries the idea of the instruction that comes through discipline and chastisement.[17] Even though Proverbs is gender-equivalent on the subject of correction (both mother and father are commanded to do it [29:15, 3:11-12]), the research on moral development in the child has found some very interesting patterns.

Work by Bronfenbrenner (1961) "found that the develop-

ment of leadership, responsibility and social maturity in adolescent males is closely associated with a father-son relationship that not only is nurturant but also includes a strong component of paternal limit-setting."[18] When the nurturant
relationship exists between parent and child, the secondary
aspect of limit setting (discipline) then is crucial to the development of a mature, responsible adult. When the father plays
an important part in setting limits (moral boundaries), the
child's attachment to his father and masculine development
are facilitated only if there is an already established affection-
ate father-son relationship.[19] Even though from this literature
it would seem the father has a critical role in the moral development of the child, other research suggests the mother also
is vitally important as a disciplinarian, especially when she is
also a controller of the resources![20]

What correction does is establish the moral boundaries for
the child. It defines what is right and what is wrong. Even
though this is the lowest level of moral development according to Kohlberg (because it is defined by the parent and based
on rules),[21] this is where God begins with all of us (Galatians
3:24). Setting limits and defining the moral boundaries for the
child shows the child he lives in a moral universe. The way this
moral universe is ingrained within him is through chastisement:

> Stern discipline is for him who forsakes the way;
> He who hates reproof will die. (Proverbs 15:10)

The word translated "stern" here is *ra'*, "evil." To the child
this discipline is not good (*tob*) but bad (*ra'*); but it is designed
to give the child a jolt about reality. When he forsakes the way
he ought to be on, something painful and evil (to him) comes
out of nowhere and strikes him. The smart child will begin to
see that there is a moral universe of right and wrong out there
in Mommy and Daddy Land, and if he does not stay inside the
moral boundaries he will have another educative/corrective
experience.

The development of a moral consciousness is built around

the setting of limits and is followed up by correction for limit breaking. This is the ugly task of parenting. As seen in the previous chapter, discipline that works grants a certain mental peace of mind. But as revealed there, discipline carries no unique magic to it. Each child is different. Some have very thick skin, others seem to have little skin at all. Supersensitive kids have very hard times. They can be bruised and battered by words alone. Discipline by logical consequences (the left-outside bicycle is stolen and gone and is not replaced) may be enough for them to learn to be wiser. For the more strong-willed types, their hardened outer shell may never be pierced except by the Spirit of God breaking through to them. I have had one of each in our home. It hasn't made for an easy time. But Proverbs is realistic. It just shows us life as it is, not necessarily the way it ought to be. Therefore, being a parent also brings some other very painful realities to bear.

TWO PARENTAL REALITIES

John Bradshaw has brought the subject of shame to public television and the larger viewing audience. His books have been overwhelming best sellers, like *Healing the Shame That Binds You*. The thesis of Bradshaw's material is that "toxic shame" is at the core of most of our emotional problems: "Once shame is transformed into an identity, it becomes toxic and dehumanizing."[22]

Both my wife and I have found this concept very helpful in understanding aspects of our own identities. When we begin to feel "defective" in our core identity because of some shame-based relationships of the past, we must begin to see ourselves more in line with how God views us. However, Bradshaw focuses only on one relationship and reality: that of the parent being the shamer of the child.

Certainly parents can and do shame their children to such an extent that their very identities are in one constant state of shame. But this is only one side of the shame relationship. Proverbs focuses on the other end, the parental end, of this experience of shame.

The Shame That Stays

Proverbs teaches the reality that parents hurt too. They seriously grieve over their children's hurtful rebellion. They are bearers of their children's shame. The grief and shame experienced affect both parents:

> He [the mother] who begets a fool does so to his [her]
>   sorrow,
> And the father of a fool has no joy. (17:21)

The word translated "sorrow" is used of "the pain experienced in the hoof of a horse and of the emotional pain experienced by Jeremiah in the destruction of Jerusalem (Lam. 3:33)."[23] These two examples give us a clear picture of what parental shame feels like. It's like trying to walk with a stone in your shoe, or like coming home to find your house completely burned down. There is an abiding pain and a feeling of complete loss because the one who has passed through a mother's loins and a father's home has turned out a fool. The father cannot be happy and the mother feels pain. This shame stays and sticks to the core of a parent's identity as much as the shame of the child who has been shamed by parents.

The father bears the same pain:

> A foolish son is a grief to his father,
> And bitterness to her who bore him. (17:25)

The two emotional terms here are different, each reflecting an advanced (by modern psychological understanding) perspective on grief processes. The word *grief* (Hebrew, *ca'as*) can be translated either "anger, vexation or grief."[24] Its usage clarifies its meaning. David uses this term when he complains,

> I am weary with my sighing;
> Every night I make my bed swim,
> I dissolve my couch with my tears.

My eye has wasted away with *grief* [*ca'as*]. (Psalm 6:6-7,
　　emphasis added)

This picks up the grief element of the word.

Solomon uses it differently in his lament about the futility
of life. "So I hated life, for the work which had been done
under the sun was *grievous* [*ca'as*] to me; because everything
is futility and striving after wind" (Ecclesiastes 2:17, emphasis
added). We can almost feel the underlying anger in this usage.
Solomon is mad that life has not given what it was apparently
supposed to give.

Therefore, the grief a father bears from a foolish son is a
shame characterized by an inner vexation, an all-encompassing
feeling of agitation or angry irritation. It doesn't go away but is
under the surface at all times.

The mother's term, *bitterness* (*memer*), is rooted in the
word *marah*, which is what Naomi asked to be called after the
death of her husband and sons (Ruth 1:20). It is the bitterness
experienced due to loss. The father grieves over a son who
didn't turn out as he thought, and the mother feels a certain
bitterness because she considers the child a "lost cause." These
are the painful realities and possibilities all parents must face
at some point in their lives.

Frankly, Proverbs has so much material on this shaming
aspect of parenting that I get concerned when I see parents who
have "perfect" kids. I wonder what is really going on there? These
homes are truly gifts from the Lord, but I wonder if they are really
all that normative and should be made the models for others.

This shaming gets worse. Parental shame can in fact
become the downfall of the family, or at least the parent: "A foolish son is destruction to his father" (Proverbs 19:13). The word
translated "destruction," *hawwot*, is closer to the idea of "ruin"
and, being in the plural, may imply the repeated blows that
have come from his son.[25] Over time the continual failure of his
son to turn toward wisdom finally brings down his father. I
wonder how many fathers have turned to alcohol, compulsive
workaholism, or affairs simply because of the inner grief/rage

they feel toward sons who have humiliated them. "He who is a companion of gluttons humiliates his father" (28:7). The humiliation here is the feeling of "worthlessness"[26] that a father feels coming from his child. God commands a child to "honor his father and mother"; here, the child has so deemed his parent worthless that the parent is utterly humiliated.

I hope this section has not discouraged you, especially those who are thinking about starting a family. If anything, this material should encourage those who have been through the difficult times with children and feel the shame that stays. It should encourage you that you are normal to feel what you feel. This "toxic shame" is the natural, normal result of having the kind of children we did, no matter what we tried to do to have them turn out otherwise. I have felt this pain. I still feel the shame and humiliation not only from my own children, but also from a less-than-understanding community. Even the church, in making the nuclear family such a high priority, has sometimes unwittingly denied the reality that childhood and adolescent rebellion are normative. In responding negatively or overreacting to normal parenting "stuff," it has driven many away altogether.

But there is some good news in this treatment of the parent. Some parents find incredible joy and happiness in their parenting.

The Joy That Rewards

Proverbs also affirms a genuine reward for seeing righteousness and wisdom in our children. This is also one of the realities of parenthood.

> The father of the righteous will greatly rejoice
>   [rejoicingly rejoice],
> And he who begets a wise son will be glad in him.
> Let your father and your mother be glad,
> And let her rejoice who gave birth to you. (23:24-25)

The greatest joy parents can have is to see their children walk in truth (3 John 4). So it is here. These kinds of parents, when they see wisdom and righteous living in their kids, can celebrate. Not so much for doing anything right, but simply because of what they see in the kids.

The best season of life, as far as I am concerned, is the season of forming adult-to-adult relationships with your kids. Cinny and I enjoy being with our adult children more now than probably ever before. We will drop everything and drive cross-country to be with them. To see your kids emerge out of your home and live as responsible, sensible adults with serious convictions is the most I believe a parent can ask for. Whether they married wealthy or not, whether they are in the "right careers" or not—none of it matters. Seeing wisdom, character, commitment to a righteous life—these are the important things.

The ultimate reward for mothers is the tribute that finally and deservingly comes to their labor. King Lemuel simply gives his quiet tribute to his mother by saying, "Here's what Mom taught me; it's good stuff for kings and others; learn it and do it" (see Proverbs 31:1-9). As a part of this tribute, he concludes with the greatest Mother's Day acknowledgment an adult child can give his mother:

Her children rise up and bless her; . . .
"Many daughters have done nobly [married well?],
But you excel them all." (31:28-29)

Our children are aliens. I have had to learn this. Though I have prided myself in thinking that my kids are like me, the older I have gotten the more I have seen that they are utterly and completely unlike their dad. Oh, there are resemblances in face and form, and some quirks. But for the most part they are alien to me, and I to them. They are God's good gifts that have been given to me to take care of for a while, and then they depart to go on to other things. They are simply arrows in one's quiver until they are shot to the world (Psalm 127:4-5). Some hit their intended targets, some don't. Maybe one of our problems today is that we just have fewer of them. When couples had ten or twelve children, with two or three not living even to their adult years, perhaps not so much was riding on each kid. They could just be kids. If one didn't turn out, no problem, there were plenty more coming. Almost every family had its "black sheep" or child no one talked about. I have asked bow-hunters how many arrows they usually carry. Most say five or six. But it really depends on how good a shot one is. Some parents may hit the target with one child. Others, it may take a few more. Even for those who "miss the mark" there is hope.

Researcher Stanton Peele writes,

> It seems that most parents find it more stressful to deal with an adolescent or young adult in the home. (My father described this process for me when I noted that his health had improved between the ages of sixty and seventy. He told me, "Yes, and I felt better when I was sixty than when I was fifty, and I looked and felt worst of all when I was forty. You know why? That's when you and your brother were still living at home.")
>
> The bottom line to all this might not be surprising, were it not so strenuously denied by the disease industry: (1) people respond to positive options with healthy behavior; (2) people strive to right their lives and to overcome problems and frequently succeed over time; (3) age is an important ingredient in determining people's habits, in the large majority of cases leading to improved coping and self-contentment.[27]

It's hard to believe that just growing up brings about a certain wisdom. But apparently, even straight "secular" research is saying that most kids do straighten up and eventually come home. What is it that causes them to come home? Perhaps Helmut Thielicke's sermon "Waiting Father" sheds some light:

> It was because the father and the father's house loomed up before his soul that he became disgusted with himself. . . . It was his father's influence from afar, a by-product of sudden realization of where he really

belonged. So it was not because that far country made him sick that he turned back home. It was rather that the consciousness of home disgusted him with the far country, actually made him realize what estrangement and lostness is.[28]

Of course, it is the waiting that is so difficult, especially when we wait in pain. Our ultimate goal and strategy is not to draw our wandering, rebellious children back by our own powers. But to wait upon what God will do in both their lives and ours. As Lewis shares in her book, "A friend whose hurt I've shared summarized. . . . 'We're so busy being parents. But what God really wants is for us to be His children.' My friend is right."[29]

John Charles Ryle puts it another way:

Let us learn not to expect too much from anybody or anything in this fallen world. One great secret of unhappiness is the habit of indulging in exaggerated expectations. From money, from marriage, from business, from houses, from children, from worldly honours, from political success, men are constantly expecting what they never find; and the great majority die disappointed. Happy is he who has learned to say at all times, "My soul, wait thou only upon God; my expectation is from Him" (Ps lxii. 5).[30]

Rodney Clapp is also right. We become parents so that we might be the kind of people who are more capable of welcoming strangers!

The Wife

There is no animal more invincible than a woman
nor fire either, nor any wildcat so ruthless.
ARISTOPHANES

▼

He who finds a wife finds a good thing
and obtains favor from the Lord.
PROVERBS 18:22

I have a friend who once told his girlfriend, "Marry me and we will have one adventurous life together." Thirty years later, as we compared notes on our lives, we realized neither of us had had any idea where this "adventure" called marriage was taking us. Had we known, both of us might have stayed single! This is not said in any way to disparage the woman I married. The statement just gets at the realistic view of marriage that twenty or thirty years provides.

I would marry Cinny all over again, but for an entirely different set of reasons than when we were young. Then I liked her personality, her figure, her commitment to Christ, and her radiant zeal for life. But today the things I value in her go much deeper because I've seen her suffer through the challenges of rearing children, multiple relocations, graduate school, lean economic times, crazy church problems, and dealing with me everyday. I value her support and continued caring.

In 1994 we celebrated our twenty-fifth wedding anniversary. As an event, it wasn't all that spectacular. We are both just

151

thankful we are still together in spite of everything. Many of our friends split long ago. Some more recently. Each time I feel a deep sense of pain. Two breakups in particular really hurt because I genuinely cared about both the men and the women. They were our friends.

Divorce statistics vary. Most of the secular media puts it at around 50 percent. This is probably inaccurate. Researcher George Barna says the calculation is twice as high as the reality.[1]

Just the same, every divorce hurts. Inside the church and out, people are reevaluating why marriages are not fulfilling lifelong commitments. What is being questioned is the "social exchange" theory of marriage—the simple exchange of support (financial) and sex. This theory assumed a person would select a mate who brought as much to the relationship as that person.[2] The man promised support, "to have and hold as property," while the woman promised sex, "to love, honor, and obey"—the ultimate bed and breakfast arrangement.

However, after the French enlightenment, the passions of young men and women were not solely bound by this legal/financial contract. Couples began to marry based on mutually shared affections and emotional stimulations. According to this "complementary-needs" theory, a person selected a mate whose psychological needs or personality complemented his.[3] My friend Tom Jones, who is a divorce recovery speaker, calls this phenomenon, "two fleas on a dog." Both partners are in the relationship for what they can get out of it!

Citing the dangerous expectations that such an arrangement creates in the minds of the partners, more and more observers are calling this arrangement to task today.[4]

When this "exchange" theory of marriage is assumed, our "solutions" to marriage problems only further accentuate the assumption. We look for better techniques, books, seminars, and counselors to help us pull off this faulty theoretical assumption. We feel we are entitled to a certain exchange, a certain definition of intimacy, and marriage retreats are looked at as being times of "rekindling" the flames. Rodney Clapp calls the exchange theory "contractual fidelity" as opposed to the biblical "covenantal view of marriage." He writes,

> Contractual fidelity, by contrast, assumes that intimacy is strengthened through technique. Do my spouse and I fight chronically and bitterly, hindering our intimacy? Then above all we need a seminar on conflict management. Is our sex lackluster? Give us a manual introducing new positions, better lovemaking methods. Are money worries ruining our marriage and our intimacy? Teach us how to design our budget, provide more effective investment strategies. Contractual intimacy assumes that marital commitments can be entirely submitted to the mechanics of the market. So of course it can be captured or explained by a "formula" applicable to any or all marriages. Contractual fidelity views marriage like machines, the people within them like interchangeable parts, their difficulties like mechanical breakdowns amenable to repair by technical experts.[5]

So divorce solves this problem. Many bail out when they realize they are putting in more than they are getting back. If the exchange is not equal, the terms of the contract are no longer valid. Divorce resolves and dissolves the arrangement and both parties move on. When couples separate and find other partners, who are the real losers, besides our whole society at large? George Gilder calls these remarriages "serial philandering" (eight out of ten divorced men and seven out of ten divorced women remarry[6]) in which women are the real losers. He writes,

> Monogamy is egalitarianism in the realm of love. It is a mode of rationing. It means—to put it crudely—one to a customer. . . . One generally does not act on one's lusts. One does not abandon one's own wife when she grows older, to take a woman who would otherwise go to a younger man. One does not raid the marriages of

others. . . . A breakdown in the sexual order will bring
social ills and injustices far more grievous than the
usual inequalities of money and power. A society is
essentially an organism. We cannot simply exclude a
few million women from the fabric of families, remarry
their husbands to younger women, and quietly return
to our businesses as if nothing happened. What has
happened is a major rupture in the social system, felt
everywhere.[7]

This leads to one simple proverbial fact. Marriage in modern society has gone way beyond what were the normal expectations for men and women in marriage during biblical times.
When a man spent all day plowing his field behind the rear
end of his trusty ox and came home to his woman and a warm
meal, she looked pretty good! Likewise, after she had taken all
day to make bread, mend clothes, and milk the goat, she
appreciated the manly strength her husband provided as he
chopped and carried the next day's load of firewood into her
kitchen. Today, each is looking to the other to provide for their
physical, emotional, sexual, intellectual, recreational, and social
needs. With most marriages riding on such high expectations,
it's surprising the divorce rate is not even higher!

Into this marital complex, Proverbs simply presents the
wife as she is and what she can become. Two ways of life find
their outworking in the tale of two women: the foolish wife
and the wise wife.

THE FOOLISH WIFE
We see individual foolishness in the interpersonal relationship
a wife has with her husband. This proverb sets the principle:
"The wise woman builds her house, but the foolish tears it down
with her own hands" (14:11). The contrast is between the two
ways of life women can pursue. The wisest of women (literal
translation) *builds* the home, while the foolish woman *tears* it
down with her own hands. The foolish woman lacks sense and
God's way of looking at life. She is the antithesis of wisdom.

The word translated "tears down," *haras*, means "to throw down, break or tear."[8] The word is used of tearing down cities (Isaiah 14:17), walls (Ezekiel 13:14), and the stones in a wall (Proverbs 24:31). This last passage is a visual picture of the process. The sluggard daily observes a few more stones out of place but doesn't repair them. Stone by stone, little by little, the wall is broken down by the lack of doing what he ought with his own hands. The foolish woman tears down the sphere of her own domain by her own foolish choices.

I can't help thinking of what has happened in the U.S. since the sixties. Women have always held the domain of the home as their greatest area of strength and contribution. But under the agenda to give more civil rights to women and create other alternatives, some of the first feminists looked disparagingly upon the home in order to get women out of it. On their way out of the home, they shut the door and condemned it. Many women felt guilty and apologetic if they still wanted to be there. The sixties were economically prosperous. When women enjoyed their natural skills of motherhood, an angry and stern sisterhood came alongside and viewed this as unnecessary, of low value, and socially regressive.[9] A few more stones were removed from the walls of the house.

Next, they argued that a woman had a right to choose. She could choose her right to work over her right to bear life. Choice became god. Human beings were sacrificed, and another brick was removed from the home. As more women entered the workplace the sisterhood taught that men were the enemy. Men had all the power, women had none. Women were the victims, men, the victimizers. Male hatred and male bashing followed. A recent cover of *TIME* magazine portrays a pig dressed up as a man with the cover story "Are Men Really That Bad?" The article comments, "The assumption is that men are fair game. Any man insulting is retributive: a payback for the years, the centuries, of male domination and oppression. And for the continuing Awfulness of Men."[10]

Another brick was taken out of the wall. Brick by brick, stone by stone, the home began to collapse. Fortunately, the pendulum is swinging back and the reaction is tempered. Reasonable people are reversing field and saying, "Something must be wrong!" What has happened to the institution of the family? Women need the option of being either a mother at home, a working mother, or a career woman without shame or guilt. Women don't have to destroy the home or hate men to have social and economic justice. Even many pioneer feminists, such as Gloria Steinem, are more honest about their personal struggles.[11]

The current thinking is that the feminist movement made a fundamental error in opposing the maternal and domestic strengths and instincts of women. The movement lost touch with the lives of many women who would not identify with the "victim" image or with its support of the gay alternative lifestyle. My wife, Cinny (Cynthia), and I have written more extensively on this subject in our book (predominantly her book) *The Feminine Journey* (NavPress). There we discuss the differences between the feminist agenda for equality and the biblical portrayal of the nature and seasons of a woman's life journey as designed by God.

No matter how hard one tries, it is hard to fight nature *and* divine design. Whether a woman is the CEO of a large corporation or stuck in a low-paying job in the typing pool, when she stops to buy a magazine for her commute or enjoyment, statistically she doesn't buy *New Woman*, *Ms*, or *Working Woman*. She buys *Better Homes and Gardens* (eight million), *Family Circle* (five million), and *Ladies' Home Journal* (five million). As we say in *The Feminine Journey*, "What does this mean? I believe it means that even though many women today are working and pursuing careers, and are very educated, deep within their souls is another voice. It is the relational voice that springs forth when they want reading material. Even though they may have other interests and vocations, their ultimate fantasy is that of the home, its furnishings, and the relationships cultivated there."[12]

The idea of the feminine mystique as originally coined was a mistake because it did not affirm the true feminine mystique, which was to build a house. The foolish woman is one who tears down this instinct brick by brick until the home lies in ruins. It is wisdom for a wife to secure the prosperity of the home.[13] Or as one insightful teacher put it, "When mama ain't happy, no one in the house is happy"!

Proverbs reveals three areas in which the foolish woman makes mistakes and consequently tears down her home.

Verbal Contention Tears Down a Home

Once when my mother came to visit, she took one look at a small drip coming from the bathroom ceiling and said, "Why don't you fix this thing?" I'd been putting off fixing that small leak for months. I called the plumber that day. It cost close to three hundred dollars to repair the damage of that little drip! What a lesson in the destructive ability of one little water leak. Proverbs says the same is true of the foolish woman who is constantly complaining and nagging:

> A foolish son is destruction to his father,
> And the contentions of a wife are a constant
>   dripping. (19:13)

Two things have the potential of destroying a home in this verse: a foolish son and a contentious wife.

The word used throughout Proverbs for "contention" is the Hebrew word *madon*. Notably, the root of this word means "judge or judgment in the noun form" (Hebrew, *din*).[14] It means to act as a judge or to execute judgments or to create legal strife via lawsuits. To be contentious means to be constantly judging, evaluating, arguing cases, bringing up issues, without any rest. The analogy with dripping rain is instructive. The continuous dripping of water is like the constant contentions of a foolish wife. They both end up destroying the home and driving the husband out! The Arabs have an adage that puts it into perspective: "Three things make a house uninhabitable: tak (leakage of rain), nak (a woman's nagging), and bak (bugs)."[15] The message is poignant. At least bugs can be exterminated and the roof fixed!

Lest my female readers think of me as a sexist, I will be honest enough to point out that contention is not gender specific. Hot-headed men also create their share of contention by their anger (15:18, 29:22, 26:21). But, of course, in this section, we are talking specifically about the foolish wife.

This wife is presented as unpredictable and uncontrollable.

A constant dripping on a day of steady rain
And a contentious woman are alike;
He who restrains her restrains the wind,
And grasps oil with his right hand. (27:15-16)

These are not easy verses to make sense of. The word "restrains," *tzaphan*, means "to hide or put away in safe keeping."[16] Interestingly, the Hebrew word for "north" comes from this word, implying that the northern region from Palestine was viewed as the hidden or remote areas of life. Here, the perspective is from the husband's point of view. Apparently, this contentious wife is such an embarrassment to her husband, he desires to lock her away somewhere that will give evidence of what she is. This attempt is likened to trying to hide the wind. One can close the windows and board them up, but the noise of the wind is still heard. So it is with the contentious wife. Her character cannot be concealed. Rabbi Metsudath David wrote, "Whoever thinks to conceal her character from neighbors is like one attempting to enclose the wind. The effect is only to increase the sound of its howling; similarly this type of woman would raise her voice still louder if she knew that her husband was anxious for others not to hear her."[17]

The mention of oil is the difficult part of the verse. It can be taken at least two ways. "As oil in a man's right hand," which cannot be controlled, so is this contentious woman. Or "as the fragrance of oil upon one's right hand (the hand which puts on perfume), which cannot be hidden, so is the constant criticism of this foolish wife."[18]

Over my years in ministry I have agonized watching destruction come from such women. They would call me at the church, complaining about the service, complaining about the nursery, complaining about the color of my socks, complaining about their husbands, complaining that no one in the congregation cared about them, and that even God didn't listen to them! During our time in Hawaii, when the pastorate was located close to Kaneohe Marine Corps Air Station, I realized why many marines volunteered for six months' floats (time at sea) even when they didn't have to. Being at sea was their desert and rooftop!

How does a husband deal with a contentious wife? Simple, says Proverbs, he just flees the premises! "It is better to live in a corner of a roof, than in a house shared with a contentious woman" (21:9), and if that is not far enough away from her, "It is better to live in a desert land, than with a contentious and vexing woman" (21:19). From the husband's perspective, spartan conditions are better than living with contention. And, it's peaceful on a roof when one is alone.

The point of the passage should be very instructive to women. The way a man deals with nagging and consistent criticism is by fleeing. I know many women view this as not wanting to talk things out, not wanting relationship, or just plain being a wimp. But it is the typical male way of distancing in order to find enough peace of mind to come back and reconnect. A wise woman lets her man go up there awhile without following him up the stairs, which will only drive him further away . . . to the desert if need be. The faster she advances, the quicker he retreats!

I have seen this dynamic more times than I care to write or talk about. I have seen men living in shacks after a divorce. I've gone to their apartments (the wife got the house), where there is no furniture other than a mattress, a kitchen table, and a couple of chairs. Dirty dishes in the sink, TV dinners in the ice-box, and clothes all over the place. This guy can look at me and in all honesty say, "It's not so bad. I kind of like it. It's quiet, with no hassles." I'm sure many women can't understand this.

This male/female dichotomy generally reflects the differing views between men and women on interpersonal relationships. In both use of language and overall perception women seek connection, while men seek independence and differentiation.[19] This produces the "flee and pursue" syndrome in marriages. The wife wants connection as she closes in on her husband, criticizing their current relationship. He responds in male fashion by distancing to buy time and space to think this thing through while affirming his independence as a person apart from his wife. She then interprets his distancing as not caring, thus confirming her original assessment of the relationship, which makes her even more frustrated or frightened. In response, she pursues more frontally, to which he flees more directly. Finally, he is in the desert saying, "This isn't so bad," and she's still in the house saying, "I can't believe the jerk left me!"

The mind-sets are radically different. The man prefers contentment over and against companionship. His wife would rather have contention with her companion than to be alone. The final result is that neither really gets what he or she wants. He wants companionship without contention. She wants connection with her companion! Contention becomes a destructive force in the foolish wife.

One parenthetical note needs to be clarified. Yes, I realize that men leave their wives for a variety of reasons—for younger women, or more sexually appealing women, or just to be free to do their own thing. I have counseled many of their wives through the difficult separation and final divorce proceedings. I have seen women totally deceived by their husbands and ripped off in the financial arrangements and child support. But these are not the women I am talking about here. We're looking at the foolish women, whose husbands apparently wanted to *stay* in the house but were driven out!

Finally, the contentious wife may be driven by a certain charge or excitement she gets from conflict.[20] The conflict may be what makes her feel alive. This woman may come from a background where conflict is the norm. Thus she creates what is familiar with no mental picture of positive relating. But the constant nagging may be perceived by men as violence!

The foolish wife also breaks the sexual boundaries of the marriage.

Sexual Violation Tears Down a Home

As an Air National Guard chaplain I was once attending a seminar about how to deal with sexually transmitted diseases in the military. We discussed the legal issues, the treatment of the HIV virus, maintaining confidentiality, etc. When the seminar leader finally discussed identifying other potentially infected sexual partners via a sexual history, I was somewhat shocked by his strategy. He explained, "When I have a positive I tell the individual to go home and accuse his or her spouse. In 80 percent of the cases, the person comes back with their spouse who has admitted their own unfaithfulness." Both partners often have had independent sexual histories that were kept secret from each other.

Such is the sad state of our world. One of the quickest and most foolish ways to bring down a home is through sexual infidelity.

Proverbs sternly outlines that one major purpose of wisdom is deliverance from the adulterous life: "To deliver you from the strange woman, from the adulteress who flatters with her words; that leaves the companion of her youth, and forgets the covenant of her God; for her house sinks down to death and her tracks lead to death" (2:16-18). It is surprising in this exhortation that this woman is called a "strange" woman or a foreigner, *zarah*. This term was used of foreign, non-Israelite wives as when Solomon took foreign women (1 Kings 9:1,8).

But in Proverbs she is very much in the covenant community of Israel because she has abandoned the husband of her youth (a phrase used for Israel's marriage covenant, as in Malachi 2:14) and laid aside the covenant of her God (Elohim). These passages confirm she is a fellow Israelite who falls under the law prohibiting adultery (Exodus 20:14) and is in a relationship with the God of Israel. She is a believer, but a foolish one at that, for she acts like a pagan!

In another passage she actively pursues other men while her husband is away (7:5,14). Her speech is smooth, alluring, and seductive. She paints mental portraits of her bedroom and makes her potential paramour feel special (7:15-21). The end reality, however, is that her entire household goes down with her. She has violated her marriage, her God, and herself. She is the foolish woman who tears down her house with her own hands. "Her house sinks down to death."

But why would a woman do such a foolish thing, especially if the previous premise is true about women's "nesting" instinct and their claim that they want intimacy with their husbands? This question is not answered in the biblical text. But Warren Farrell, a researcher who has interviewed over 100,000 men and women on the subject, has some ideas:

> For so many women security is the primary unfulfilled need; for most men it is intimacy or love since he expects himself to handle his security needs. . . . How can I call security a woman's primary fantasy if I am saying it is also her primary need? Because the fantasy is that her primary needs get taken care of by someone else. Or at least that a man has the responsibility to take care of them and she has the option to take care of them.
>
> Why do many women focus so much more than men on intimacy? Because within the framework from which they have chosen their men intimacy is often the single biggest missing ingredient. And because these men, by taking care of much of their primary need, allowed them the luxury of focusing on the neglect of intimacy.[21]

If I understand Warren's words, he is saying that this woman goes outside her marriage to have her intimacy needs met. What attracts her to a man in the first place is that he is a good candidate for providing home and security. This woman doesn't marry for intimacy or because of intimacy, but because she thinks her husband is the gallant knight on the white horse. Once married, she finds he doesn't like to shop with her, doesn't pick up his clothes, gets the carpet dirty when he comes in from the yard, and just doesn't talk much. He may be a great provider, thus fulfilling that primary need, but now she has the luxury to focus on her intimacy needs, which are not being met. The more she focuses on his lack or inability to meet these needs she becomes dissatisfied. Finally, she may reach the point of no return and look outside the marriage to have her intimacy needs met. Her knight in shining armor has failed, and she looks elsewhere.

What is amazing in Proverbs 7 is the subtlety that is dropped into the text when she "forsakes the companion of her youth." This phrase focuses on where she was when they first married. "Companion" is an improper translation. The Hebrew term is that of a "tribal chief," *'alluph*.[22] In other words, this man was her knight in shining armor. He was her chief, her "leader" in the tribe. She could not have been more secure than to have been married to the tribal chief himself. But something happened. Disillusionment set in, her heart went astray, and her youthful pledge was violated, rooted in her own relational dissatisfaction.

Relational Dissatisfaction Tears Down a Home

Being human is terribly humbling. We come into this world thinking we are gods and goddesses. Or at least thinking we might marry one! But the more we taste of life, the more life seems to let us down. God created us and gave us everything we needed for a fulfilling life. But we weren't very long on earth when dissatisfaction set in. For Adam, even God's created delights became rivals to Him. When the woman saw "that the tree was good for food, and that it was a delight to the eyes, and that the tree was desirable to make one wise, she took from its fruit and ate; and she gave also to her husband with her and he ate" (Genesis 3:6). The first dissatisfaction set in when Eve saw something she didn't have. As the quip goes, "Of two evils, choose the prettier." She did. Foolishness lies in letting go of something we have in order to try to obtain something we don't have. Foolishness lies in the realm of the foolish wife's relational expectations.

The woman of folly is boisterous,
She is naive, and knows nothing.
And she sits at the doorway of her house,
On a seat by the high places of the city,
Calling to those who pass by,
Who are making their paths straight;
Whoever is naive, let him turn in here,
And to him who lacks understanding she says,
"Stolen water is sweet;
And bread eaten in secret is pleasant."
But he does not know that the dead are there,
That her guests are in the depths of Sheol. (9:13-18)

Three things characterize her foolish ambitions. First, she is attracted to *the righteous life* (verse 15). She calls to those who are on that path. She wants what she does not have—the righteousness of someone else. Whether this is to bring them down or an attempt to elevate her own moral standing, the text is not clear.

I have seen this happen. Women are sometimes attracted to godly men, to pastors and those who are perceived as righteous. To many women in the congregation, the male pastor is the chief paradigm for the spiritual life. He is the kind of man their husbands are not. They wish their husbands would pray more, knew the Bible better, and could lead in devotions. Then a romantic affair develops in her mind with the man in the pulpit who becomes her surrogate husband. Emotionally, the dynamics are already there just waiting for a certain isolated encounter to set the fantasy aflame with real, live passion. This happens today at alarming rates, destroying both the pastors' and women's homes.

Following this first aspiration, she is also attracted to *the citadels of power* (verse 14). Not being content to sit in the confines of her own home, she ventures out. She sits on a seat at the high places of the city. In ancient times the high places were always places of power, whether in pagan temples where gods were worshiped or in the city gates where city politics were dispensed. Either way, she had stationed herself at the "heights of the town" to do her bidding.[23] As alluded to earlier, the foolish woman is attracted to power and men of power. Whether they be politicians, professional athletes, rock stars, or the Donald Trump types, a massive seduction comes with power. The foolish woman knows the power she has to seduce men of power. It's the power of her beauty (7:10,13) and the power of her promise of secrecy. Things done in secret are more exhilarating than the mundane sameness that produces no adrenaline rush. There lies her third desire.

Third, she is attracted to *secretly stolen pleasures*. She says, "Stolen waters are sweet, and bread eaten in secret is pleasant" (verse 17). She is right. Researchers have found that the very anticipation of meeting someone during some private sexual encounter causes an adrenaline rush that increases the heart rate, feeds the imagination, and consequently produces an orgasm that is unmatched in normal, marital lovemaking. The addictive elements are all here to creating a romantic-sexual affair that makes pale the normal marriage with a guy who doesn't pick up his socks![24] This foolish woman is discontent with the existing relationship she has and goes after what she does not have. The final line pictures a frightening reality. The guests who visit her love-nest are the ghosts of the dead!

It is particularly intriguing that this passage is a perfect parallel to what Lady Wisdom does. She too stations herself at the places of influence and power; she too cries out to the passersby and says, "Come drink from my wine and eat of my food" (9:1-6). In other words, this foolish wife parrots Lady Wisdom,[25] but with seductive and selfish motives. This difference is apparent as the mixed wine of wisdom is substituted with stolen water and delicious food is replaced by bread. It's a complete counterfeit. The foolish wife is terribly deceived by her more base passions and wrong expectations. Rather than looking outside her home for fulfillment, it would be more beneficial for her to accept the husband of her youth and keep her covenant with God. Rather than having her house be destroyed, she can accept the painful realities of life. We are limited, finite creatures, and not all our problems need solutions. Zildergeld concludes that we are not nearly as bad off and in need of fixing as therapists tell us. Much of what we now think of as problems—things that ought to be altered and for which there are solutions—are not so much problems as inescapable limits and predicaments of life.[26]

So much for the bad wife. Now for the good wife, the woman of strength.

THE WISE WIFE
In chapter 1, "The Search for Wisdom," I underscored the reality that wisdom is a rare commodity. Just as there are more fools, sluggards, wicked, and naive among us than wise men, the same is true of wives. Again, we would like a neatly packaged list of steps on how to become a wise wife. But Proverbs does not present her in this manner. Likewise, it would be nice if a man could flip through the proverbs and come up with a list of seven or eight things to look for in a potentially good wife. But again, Proverbs defies our quick, consumer-ready, user-friendly desires. What Proverbs describes about the wise wife is more evocative than educative. It raises questions at the front end of this search for wisdom.

In the beginning tribute to the excellent (strong) wife, the writer asks, "A good wife who can find?" (31:10). This rhetorical question poses the evocative nature of the wife. The assumption is that she is not a common commodity. In our search for wisdom, we can search in vain for this kind of woman. She is a rare find indeed. A treasure to be valued once her husband realizes what he has in her. Her "goodness" of character lies in her overall strength in domestic, commercial, charitable, and business life. As such she is depicted by the term used of heroism (*ḥayil*), which usually has to do with "mighty men of valor" (Joshua 1:14).[27] This wise woman is a woman of strong character, or a "steel magnolia" as my wife calls her.[28]

> He who finds a wife finds a good thing,
> And obtains favor from the Lord. (18:22)

Proverbs doesn't tell us where to find one, or what she looks like, or what a woman can do to become one, she just is. When she is found, she is a beneficial asset, upon which God's favor rests. "The word for 'good' describes that which is pleasing to God, beneficial to life, and abundantly enjoyable."[29]

A Wise Wife Is a Crown to Her Husband

A man has two crowns in the book of Proverbs. Older men (*zaken*) have the crown of grandchildren (17:6); husbands have a crown in their woman of strength (*eset hayil*): "An excellent wife is the crown of her husband, but she who shames him is as rottenness in his bones" (12:4). This wise woman of strength is the wreath of honor around her husband's head.[30] In the parallelism, the crown is contrasted with the foolish wife who "puts to shame" her husband's standing in the community.[31] She is as rottenness in his bones. If bones represent the substantial framework of the body, then as rottenness caused by decay slowly eats away at the health of the bones, so a foolish wife gnaws away at the marrow of her husband's life and finally undermines it.

The wise wife has the moral and spiritual fortitude not to eat away at her husband's well-being by shaming him; instead she exercises discretion in her judgments and good taste in keeping with her beauty.

As a ring of gold in a swine's snout,
So is a beautiful woman who lacks discretion. (11:22)

We know the wise wife has a certain beauty, but her outward beauty is ultimately vain (empty) because it will eventually fade. The reason she surpasses all the nobles' daughters is because she fears the Lord and for this she is praised (31:29-30). But physical beauty is out of character when not matched with discretion. The word translated "discretion" (*ta'as*) has to do with the taste buds. It means to have a discriminating taste or to examine something by tasting it.[32] Just as a gold ring does not fit the character of a pig, so a lack of taste or appropriateness does not fit the character of a beautiful woman.

The wise wife is a crown to her husband because she has not only beauty but refinement. She knows what is appropriate and what is not.

> House and wealth are an inheritance from fathers,
> But a prudent wife is from the Lord. (19:14)

A man may receive property and wealth from his father's estate, but when he has the benefit of a prudent wife (*sakal*: insightful or good sense), he knows that she is a good gift from the Lord. This kind of wife was not found through the wise choice of her husband; she is his apparently purely because of the good graces of God. Consequently, as the crowning honor of his life, he values her more than rubies (31:10), trusts in her and lacks nothing (31:11), and praises and honors her at the gates for her exceptional character (31:28-31).

But this wife is not only a crown to her husband, she is also a cistern.

The Wise Wife Is a Cistern to Her Husband

From the opening chapters of Proverbs, Solomon is conducting sex education with the young princes. He tells them of the deceiving lips of the adulteress being so smooth and sweet as to deceive the naive (2:16, 5:3). But there is more to this education than merely a negative "don't." There is also the very positive "do." Solomon tells his young sons where to find their sexual enjoyment. He exhorts,

> Drink water from your own cistern,
> And fresh water from your own well.
> Should your springs be dispersed abroad,
> Streams of water in the streets?
> Let them be yours alone,
> And not for strangers with you.

Let your fountain be blessed,
And rejoice in the wife of your youth.
As a loving hind and a graceful doe,
Let her breasts satisfy you at all times;
Be exhilarated always with her love.
For why should you, my son,
Be exhilarated with an adulteress,
And embrace the bosom of a foreigner? (5:15-20)

The term "wise wife" is not used in this extended passage as a comparison with the excellent wife (31:10-31) as the ultimate personification of wisdom. However, the context seems to argue that whereas the adulterous woman (the fool) desires to steal away the young men, the "wife of one's youth" (5:18) is to be the refreshing source of sexual pleasure. The husband should not seek out pleasure in the streets but go to his own private cistern or well.

In ancient Israel the privately owned cisterns were usually enclosed inside the walls of a home, collecting rain water and perhaps drawing from underground springs. As water satisfies the physical desires of thirst, so the wife of one's youth (the wise wife) should seek to satisfy her husband's sexual desire, and vice versa. The image that is intended by "let your fountain be blessed" could be either his wife as the cistern and source of pleasure or his own flow or ejaculation.[33] Either way, the passage establishes the principle that the wise wife is the continual, monogamous source of pleasure for her husband.

To close out the metaphor, Solomon cites the animal kingdom to drive the point home. Most translations don't do justice to what is going on in the Hebrew text. The two animals mentioned are probably the Palestinian "roe-deer" or "ibex," which was regarded as a symbol of beauty and grace in ancient times,[34] and the gazelle, which is so frequently mentioned in the Song of Songs (2:17).

Since the first line is plural, it could be either "hinds in the act of loving" or "loving hinds." Since the context is sexual, we assume Solomon is using the animal world to give a clear picture of the wise wife and her husband. As two gazelles in the act of loving, so let her breasts satisfy you at all times. The second part picks up the gentleness and grace of a doe, perhaps being nursed by its mother. Just as a woman's breasts are a very sensitive and delicate part of her body, so this husband should approach them as a gentle and gracious doe. Solomon illustrates for the young husband and wife how he should approach his wife and that she must see herself as this source of pleasure for him.

In closing, we return to where we started and go beyond it: "The wise among women builds her house" (14:1), but also the wise woman "extends her hand to the poor; and she stretches out her hands to the needy" (31:20). She is not an island, her home is not her boundary but a base of operation. Her world is larger than her own home, but she never sacrifices her own home for the sake of the bigger world. After all, she is a wise woman!

The Fool

A fool in a gown is none the wiser.
KENNETH AIKEN
PROVERBS

▼

A fool's mouth is his ruin.
PROVERBS 18:7

I live in the Philadelphia suburbs. However, having one's home in this historic area does not make one an expert or even knowledgeable about what really happened here two hundred years ago.

People come from all over the world to see Independence Hall, the Liberty Bell, and Valley Forge. Even the tours of these places largely focus on our desire as a people to be an independent nation free from the restraints of the British. They speak of the "genius" of Jefferson, Madison, Adams, Franklin, and even Washington. The presentations cast these men as young, educated, articulate rebels, fighting for a way of life free of British tyranny.

What is fascinating, though, is that on the day these signers of the Declaration of Independence threw out the thirteen British constitutions governing each colony, they went home and began writing new constitutions for their home states. These were not men who wanted no authority over their lives, but men who were wise enough to recognize there was only

171

One who was wise enough to govern them. Therefore, almost all of the new thirteen states' original constitutions, by today's standards, look more like a doctrinal statement for a theological seminary or Bible school than a state constitution. Take for example the Massachusetts Constitution authored by Samuel Adams: "(All persons elected must) make and subscribe the following declaration, viz. 'I do declare; that I believe the Christian religion; and have firm persuasion of its truth.'"[1]

These men considered it wise in forming a new government to recognize God as their ultimate authority, and to have men in government who would not only subscribe to a certain belief about God but also seek to obey Him. Today such beliefs are considered "foolish" and a violation of the separation of church and state, a concept apparently never envisioned by our founding fathers. When our country was founded it was considered "foolish" not to have a government that recognized God's superintendence over the lives of its people. Today, over two hundred years later, it is "foolish" to even talk of God as being relevant in the public sector of life.

From the perspective of the psalmist, it is the fool who says God has no relevance to life (Psalm 14:1, 53:1)—"The fool has said in his heart, 'There is no God.'" Of course God exists, but the fool has no place for Him in his heart. He has concluded that God is not relevant: Therefore, he lives as if there is no God.

In studying the character of the fool, we can simply look at our own nation today. At critical points in our history we have made some foolish decisions by allowing fools to determine the destiny of our country, our schools, our major denominations, and probably even our individual churches. Therefore, it is paramount that we understand how to recognize the fool and the foolishness we may tolerate in our own hearts. Just as P. J. O'Rourke has called Washington "A Parliament of Whores,"[2] so I believe our "more perfect Union"[3] has become a communion of fools.

WHAT DOES A FOOL LOOK LIKE?

In the book of Proverbs, three different Hebrew words are translated by the English word *fool*. The first, *'ewil*, has root meanings that have the idea of "growing thick of fluids."[4] This "thickness" may manifest itself in "moral perversions rather than in mental stupidity."[5] In other words, the fool is foolish not because he lacks mental abilities but because he refuses to submit to any authority higher than himself. In Proverbs he refuses to submit to anyone else's commands.

The second word translated "fool," *kesil*, brings out the idea of "lacking foresight" or having "a propensity to making wrong choices because he has never adequately matured."[6] In other words, this fool has never really grown up. He still thinks and behaves like a stunted teenager in adult life. Because of this immaturity he continues to make seriously wrong moral choices.

The last word, *nabal*, picks up the ideas of being "empty-headed" and "lacking moral sensitivity."[7] Therefore, the quick snapshot of the fool reveals the paradoxical concepts of being both thick-headed and empty-headed at the same time. His thick-headedness is revealed in his stubborn refusal to listen, learn, and submit to wisdom. His empty-headedness is reflected in his adolescent behaviors and attitudes. He appears to lack the common moral judgments that even average human beings display. More particularly, we can see the first element of his foolishness in his contempt for learning.

He Hates Learning

The most obvious characteristic about the fool is his utter hatred of learning. Sister Wisdom cries, "How long . . . will . . . fools hate knowledge?" (1:22). The fool can look at a body of knowledge, scientific research, or biblical revelation and conclude, "I have no use for it."

Consider the effect the government's warning labels on cigarette packs has had on smokers. The number of tobacco-related deaths every year is estimated at over four hundred thousand.[8] Addiction researchers agree that nicotine is as addictive as heroin, cocaine, and alcohol, and one in particular says smoking, of all addictions, is the most difficult to stop.[9] But every day "fools" buy another pack or carton thinking the research does not apply to them or that they are somehow immune to the ill effects. The fool ignores and deep down resents people with knowledge telling him how he ought to live his life. He doesn't want to orient his life around learning, wisdom, or knowledge, but around what he wants to do. Pure and simple, nothing else.

The fool, though, does have his reasons for resisting the wisdom-producing effects of knowledge. First, serious learning involves correction and having to face one's failures. We learn that . . .

> Understanding is a fountain of life to him who has it,
> But the discipline of fools is folly. (16:22)

Because the fool fundamentally rejects the obtainment of knowledge, even when he is corrected about something he rejects the correction. Therefore, he never learns from anyone about anything.

Most of us probably remember more from our failures than from our successes. The reason I love the Hebrew language today, and am able to write this book based on these Hebrew characters in Proverbs, is because I suffered through a painful process of having my mind disciplined by one notable professor.

Dr. Bruce Waltke was and still is one of the most humble Christian gentleman-scholars I have ever had the privilege of studying under. He is as brilliant in mind as he is humble in spirit. But my first course with him was a most painful experience. On quizzes of 100, I averaged scores of 20 to 40! Not really promising or rewarding! I flunked the midterm exam. Everything came down to the final, which I passed with a C-minus. Among my fellow students, very few wanted to take any electives from him. Why voluntarily endure so much pain and suffering? I merely accepted the reality that I would get

C's from this man, but for what I learned from him in the process it was worth it.

Now I thank God for the painful discipline I endured and the love I still have for the Hebrew language. At least in this one small area of my life, I think I learned the lesson that it is foolish to try to stay away from pain and truly learn something. Wisdom involves learning, and learning means suffering through failure and correction. But the rewards are great. When the fool looks at the discipline required for learning something, he concludes it is too much "above" him. "Wisdom is too high for a fool" (24:7).

But there's another reason the fool hates knowledge: He believes he has all the knowledge he needs! He believes he is okay. He is a firm believer in the "I'm Okay, You're Okay" philosophy (later we'll see that he doesn't believe that anyone else is okay). Obviously, people who believe they have all the knowledge they need don't need to learn anything more. Proverbs states outright,

> The way of the fool is right in his own eyes,
> But a wise man is he who listens to counsel. (12:15)

When a fool looks at his own life, he directly concludes that he is right and therefore doesn't need the advice of others. The wise man, on the other hand, opens himself to the counsel of others and listens to it. One writer observes, "The fool knows no other standard than his own opinion, and however clearly and truly one may warn him that the way which he has chosen is the wrong way and leads to a false end, yet he obstinately persists."[10]

What makes our nation a nation of fools today is this self-oriented, self-defined, self-justifying, totally subjective determination that "rightness" is whatever we are into or like. The individual then becomes the standard by which all other behavior is evaluated as right or wrong. To think that one human being can have all the truth or be the judge of all reality is not only foolish and impossible but downright preposterous. The end result is the kind of foolishness we see daily on the afternoon talk shows that showcase the bizarre as normative and the deviant as misunderstood. If one feels an inclination to be gay, or an adulterer or cross-dresser or voyeur, or has feelings of being obsessed about one's sister's boyfriend who suffers from the Peter-Pan-Tinkerbell-Captain-Hook Syndrome, then one is true and right. All inclinations are equal. Descartes' axiom "I think, therefore I am" has become "I feel, therefore I am right" in the fool. Proverbs calls it correctly. To make yourself the judge of all reality is to be a fool.

There exist in Proverbs some other reasons why the fool hates knowledge. Apparently he never submitted to it during his childhood years. Our writer gives us two proverbs in this regard:

> A fool rejects his father's discipline,
> But he who regards reproof is prudent. (15:5)

> A wise son makes a father glad,
> But a foolish man despises his mother. (15:20)

What is interesting about these passages is that the parents had apparently tried to discipline their child but the child never responded positively. This teaching goes against the grain of the current, popular psychotherapy movement that imputes any problem in the child to the parent. In Proverbs, equal responsibility is placed upon the child and the parent. Recently, in a precedent-setting court case, a father won damages from the court when it was shown that his daughter's memories of abuse (by her father) had been false memories "implanted" by therapists.[11] I think this is a needed change of direction from the almost universal granting of innocence to children against their parents that has taken place in the past.

The fool also has difficulty submitting to knowledge because he has so many divided interests. We are told:

> Wisdom is in the presence of the one who has
> understanding,
> But the eyes of the fool are on the ends of the earth.
> (17:24)

In short, the person of wisdom can narrow down and focus on one goal, and then go about moving toward accomplishing it. Cohen says, "The fool is unable to concentrate his mind, so that his gaze keeps wandering in all directions."[12] Apparently, the fool has great ambitions but can't pull them off because he can't buckle down to doing *one* thing. Wherever the fool is, he is thinking about being elsewhere. His eyes are on "faraway" things rather than the things sitting right in front of him.

But the main reason the fool hates knowledge is simple pride! He is too full of himself to learn from someone else. Our sophist concludes, "In the mouth of the foolish is a rod of pride."[13] The word for "pride" here brings up imagery of a swelling sea and a head lifted up in triumph.[14] The proverb itself is very graphic. Imagine a large rod sticking out of someone's mouth. It's a rod of pride. In other words, every time this individual opens his mouth, his own swelling pride comes out. A person so full of himself is not going to learn from someone else. What a tragedy!

It would seem reasonable a man so full of himself would have no difficulty managing himself (since there is no one else in his life of importance). But this is not the case. He has difficulty controlling himself.

He Can't Control His Temper or His Tongue

In a somewhat humorous analogy, Aiken says, "His mouth is a minefield and everytime he opens it he puts his foot on a mine."[15] On this point, the wisdom literature of the Bible parts company with much of modern psychotherapy. Since the sixties, much emphasis has been placed on the validity and value of "venting" whatever feelings a person has. Now, I don't question the need to have others in our lives to dump our deepest feelings on, and to have them validate us or listen to us with a sympathetic ear.[16] But some, I suspect, have concluded that to be a truly mature, open, and honest human being we must speak our mind to any and every person who comes across our path. Proverbs instructs, "This is not wise, this is what fools do." Our writer carefully warns:

A fool always loses his temper,
But a wise man holds it back. (29:11)

A fool's vexation is known at once [the same day],
But a prudent man conceals dishonor. (12:16)

In other words, the fool is known by his lack of self-control. He can't control his own spirit long enough to get through the day. He has to let everything out at once.[17] Whatever is affecting his spirit, everyone around him knows it because he does not have the ability to keep his feelings inside.

What is worse, once whatever it is that is agitating him is out, it becomes a weighty issue for others around him to deal with. The wise counselor affirms,

A stone is heavy and the sand weighty,
But the provocation of a fool is heavier than both of
    them. (27:3)

Anyone who has tried to move stones, or has put more sand in a bag than he could carry, knows the reality of this verse. Once the fool has lost his temper, exploded, and told everyone around him what he thinks of them, the weight of his anger is multiplied by the number of people within earshot.

I know. I have seen it happen. A large evangelical congregation felt their church was the greatest and were not aware of any problems, but one Sunday during worship the pastor, in one extended outburst of vexation, told the assembly they were too sinful to receive Communion that morning, walked out the side door, and never came back! Some parishioners cried; most just sat stunned and motionless in the pews. Finally one man stood up and spoke for everyone, "What in the h—

is going on here?" For almost one year the vexation of one man was multiplied times the number of those who chose to remain during difficult times. It became a heavy weight for all involved. In my opinion, this godly pastor made one very foolish mistake and caused many innocents to suffer because he couldn't control himself.

This lack of control within his own spirit is what causes the fool to be so contentious.

> Keeping away from strife is an honor for a man,
> But any fool will quarrel [burst out]. (20:3)

I am amazed at the countercultural direction of the wisdom literature. I opened this chapter by voicing my opinion that our country has become a nation of fools. This is evidenced even more in the therapeutic model of reality and relationships that is currently in vogue. The goal, if not the definition, of healthy relationships and healthy individual psychology is to lay open the hidden areas of a person's life. Even the news media illustrate this when they "cover" a story. To cover usually means to keep private and not expose, but when the press covers a story, it is for all the world to see! To cover now means to expose or do an exposé.

In this verse, what is honorable is keeping your mouth shut and being at peace from the divisive agitations of the world. It means refusing to be drawn into a quarrel or conflict. The opposite is even more striking. Every fool "discloses oneself." The verbal idea in this word, *gala'*, is to "expose, or lay bare." Other usages suggest the idea of "showing the teeth, and snarling."[18] This idea approximates some of the "person-centered therapies" that were once thought to be very helpful in getting people's pent-up aggression out and facilitating mental health. Two Christian psychologists caution us about such therapy:

> Thus one of the greatest assets of the person-centered
> therapy is its strong emphasis on awareness of feelings.

But this is also a liability. Awareness is an end in itself in this system; awareness *is* health. As Van Belle (1985) has observed, greater awareness of emotional response might lead to a sense of emotional relief, freedom, improved self-awareness, personal autonomy and inter-personal competence. But there is no guarantee that "healthier" more emotionally "in-touch" persons will anchor themselves in any abiding structure outside themselves, because as we noted the self is formless in person-centered therapy theory. (emphasis added)[19]

I agree. I do think there is value in being aware of one's feelings, but giving uncontrolled expression to everything we feel is not wise. The fool disagrees! Like water once out of a dam that cannot be returned, so is the anger of a fool once released.

The beginning of strife is like letting out water,
So abandon the quarrel before it breaks out. (17:14)

As much as the fool is known by his temper, he is also known by his tongue. In fact, he is so characterized by his tongue in Proverbs that when he has enough sense to keep his mouth shut (a rare occasion indeed), he is deemed wise!

Even a fool, when he keeps silent, is considered wise;
When he closes his lips, he is counted prudent. (17:28)

Again, the value of not bearing one's whole feelings is viewed as wisdom and not psychological denial by the writer of Proverbs.

Do we think we have more wisdom about such things than the ancients? Anybody who has lost jobs or friends sim-ply because he was too "honest" knows the answer. If nothing else, the careers of politicians who have been ruined by "kiss-and-tell" affairs should tell us about the reality of "openness." We love to be voyeurs peeping in on other people's dirty laundry, but we don't want anyone looking in on ours. The fool doesn't worry about such things. He is the perfectly modeled modern man and woman who values openness and says whatever is on his mind or heart. But when he talks, his speech betrays him. His communication evidences some distinctive patterns. He has two favorite subjects.

The content of the fool's speech is, first of all, characterized by talking about other people in the negative. Indeed, his favorite topic of conversation is slander about others. Consider two verses from chapter 10:

> He who conceals hatred has lying lips,
> And he who spreads slander is a fool. (10:18)

> The wise of heart will receive commands,
> But a babbling fool will be thrown down. (10:8)

When taken together, these verses suggest that at a party or social event, the fool is the one doing most of the talking. The word translated "babbling" means "the fool of lips," or being much lipped. The imagery gives us a very graphic portrait of the fool. When we observe him, he is the one who is much lipped, always talking, primarily about others in slanderous tones.

In one sense I hated being a pastor. I don't know how many times I would be on my way to the worship service, thinking about leading my people in the worship of God, when some dear soul would stop me and say something like, "Pastor, I just thought you ought to know what is going on in so-and-so's life." As a young man in the ministry I would stop and listen, not wanting to be perceived as a pastor who couldn't care less about what was going on in someone else's life. But over the years, I began to realize that about 90 percent of what I heard was pure slander, conjecture, or jealousy! Most of the accusations were against leaders in the church. Finally, I realized I was caving in to a clear biblical prohibition: "Do not receive an accusation against an elder except on the basis of two or three witnesses" (1 Timothy 5:19). Now, I just ask, "Are you wanting to make a formal charge against this elder or person, and do you have some additional witnesses?" The accusers are usually quite quiet, and leave as swiftly as they approached. The fool is a slanderer and, as we shall see later, we are foolish even to listen to the fool! But the fool has an even more favorite subject of conversation. Himself!

In Proverbs 14:3, we found that what is sticking out of the mouth of the fool is his own pride. By implication, we can suppose his even more favorite topic of table conversation is himself. Literally, his mouth is his own ruin:

A fool's mouth is his ruin,
And his lips are the snare of his soul. (18:7)

Whether it is speaking about himself or others, the more words that come out of his mouth, the more the character of his soul becomes self-evident. His words deny whatever glorious reputation he is trying to gain from his listeners.

Cinny and I once had several couples over for dinner. On the day of the dinner party our boss asked if a fairly well-known (to us) psychologist could join us for dinner. Since our guests did not know who this special guest was, we just introduced everyone without much comment. During the meal, one of the men literally dominated the conversation with his particular political views, accounts of his world travels, and his salesman-persuasive personality. He was a man very much caught up with himself (and obviously very insecure). The real topic of conversation that night was him! Over dessert, he must have finally gotten a pinch under the table from his wife, because for a moment he got out of himself long enough to look across the table and ask our new friend, "What kind of work do you do?" It was one of those moments you wish you could have captured on film. The special guest looked up, swallowed, and said, "I'm a psychologist!" Our self-evidenced fool turned a little red, apparently realizing he had monopolized the entire evening, and said nothing more. So it is with the fool.

Given enough time, his tongue brings upon himself his own ruin. The wise man at our table that night was the psychologist, who had more wisdom and insight about many of the things the fool was speaking about. But he was gracious and quiet and allowed the fool to speak until he buried himself. Proverbs contrasts these two men:

Wise men store up knowledge,
But with the mouth of the foolish, ruin is at hand.
    (10:14)

Cohen says the opening verb in this verse means "'lay up knowledge' rather, 'conceal knowledge.' They are not talkative and make no show of what they have learned. When they speak, it is with due deliberation."[20] Cohen is correct, the verb *store up* is *tzaphan*, which means "to hide, or treasure";[21] in the imperfect tense it has the idea of ongoing activity or aspect. The wise man is continually adding to his treasure of knowledge and does not need to dump it on every passerby. The fool, on the other hand, lacking this quality and the true knowledge that goes with it, has his own ruin lying close at hand.

If the fool doesn't do well with his mouth, we are also told in the wisdom literature that he doesn't do well with money or honors either.

He Can't Handle Success
As Americans we have a deep-seated belief in meritocracy. We believe those deserving of merit will end up on top (ruling). We are told early on by parents, teachers, and even Sunday school teachers that if we work hard, get a good education, and are honest and kind, we will end up with the American dream. As our teens so aptly say, "NOT!" But this belief is at the core of many of our "adjustment reaction" problems when life doesn't work out as we thought or planned.[22] One thing the wisdom literature alerts us to is that life is not always fair. Ecclesiastes tells us that it can rarely be figured out, because of all the paradoxes, ambiguities, and senseless things that

happen. One of these seemingly unfair, senseless things is that even fools obtain honors and money. But when they do, they can't handle it.

Honors Do Not Dress the Fool

When I fly I usually glance through the airline magazines for something interesting to read. Most of the time I get more interested in the advertising than the articles (by marketing design, I'm sure!). One thing I see in almost all airline magazines are ads for "alternative education programs." These used to be called "mail-order diploma mills," but today they are big business and go by other names. Degree-completion programs, life-learning credit institutions, distance education— these are the new concepts. Sometimes I tear the ads out and send my name in just to see what I will get. One school assured me that I could study anything from law to business to medicine and get advance credit for almost everything I'd done with my life up to this point. Not bad! I can become a doctor by receiving credit for putting Band-Aids on my kids! Such a deal.

But, as I look around at people traveling and reading these magazines with me, I see mostly businessmen and business-women, fairly well-off, and certainly not fools. Why would these schools run these very high-priced ads in magazines mostly read by business travelers? Perhaps the thought of getting a Ph.D., M.D., D.D., or CPA rating for doing very little work strikes very deep to the fool within all of us. Americans have always been suckers for any kind of snake oil as long as it was packaged right! Now, as much as I do believe there is a place for *legitimate* institutions like these and that they have value in educating the self-motivated and highly disciplined person with lots of money, there is something very inappropriate in thinking about a successful person in terms of mail-order degrees. I also wondered if the pilot of the plane had gotten one of these by making model airplanes when he was a kid.

This illustrates the phenomenon of what happens when we reward the fool with honors. Proverbs says,

Like snow in summer and like rain in harvest,
So honor is not fitting for a fool. (26:1)

Like snow in the middle of July or a rampant downpour while
farmers are putting the sickle to their crops, so it is to give honors to a fool.

Two concepts flow from this analogy. First, there is a clear
inappropriateness to these events. Snow doesn't fit summer,
nor rain the harvest time. They are out of season (for biblical
culture). The Hebrew language gives a very meaningful word
picture here with *fitting*. The Hebrew expression *na'ah* carries the idea of "beauty," as is used of a beautiful woman (Song
of Solomon 1:10, 2:14, 4:3).[23] Solomon uses this term to com-
pliment the radiant beauty of his wife, which seems to fit
within the context of the rest of his relationship with her. Her
beauty is in keeping with her character. With the fool, this is
not the case. As men, we can read *Gentleman's Quarterly*,
even buy the clothes we see advertised there, but Wisdom
says, "Clothes do not make the man." Dress a fool in thousand-
dollar suits and he is still a fool. Dress a foolish woman in
gowns, and she is still a fool!

Second, to give honor to fools is destructive. A frost in
summer will kill all growing things, just as a hard rain will
destroy a year's harvest. In the final analysis, even though the
fool is rewarded at times, the honors that come to him don't
fit him and are ultimately destructive to his life.

Some of the first American millionaires, who made their
money during pre-income-tax days, so wanted the royalty of
Europe to view them as honorable and royal that, between the
1880s and 1920s, they headed off to the European capitals and
southern Mediterranean gambling spots for the specific purpose of losing large sums of money. How else could they prove
they were just as wealthy as the nobility of Europe except by
walking away from what was considered a fortune by the average person? Economist John Maynard Keynes concluded that
the Europeans were not impressed, and the rich Americans
were never accorded the "royal" status they were seeking. We

might conclude that the Americans' wealth did not fit them. Money and honors can never truly buy what is lacking in character.

Proverbs 26:1 should alarm us as to how often we in the church honor fools. Oh, I don't think we do it consciously. But sometimes we are so busy promoting our heroes and heroines that we never stop to ask the important questions about character. I have seen this happen when famous people come to know the Lord and we immediately put them on the speaker circuit to give their heartwarming testimony all over the country. Who in their right mind would not want to go hear Oprah, Howard Stern, Phil Donahue, or Madonna, should one of these come to know Christ and have his or her life significantly changed? Would anybody ever suggest that perhaps they are too young in the Lord to have biblical wisdom and we are only pandering to their already substantial celebrity status? In having them speak are we in fact honoring fools? As I look back on some of my early heroes in the faith, who got on this circuit and received accolades and honors for doing so, I am painfully aware that most are no longer around today. Some have dropped out of sight, others had affairs, still others moved on to more promising careers or even to other faiths. To honor fools is both inappropriate and harmful. They can't handle it. Fools don't do any better with money.

Money Doesn't Buy Him Beauty

A popular saying among women used to be, "A woman can't be too thin or too rich." Well, we all know now that women who have lived by this philosophy have starved themselves to death (Karen Carpenter) through the destructive process of bingeing and purging. However, I doubt if any men or women could say the second part of the statement is no longer in vogue. Deep down we are all still envious of the lives of the rich and famous, and if they do have problems, we assert that "problems with money are still easier to deal with than problems without money."

Proverbs seems to imply that fools can and do get money,

but once they have it, it doesn't wear well on them. A life of luxury is just as unfitting for fools as a Ph.D.! Wisdom says,

> Luxury is not fitting for a fool;
> Much less for a slave to rule over princes. (19:10)

It's hard for us to admit that fools can live luxuriously and by all appearances "have it all." The word used here for "luxury" is *'anog,* which emphasizes the ideas of "softness, delicate things, and anything which gives pleasure in abundance."[24] It is used of the sexual pleasures of men and women (Song of Solomon 7:7, Ecclesiastes 2:8), luxurious houses (Micah 2:9), and abundant prosperity (Psalm 37:11). But the wealthy mansions around the world contain far more: dainty, fragile, period antiques; soft, silken clothes and tapestries; the best that money can buy, up to and including whatever the sexual pleasures of the household might be. All these, the sophist says, do not fit the fool, yet he has them! Here lies the certain irony of life. They do not fit the fool because his character is not such that these rewards are in keeping with who he is. They are more the rewards of wisdom, but the fool has them! Perhaps, because the fool lacks wisdom, his money ultimately disappears, having been consumed by his pleasures rather than being used to God's glory.

My son-in-law is a professional baseball player in the minor leagues. He has gotten to know quite well several of the "bonus babies." These are mostly young superstars—some are nineteen years old—who are given five-hundred-thousand-dollar signing bonuses. Jason has told me how many of these players, after just several years in the minors, have nothing to show for their money. It's all gone! What did they spend it on? Cars, stereos, clothes, gifts to friends, you name it! With so little wisdom around in our culture, is it surprising they wouldn't be wise enough to invest that money in a growth account and let it draw from 12 to 18 percent interest? They would be set for life, whether they ever play in the majors or not. No, many are foolish.

The fool doesn't handle money or honors too well. Given

enough time, the success that does come to him destroys him.

But the fool is also recognizable by a certain attitudinal complex. The fool reveals a very clear temperament in response to life situations.

The Fool's Reward

A fool may make money,
but he needs a wise man to spend it.
A. B. CHEALES[1]

▼

Like a dog that returns to its vomit
Is a fool who repeats his folly.
PROVERBS 26:11

I don't know how many times I have had to go to someone to get some misunderstanding straightened out. Sometimes people have had to come to me, either because I was totally unaware of their problem with me, or I was just too "chicken" to go to them! At any rate, in doing this kind of conflict resolution, I have seen one disturbing phenomenon. We can do the right thing in confronting, seeking resolution, and trying to mend past relationships and still have the attempt explode in our faces. When this happens, one (or more) of the parties involved may have been and probably still is a fool. Our proverbial writer makes it clear:

When a wise man has a controversy with a foolish man,
The foolish man either rages or laughs, and there is no
    rest. (29:9)

Even though the wise man may want to maintain peace and harmony, when he must press charges he faces a response

189

of either anger or laughter.[2] Ross notes, "It is a waste of time to try to settle a dispute calmly or rationally with a fool . . . To go into court with a fool, you have to reckon 'with unreasonable and objectionable behavior and a complete lack of proportion.'"[3]

The fool's attitude and response to conflict are clear: He either reacts with a self-justifying anger or laughs the offense off as an insignificant nuisance. In many ways, we see here the criminal mind in formation. One who laughs at the law thinking he is above it or does not take the law seriously is sowing the seed of criminal instinct so often seen in both Mafia and political leaders. But the fool does more than just laugh at those opposing him.

He Mocks at Forgiveness

In a difficult passage to translate (14:9), we also see the fool as one who, having experienced an offense, will not initiate or accept the forgiveness necessary for reconciliation. The verse says, "Fools mock at making amends for sin, but good will is found among the upright."[4] The word used for "making amends" is *'asham*, which means "a trespass or guilt offering."[5] As the fool looks at the available forgiveness for his own sin and others', his response is not one of contrition and thankfulness but of holding it in contempt. Apparently, to accept the forgiveness that God has provided in the guilt offering would mean having to give up his grudge and no longer hang onto his adversarial relationship with the offended party. In fact, the fool probably sees in this simple forgiveness a serious weakness of character rather than strength. As Ross clarifies, "The parallelism suggests that the idea is that fools ridicule reparation whereas the upright show good will."[6] It is wise to accept and initiate forgiveness, but the fool is not capable of doing so. Therefore, his offended relationships are never repaired.

I wonder what the cost in time, energy, and wasted human industry is for even Christian organizations when they fail to repair the damage of offended brothers and sisters. I have seen so many gifted individuals who leave churches and organizations offer as their reason the dishonest cliché "The Lord is leading me elsewhere," when in reality they are leaving because of unreconciled relationships. I fear for the judgment seat of Christ, when our every word and deed is accounted for in light of how well or poorly we have treated each other (Matthew 25:31-46, 1 Corinthians 4:5). We are very foolish to let pastors, parishioners, and friends leave our circle of employment or accountability without seeking to reconcile the relationships. At the same time, when resistance to such activity is found, we know very graphically we are dealing with a fool! The fool either outwardly or inwardly mocks at such "ridiculous" suggestions. But another toxic attitude is also firmly imbedded in his temperament.

He Enjoys Wickedness

There is a vulgar scene in the movie *Schindler's List* when the Nazi commandant of a Jewish labor camp picks up his telescope-equipped rifle and randomly picks out Jewish laborers in the open gathering space. He moves the scope from person to person in whimsical fashion, then fires, and a randomly "selected" human being falls to his death. As the commandant reenters his quarters, the camera depicts a small upward turn on the officer's mouth. A hint of a smile at killing innocent human beings! Killing Jews was his sport! So it is with fools.

Sister Wisdom informs us,

Doing wickedness is like sport to a fool;
And so is wisdom to a man of understanding. (10:23)

What makes this commandant so evil, along with the entire Nazi extermination (Final Solution) operation, is the intense, well-coordinated planning that was required to do it. Planning always reveals intention, so the real core of the fool's wickedness lies in his designed intentionality. The words *doing wickedness* in the text pick up the Hebrew term *zimmah*, which in its verbal use has the idea of "planning to do something." In this noun form, the word takes on the meaning of well-planned and intentioned evil.[7] In other usages, it involves a full range of sexual offenses (incest, Leviticus 20:14; pushing one's daughter into harlotry, Leviticus 19:29; marital infidelity, Job 31:9-11) and the crimes of blood-thirsty men (Ezekiel 22, Psalm 26:10). Toy concludes, "It is the fool's moral superficiality that enables him to enjoy sin—he has no deep sense of its sinfulness; . . . such conduct is easy for him—the assumption is that wrongdoing may become part of a man's nature, his normal and joyous activity."[8]

The fool's attitude toward things criminal, the legal process, and the forgiveness of such things is most instructive as to his moral nature, or lack of it. The fool is most deficient in moral reasoning and more importantly in moral actions. He mocks, laughs, and makes sport at the things deemed criminal by both God and societies seeking to live by moral principles. Again, I restate my opening premise. Read the front page, middle page, and back page of most of our nation's city newspapers and you will find both the criminal actions of fools and often the actions of the fools defending them. In fact, the only thing the fool does consider wrong is to depart from doing his evil:

> Desire realized is sweet to the soul,
> But it is an abomination to fools to depart from evil.
>   (13:19)

Our society has come so far that even our supposed moral education is having surprising results. One of the consistent answers on values-clarification exercises on the subject of stealing from a Woolworth's is, "Woolworth's counts on losing money from people stealing things. They charge me for that when I buy things there."[9] In other words, we have already paid for the merchandise, so just go ahead and steal it! We are a nation of fools.

So what do we do with a fool when we encounter one?

HOW TO HANDLE A FOOL

Two experiences come to mind where in my opinion I was dealing with fools.

The first was when I was in graduate school working as a teller in a bank. Most of our tellers were divorced women who had understandable gripes about their ex-husbands. The bank had an employee lunchroom with about four tables in it. I walked into the room one day at lunchtime and noticed there was only one table empty. Taking my seat, I realized my fellow workers were in their men-bashing mode, venting how bad all men are. Men are all such, ahem, *jerks*, was the upshot. Realizing I was the only representative of my gender present, I felt I could hold my tongue no longer. As I was considering how to enter this debate and defend my male status, they got up to leave. As they walked by me, I took one by the arm and said, "I just want you to know that I love my wife and kids very much, and I know there are many other men out there who feel likewise." En masse, the women stopped and looked at me. Finally, one spoke for the group. "Men *are* such [jerks]." The implication? "Who asked you, buddy?" As they walked out, I said to myself, "I'll never try that again. Better just to keep my mouth shut."

A few years later I was on the campus of the University of Hawaii (somebody has to be there). I was supposed to meet one of my parishioners who was a professor there. In a little courtyard where students gather for lunch, I sat down to wait for my friend. After a few moments, a couple of women students walked up to my table and asked if they could sit there to eat their lunches. I said, "Sure." As I waited and looked around for my lunch appointment, I listened in on the two girls' conversation.

Their lunch-talk quickly gravitated to what they had done over the past weekend. After speaking of parties and the guys they met, one girl began to describe the sexual orgy that resulted at one of the parties. I was turning a little orange, while continuing to look around pretending that I wasn't hearing what they were saying. The conversation continued to other sexual exploits that, even though I had not had a "sheltered" college experience, totally shocked me. I reached into my briefcase and pulled out a Bible and laid it in front of the girls. I interjected, "Do you know what this book has to say about sex?"

The cute, little blonde who had initiated the conversation answered, "No, what does it say?"

I found Proverbs 5:16-18 and read:

"Should your springs be dispersed abroad,
Streams of water in the streets?
Let them be yours alone. . . .
Let your fountain be blessed,
And rejoice in the wife of your youth."

They looked at each other and said, "That's really neat. I never knew that was in the Bible." They then excused themselves, asked where they might get a Bible, and took off.

As I sat there still waiting for the professor, I was very glad I took the opportunity to open my mouth and say what I did in a somewhat awkward situation.

Such is dealing with fools. Do we speak to them or not? If so, when? One extended passage (26:4-11) gives us seven guidelines.

Answer a Fool Carefully Yet Firmly
The first element of advice the sophist gives us is,

Do not answer a fool according to his folly,
Lest you also be like him.
Answer a fool as his folly deserves,
Lest he be wise in his own eyes. (26:4-5)

Wait a minute, isn't this a contradiction? We are not supposed to answer a fool, but we are supposed to answer a fool? Ross explains, "The meaning of the two together is that one should not lower himself to the level of a fool but that there are times when the lesser evil is to speak out than be silent."[10]

This was my dilemma in the two experiences noted above. In the first, I tried to answer the outspoken tellers, and in a sense became like them. The attempt went nowhere, and I was the one who ended up looking like a fool. In the second, at the University of Hawaii, I felt I needed to say something, lest these two young girls walk away thinking their sexual views were not only right in their own eyes but were the only real option! I believe in that moment I made them think about another view of sexuality, which might lead to even more wise responses for them.

So when you believe you might be in the presence of fools, think about whether or not this is the time and place to answer them. In other words, answer them carefully. But when you have made your decision, jump in with both feet. I don't necessarily suggest throwing a Bible in front of someone, but once you have decided to make your move it must be done decisively and firmly. Otherwise, the fool will think your silence is approval!

Don't Give Him Responsibility

The second suggestion for dealing with a fool is:

> He cuts off his own feet, and drinks violence
> Who sends a message by the hand of a fool. (26:6)

Sending a message by means of someone's legs and feet is placing a responsibility upon that person to go to a certain place and deliver the message by the prescribed time. If a messenger is considered to be the feet of the sender, the latter, as it were, disables himself by failing to accomplish his purpose.[11] Giving a fool responsibility is only injurious to the one who sends him to the job, whether he be an errand boy or president of the United States.

Sometimes I think the sequence-processing element in my brain is a little dysfunctional. My wife can tell me as I walk out the door, "Now, on your way to the store, could you pick up the cleaning, and then go to the hardware store and get some paint for the bedroom?" I can make it to the cleaners and the store, but somehow the hardware store gets lost in the synapses in my brain. If I don't have a list (and it's still difficult with one!), I'm in big trouble. So it is all the time with a fool. He not only doesn't do the job, he probably can't find his way back to the office!

Don't Waste Your Time Trying to Educate Him

There is an eternal optimist in every group who thinks he can reform the worst of characters. This next verse is for him.

> Like the legs which hang down from the lame,
> So is a proverb in the mouth of fools. (26:7)

A proverb is a pithy, smartly packaged educational device. Our writer tells us that the proverb has no place in the mouth of the fool. For a lame man, legs are, practically speaking, useless. They do not serve the purpose for which God gave them. So it is with the best of educational devices. Send a fool to Harvard, give him a Ph.D., make him a Rhodes scholar, give him the best of education, and all you end up with is an educated fool. Allan Bloom has enlightened us to this exercise in futility in his book *The Closing of the American Mind*; even the best of faculty members at the University of Chicago only know a lot about little and can't even converse about things outside their field.[12] The education of fools is as useless as legs to a lame man! Wisdom says, "Don't waste your time trying to educate them."

Don't Grant Honor to a Fool

Ross says, "Honoring a fool is not only counterproductive, it is absurd . . . because what was intended could not be accomplished—he would still be a fool."[13] His comment is based on 26:8—

> Like one who binds a stone in a sling,
> So is he who gives honor to a fool.

As noted earlier in this chapter, honor just does not fit the character of a fool. So why would anyone want to bestow such a thing on him? It is comparable to tying a stone in a sling, making the weapon utterly useless and rendering it incapable of functioning as it should. Imagine the fearless David going out against Goliath with a sling with the stones sewn into the cloth! That's what it's like when fools are given responsibility and honor.

When will we learn that much of our hero worship is nothing more than the honoring of fools?! Unfortunately we have devised a system of organizational management that seems bound to promoting fools to places of authority, just because no one really wants to suffer the consequences of "discrimination" or having to prove less than satisfactory performance. The only solution open to us to remove them from our office is to promote them higher and reward them with the honor of a new title and a more important job description. Such is the case in corporate America, education, the military, and government.

Don't Give Him Skilled Jobs
The rule here is that the greater the skill needed, the greater the threat the fool brings to the job. Our next passage declares,

> Like a thorn which falls into the hand of a drunkard,
> So is a proverb in the mouth of fools.
> Like an archer who wounds everyone,
> So is he who hires a fool or who hires those who pass
> by. (26:9-10)

As the drunk does not feel the thorn entering his hand, so the fool does not feel the reality of the truth that may end up in his own mouth. The fool does not know what to do with the proverbial truth in his own mouth. He has been dulled to moral veracity, so wise communication has no place in his life. Ross again notes, "It is painful to hear fools use proverbs . . . he will misuse it and misapply it."[14]

One should not make a fool the company spokesperson or a public-relations person. A fool's communication skills are such that he will only get the company into trouble. The trouble is likened to an archer slinging arrows in every direction. What a picturesque portrait of what happens when we hire the fool to do a skilled job. Hitting the bull's-eye of a target or an oncoming enemy is a very skilled task. It demands practice, concentration, manual dexterity, and timing. Apparently, the fool lacks all the above and wildly lets loose his arrows at every passerby. In short, don't let a fool be your communicator or defend your country. These are highly skilled tasks, and employing the fool for these tasks will only result in benefits for the opposition and your enemy.

Don't Expect Him to Change

I have thought for some time the counseling field is not so much about change as it is about awareness and the acceptance that the people we are trying to change will never change! On this subject, our writer of wisdom is especially insightful. He writes,

> Like a dog that returns to its vomit
> Is a fool who repeats his folly.
> Do you see a man wise in his own eyes?
> There is more hope for a fool than for him. (26:11-12)

Those who have seen their sweet, little "man and woman's best friend" throw up on their favorite carpet or even on their lawn, only to have it immediately start licking up its own vomit, have seen this fool's reality. The fool returns to repeat his foolishness over and over again. In other words, he is largely unreformable. It is futile to try to change such a one. Oh, I know Jesus can change anyone. I will get to that in a moment. But for now accept the reality that fools don't change, and *you* are not going to change them. In a use of Semitic irony, our writer says the fool is more easily changed than the utterly self-conceited person (an impossible situation is implied, even though it does hold out some element of hope for the fool).[15] From the perspective of our wisdom writer, the character of the fool is set because he is not open to learning and discovering wisdom. For him there is no search, because he already has all he needs.

Stay Away from the Company of Fools
It is clear from Proverbs that who one spends time with is the clearest illustration of the kind of person an individual is. Our counselor cautions,

> He who walks with wise men will be wise,
> But the companion of fools will suffer harm. (13:20)

The point is clear, it's not nice to fool around with fools, because it increases the likelihood of becoming a fool. Aiken says, "The fool is generous in sharing his folly with his friends and Israel's sages were sure that to keep company with him was the quickest way to become like him. Hence, their repeated warnings to watch the company we keep (eg 22:24-25; 23:20; 28:7). Neither by word nor example is wisdom to be learned in the company of fools."[16] This again places the power of choice upon the young person or adult who sincerely wants to grow in wisdom. The choice of whom we "hang with" is the most determinative for our own character. Parents can't do it alone, teachers can't either; only the individual can choose who he wants to be with. A medieval Jewish moralist wrote, "Wouldst [you] know all about a man? Ask who his companion is."[17] A Hebrew wordplay is found on the words *companion* (*ro'eh*) and *suffer harm* (*yeroa*). By the switching of vowels and consonants, there is a subtle reminder that with every companion (*ro'eh*) there exists a potential (*yeroa*) harm.

Now, we come back to the most important question, Can the fool with all his foolishness change? Or what do I do with the foolishness I see in myself?

WHAT DO I DO WITH ALL MY FOOLISH SYMPTOMS?
I don't know about you, but in chapters like this one I get to feeling a little discouraged toward the end of it. I see so much

of myself in many of the fool's characteristics. But I do want to hold out the reality that even fools can change. Hidden in Wisdom's admonition "How long, O fool, will you hate knowledge?" is a suggestion that change is possible. The rest of the passage gives us the dynamics of this change. Wisdom simply says, "Turn to my reproof" (1:23).

Change of direction always starts with the recognition that one has been going in the wrong direction. What our feminine sage is asking of the fool is to turn to her "reproof." The word has serious overtones meaning "exposure of one's sin" and "confrontation of wrongs committed."[18] The fool then must own up to his life and lay it open before the scrutiny of the light of God and Scripture. Without this willingness, apparently, there is little hope for the fool. But there is more.

Our sage goes on,

"Turn to my reproof,
Behold, I will pour out my spirit on you;
I will make my words known to you." (1:23)

Wisdom promises to pour out her own spirit upon the person who submits to her. McKane observes, "Wisdom likens herself to a copious gushing spring. Just as its waters gush with lavish abundance, she will cause her spirit to overflow generously on those who acknowledge her authority and incline to her instruction."[19]

After repenting, the fool must receive the ministry of Wisdom's spirit. This is obviously the element that is impossible in most moral education and penal institutions today. How can hardened criminals be changed? What can break through the calloused recesses of the human spirit to bring about significant, empowering change. Only the Holy Spirit of God. Saint Paul informs a group of believers that the essence of the human heart in its natural condition is "foolishness" (1 Corinthians 2:14). By merely being human we have a certain foolishness in our souls. His "cure" for this condition is only one: the life-imparting Spirit of God. Paul counsels, "For to us God revealed them through the Spirit; for the Spirit searches all things, even the depths of God. For who among men knows the thoughts of a man except the spirit of the man, which is in him? Even so the thoughts of God no one knows except the Spirit of God" (2:10-11).

I don't understand the work of God's Spirit in my life as much as I used to (when I had everything theologically figured out!). But after some twenty-five years in ministry and dealing with people, I am certain about one reality. It is only the Spirit of God that changes people! Only God Himself as Spirit can crawl into the mysterious, complex, paradoxical elements of the human personality and cause people to see themselves as they really are, and impart a new "want to" to bring about change.

The third step in this transformation is the reception of words that wisdom imparts. What makes Judeo-Christianity (and Islam) uniquely different from other religions is how spiritual elements are inseparably bound to verbal elements. The Spirit of God reveals the words of God. Wisdom says, "I will make my words known to you." In this statement there may be some hint of the Messianic Age as seen by Isaiah the prophet (Isaiah 44:1-8), but most Christians realize our Lord gave the promise of His Spirit coming on us and making His words known to us (John 14:26, 16:13). Jesus, being the very wisdom of God (1 Corinthians 1:24), gifts us with His own Spirit in order that we might know His words, and have a grounded relationship with Truth. Without the words of Christ as revealed in the Scriptures, the fool just continues to be repentant but without instruction. In a sense, he is more like the naive, open but without knowledge. The words of Scripture build a foundation underneath his new commitment.

So there *is* hope for a fool and the foolishness we see in ourselves. When we find it, we must repent of its place in our life, allow the God of the universe to invade the area, and then see what Scripture has to say about our particular foolish sin.

• T H I R T E E N •

The Wise

Wisdom comes in small packages.
PARAPHRASE OF PROVERBS 30:24-28

▼

The wise will inherit honor.
PROVERBS 3:35

I n our continuing search for wisdom, we have finally come down to taking a direct look at the person who is called wise. In one sense we have already studied the wise by looking at all the other characters. Certain elements of wisdom are affirmed in the opposite as they are contrasted with the simple, sluggard, fool, wicked, etc. But now, the search has brought us directly to the wise.

As mentioned in the first chapter, the word translated "wise," *hakam*, does not have the idea of intellectual obtainment but pertains to a practical facility, expertise, or skill. One scholar explains, "A man is called wise if he is versed in a particular skill—in the technique of fashioning metals (I Kgs 7:14), in goldsmith's work and wood-carving (Ex 31:3), in spinning (Ex 35:25)—or if he is a skilled seafarer (Ezek 27:8; Ps 107:27) or a statesman and soldier (Isa 10:13). For most of these crafts and professions the 'father's house' will have been the 'school.'"[1]

From this background, I define the wise person as the man

or woman who has the skill of living his or her life rightly before both God and men. In other words, Proverbs views wisdom not in Ivy League collegiate terms, but in the raw, mundane living terms of everyday people carrying on their everyday jobs. Whether they are successful by the world's standards or not, these proverbial wise characters are successful at life, a science that has been surprisingly lost and rarely found.

The wise man is the person who, under the fear of the Lord, has learned some of the secrets for a successful life. Fundamentally, the secrets are not all that concealed. The "secret" of successful living lies not in finding the right formulas, or going to the right schools, or even working the right kind of program. It comes by being a certain kind of person. As science-fiction writer Ray Bradbury has said, "What I do is me, for that I came."[2] I feel the same way. What I do is me, it always is. I cannot separate who I am from what I do, or the other way around. Wherever I go, it's me who's there. Whatever I do, it's me who does it!

Such is the essence of all character, and especially of this thing called wisdom. Aiken summarizes this word for wisdom (*chokmah*) as follows: "Wisdom is skillfulness in dealing with the matter at hand so as to get the best results. In Proverbs the matter at hand is life itself, and the best result is the good, harmonious and successful life. So for men 'to know wisdom' is for them to have the skills needed to make a success of their lives."[3]

So what does this unique person look like?

THE WISE IS A PERSON OF UNIQUE CHARACTER

I have often thought there might be some usefulness in having all the members of a church wear military-type uniforms with appropriate designated rank made visible. One of the confusing things about modern religious life is that sometimes we are confused about who is really in charge and whom we ought to salute. In my pastoral theology courses, I teach that it takes a new pastor about two years just to figure out whom he should salute (who really has the power) and whom he shouldn't. The reality rarely fits the official leadership structure. The functional generals are usually hidden somewhere!

This illustrates the need we all have to clearly know who is really in charge. As we have seen, even the wicked can be outwardly religious, offering sacrifices and going to prayer meetings, all the while killing people with his tongue, threats, and bribes. The first thing we see in the character of the wise person is his genuine submission to God and His commands.

The Wise Recognizes Who Is in Charge

I think the disciples of Jesus were so fogged up about what was going on around them that they missed one of the biggest put-downs Jesus laid on them. The Jews hated the Romans, and especially the occupational army Caesar had sent to Palestine to quell the obstinate Jews from time to time. In Galilee, the Roman military outpost was stationed in the Roman colony of Tiberias, just a few miles from Capernaum.

When Jesus came to the little fishing community, a Roman centurion (officer) was waiting for Him. His trusted household servant was paralyzed with a high fever, and he had come in need of the healing ministry of Jesus. Hearing of the servant's condition, Jesus said, "I will come and heal him."

The centurion, recognizing the existing tension between the Jewish community and the Romans, said, "I am not worthy for You to come under my roof." An interesting response to say the least, since for a Jew to enter a Gentile household would make him unclean by the orthodox standards. Therefore, the centurion merely said, "Say the word, and my servant will be healed." Where did he get this kind of logic and insight? From all places, his own military experience. "For I, too, am a man under authority [Pontius Pilate, the governor in Caesarea], with soldiers under me; and I say to this one, 'Go!' and he goes, and to another, 'Come!' and he comes, and to my slave, 'Do this!' and he does it."

Jesus stood amazed by the insight of this nonreligious, Gentile, sword-bearing warrior. He turned and said to those following Him (His disciples), "Truly I say to you, I have not found such great faith with anyone in Israel" (Matthew 8:1-10).

Wow! This was more than insight, this was faith in Jesus' divine capabilities based on the recognition of his much superior authority. The centurion knew whom to salute. So does the wise man. He is known by his submission to God:

> Do not be wise in your own eyes;
> Fear the LORD and turn away from evil. (Proverbs 3:7)

In the parallelism, the one who is wise is the one who turns away from evil and is not wise in his own eyes. He recognizes the One to whom he needs to submit. This is the beginning of wisdom (9:10), and the wise man has both started down this road and wants to stay on it. To depart from it and be wise in his own eyes is to depart from the way of wisdom.

Once on the path of knowing who is in charge in his life, the wise then listens to the commands that come his way. As a good soldier who does not question orders, the wise man "receive[s] commands" (10:8). The fool babbles on, while the wise man adjusts his life to the commands of God. The wise man receives the commands for what they are, the very keys to success and happiness in life.

God makes it very clear His commands are not designed to make us miserable or take away all our fun; they are about life, and having a good life: "So the LORD commanded us to observe all these statutes, to fear the LORD our God *for our good* always and for *our survival*, as it is today" (Deuteronomy 6:24, emphasis added).

When I think of the millions who will die from the deadly AIDS virus, I see certain commands of Scripture in a different light. If the researchers are correct in saying the virus is naturally occurring in monkeys, and the only way it can be transmitted to humans is through sexual contact or coming into contact with infected blood, then it puts a far different spin on passages in Leviticus against bestiality, homosexuality, and contact with blood (Leviticus 15:18-19, 18:22-23). Could it be that our God was trying to spare us such diseases? Our rebellion against Him and His laws, and our refusal to be wise about such things, is costing millions their lives today. The wise man submits to the truths God has given in order to have a life!

On the same theme,

> A wise man is cautious and turns away from evil,
> But a fool is arrogant and careless. (14:16)

In light of the above, no comment is required. Without caution today, one can be dead!

In opposition to the fool, sluggard, and scoffer, who like the way they are and have very little use for knowledge, the wise individual can never get enough. He is a lifelong learner.

The Wise Are Always Looking for More Truth

A young boy once asked his eighty-year-old grandfather why he was reading Plato. The octogenarian replied, "Why, to improve my mind, of course."[4] This anecdote strikes us as humorous rather than inspiring, because we may not expect eighty-year-olds to still be productive, learning, and wanting to further expand their minds. But our Solomonic sage says,

> A wise man will hear and increase in learning,
> And a man of understanding will acquire wise counsel.
>   (1:5)

> Wise men store up knowledge. (10:14)

> The mind of the prudent acquires knowledge,
> And the ear of the wise seeks knowledge. (18:15)

On this last verse Ross notes, "Those who are wise eagerly search for knowledge. By paralleling, 'heart' and 'ears' the verse stresses the full acquisition of knowledge . . . Kidner says, 'Those who know most, know best how little they know.'"[5] The picture is of one who is listening (has his ears open) for truth and knowledge anywhere. He is not satisfied with having the knowledge he has, but is always trying to build on it. It must occur to him that he still does not have a corner on wisdom and the truth.

There are two unfortunate realities to this characteristic of wisdom. The first has to do with how we view our relation to the external world of knowledge. For several decades now, I think we have had a sort of superiority complex when it comes to comparing our "knowledge" with the knowledge of the "world." Totally apart from the inherent heresy of thinking there are two kinds of knowledge (Christian versus nonChristian), which amounts to the ancient teaching of gnostic dualism, the reality still exists that we have not gotten over this way of regarding knowledge. Even as I write, my publisher has called to ask me to draft a response to someone who seriously questions one of my previous books because I quoted a "secular" author.[6] In my opinion, this illustrates a very narrow view of truth, and one with which the wise man would not have much compatibility. If our world is one world, created by God (Psalm 24:1), then there is truth to be found in every part of it. In this sense, I think, as regenerate believers desiring the wisdom of God in every field, we ought to be the best researchers, thinkers, logicians, writers, and scholars. Unfortunately, those with far less reverence for truth and God have out-thought us simply because we have had a too narrow view of truth.

A second element that grows out of these verses also concerns me. We who submit ourselves to the lordship of Christ sometimes believe somehow that the truth came down to us already packaged, neatly packed, with bows and ribbons. How the truth got packaged as our neat little systems of theology rarely occurs to us. Therefore, in doing theology, which we really don't do, we are only defending the neat packages we were given at our spiritual births, or in our training. This breeds a lack of wise men who think, search, and carefully examine the assumptions, data, historical conditions, and personal biases of the packagers. I am a firm believer in the value of systematic theology and still hold to a particular approach to theology, but to equate my understanding of the truth with the truth itself, I believe, is raw arrogance. The full truth is always beyond me and is found only with God. Therefore, to be a wise disciple of Christ is to be a lifelong learner. Having come to know the Truth (Christ), I commit myself to learning from Him the rest of my life. Otherwise, I am a fool, thinking I have all the truth I ever need!

What creates the conditions for more knowledge in the wise man is teachableness in his character.

The Wise Know They Can Be Wrong

My father could fix anything. Some of my most memorable moments with him were the times we took on some project around the house together. But some of the worse moments were when we would work on the car together. My father had taken cars completely apart and put them back together for fun on weekends when he was growing up. The only thing I ever took apart was my bicycle, and still I needed Dad's help to get it back together. So working on cars was not exactly my area of interest or expertise.

Our "working together" would usually commence with my mother coming into my room or the television room saying my dad needed my help. Reluctantly I would go out to the garage, only to find my dad completely under the car with tools and parts scattered everywhere. He would throw out names like "crescent wrench" and "ball-pin hammer" and "one-quarter-inch machine screw," and my job was to find it and hand it to him under the car. I know I should have taken a course on such things somewhere, or at least asked him to give me a comprehensive lesson on auto tools. But I never did. So, he was always a little displeased with my performance, and frankly, I always wanted to be elsewhere. Now, every time I almost have to sign the deed of my house over to a mechanic, I wish I would have listened more closely to my dad's instruction. The bottom line: I wasn't teachable. I didn't think I needed to learn about all that car stuff, so I didn't.

So it is with the fool. The wise son, and wise adult, is teachable—open to counsel and correction (13:1). Proverbs shows,

The way of a fool is right in his own eyes,
But a wise man is he who listens to counsel. (12:15)

A certain grown-up maturity is evidenced in realizing that one does not have all the truth and needs to hear the wisdom and counsel of someone else. Being something of an only child (my sisters were nine and seven years older), I have always fended for myself. As a boy, I built model airplanes. I would read the directions, work alone, figure it out, do the required tasks. I often made mistakes, but I corrected them. Usually I got all the parts together, and the product looked like the airplane on the cover of the box. There were many strengths in learning to work alone. My last resort was usually going and asking someone for advice. I just assumed I could figure things out without any help.

As an adult this approach has been disastrous, especially when it comes to getting somewhere. Cinny is always quick to ask directions; me, never. It takes all the fun out of life, and besides, who knows what you might accidentally run into?! Sure! When we are both late and lost, the last thing I need is a lecture about my unwillingness to ask directions! But Cinny is correct. In this area of life I am a fool.

The wise man not only values advice, he also learns to love the one who corrects him.

Reprove a wise man, and he will love you.
Give instruction to a wise man, and he will be still
    wiser. (9:8-9)

The wise man is apparently not hung up on where he learns wisdom. No matter what the source, he is open to learning something new, which includes even the hard exposure to life's reproofs.

My premier mentor in the ministry has been Dr. Howard Hendricks. My walk with Christ throughout the years has been inextricably linked to this man. My first year in Christ, as a graduate student, he taught me how to study the Bible. My first year of marriage, Cinny and I were exposed to his Christian Home material at a summer conference. I then became a student under him at Dallas Seminary. I took every course he taught. Later I joined the faculty and team-taught courses with him. After one of these sessions, we were in his office talking about how the classes were going, and I asked, "Prof, how am I doing?"

He looked at me, smiled, and said, "How straight do you want it?"

I realized he wasn't making a joke, so I swallowed my pride and self-esteem, took another sip of coffee, and answered, "Really straight, Prof."

I could almost see in his eye that he had been waiting for this "teachable moment" for a long time, but he wanted me to raise the question. Leaning forward in his chair, he said pointedly, "You're good, really good, but . . . but that's your greatest weakness. You can sit on your gifts and be right where you are today twenty years from now. You have a tendency to pull things off by just riding on your personality!"

Ouch! It was both the wounds and encouragement of a mentor and friend. These words still motivate me, even in trying to do a credible, God-honoring job in writing this book! To learn, we must be teachable; to become wise, we must know we haven't arrived yet. We must open ourselves to counsel, correction, and continued learning. At every turn on our journey we must be open to asking the big question, "God, what are You teaching me through what's going on around me?"

Imagine what it must have been like for a young teenager to be told by his dad, "Go check on your brothers," and when he gets to where he thinks they are, he finds they have moved on. Getting lost, he asks a passerby if he had seen his brothers. The man acknowledges the direction he last saw them traveling. Finally, the boy discovers his older brothers, who, rather than welcoming him, throw him into a pit and sell him to some passing traders. These travelers take him to another country and sell him to a wealthy man to be a household servant. When he attempts to avoid his master's wife's sexual advances, she becomes offended by his rejection and has him thrown into prison. As various prisoners come and go, he asks them to remember him when they get out, but they forget about him. Finally, the chief executive of the country can't sleep because of his disturbing dreams. One of the court servers who had done time with the boy is reminded of his giftedness in figuring out what God says in dreams. Joe is brought out of prison, and Pharaoh is so impressed by his abilities he makes him prime minister.

Meanwhile, back at home, a major economic downturn has taken place, which causes the boy's brothers to come to his new nation's palace asking for food. So much time has transpired, no one recognizes who the prime minister is.

At this point in the story, we have traveled through almost thirteen chapters of biblical narrative where God is rarely mentioned. It is at this point that I ask the question, "What was going on inside the heart of Joseph during these chapters?" I know what would have been going on in my depraved heart. I would want a little payback, a little just dessert, a pound of flesh or the death penalty for the whole bunch of brothers who did me in!

But apparently, through this period of time Joseph was asking the question only the wise man asks, "God, what are You doing in this?" Therefore, in the final statement to his brothers Joseph replies, "And as for you, you meant evil against me, but God meant it for good in order to bring about this present result [reconciliation], to preserve many people alive [you and all the people of God]" (Genesis 50:20).

That's the response of a wise man! It is also the response of a very self-controlled man!

The Wise Are Self-Controlled

Anyone who has ever had his tongue get him in trouble knows where the locus of self-control lies. As Saint James makes perfectly clear, "If anyone does not stumble in what he says, he is a perfect man, able to bridle the whole body as well" (James 3:2). The essence of a self-controlled temperament lies in the ability to keep one's conversation from gravitating to the lower grades of human interchange. The wise man of Proverbs is regarded as wise for no other reason than this one.

The lips of the wise will preserve [guard] them. (14:3)

The heart of the wise teaches his mouth,
And adds persuasiveness to his lips.
Pleasant words are a honeycomb,
Sweet to the soul and healing to the bones. (16:23)

The wise in heart will be called discerning,
And sweetness of speech increases persuasiveness. (16:21)

The wise man is judged wise because his mouth is under the control of his own spirit. His own heart guides the words and style of communication that proceed from his mouth. Because of his carefulness of speech, the judgment he receives from others is that he is very discerning. Careful speech not only builds character but a reputation as well.

The tongue becomes the indicator for the whole of a man's life. Hence, our sage can say,

A fool always loses his temper,
But a wise man holds it back. (29:11)

Like the fool, the wise man is no unimpassioned soul, unexposed to the conflicts of life. Both wise man and fool are exposed to the same things, but the wise man has learned what to do with his anger and his desire to say something when he shouldn't. In that moment, the wise is able to weigh the alternatives quickly, think of the long-term outcomes of his words, and walk away to deal with his feelings later. But what is even more alarming for those of us who have "blown it" with our tongues is that the wise man's speech is likened to honey. His sweet persuasiveness calms the opposition and can actually turn their venomous words around, so that instead of producing animosity, his words bring healing.

The wise of heart have the ability to persuade without

manipulation, which is a rare quality. In fact, it is this ability of positively influencing other people that marks one of the major achievements of the wise.

THE WISE IS A POSITIVE INFLUENCE ON OTHER PEOPLE

Someone once said, "The greatest of influences are those of unconscious commoners." Since the era of scientific management hit, we in the West have been presumptuously holding to the belief that all things animate and inanimate can be manufactured, designed, worked out, and made to be precisely definable, obtainable, and measurable. To these purely rational processes, the words of Jesus about the nature of His Kingdom strike us as rank agnosticism and mysticism: "The kingdom of God is like a man who casts seed upon the soil; and goes to bed at night and gets up by day, and the seed sprouts up and grows—how, he himself *does not know*" (Mark 4:26-27, emphasis added).

It's hard for us to accept the reality that something can grow without our constant intervention and intentionality. But the agricultural reality, like the Kingdom reality, is such that our intervention may in fact be more detrimental to growth than facilitate it. The impact the wise man has on his fellow humans is a portrait that shows the wise as having a profound influence on those around him simply by being the kind of person he is.[7]

The Wise Mentor by Being Who They Are

"Mentoring" describes what we used to call "discipleship." I'm not sure if there really is a technical difference, but regardless, the impact of one person upon another has been shown to be one of the most important factors in the development of current leaders. Several studies have shown leaders in business, the military, education, and the ministry have all had key mentors at critical points in their development.[8] These leaders point to such things as the mentors' encouraging perspective, their belief in their protégés, their tolerance and patience, and their own talents and gifts that attract the younger to them.

My conclusion from looking at this data is that the mentor is merely being the kind of person he or she is, which is the "mystical" element that draws the "mentee." It is this character issue that is often missed by those trying to implement mentoring as a program. The wise man is a man of influence simply by being the kind of person he is. It is his common, unconscious character that makes him the teacher, mentor, healer, and peacemaker in his culture.

The Wise as Teacher

At the seminary where I teach, we define a mentor as three things: a brain to pick, a shoulder to cry on, and a kick in the pants. The teacher element of this definition is in "a brain to pick." When students ask me how to recognize a good mentor, I say he is a person who, even in casual meetings, is throwing out ideas, concepts, and connections so fast you have to grab a piece of paper and write down some of his insights. When that happens, and it is rare, you have found not only a mentor but a wise man. "The lips of the wise spread knowledge" (15:7). The word used here for "spread," *zarah*, is the Hebrew word for "scattering as in winnowing with a fork or fan."9 Get the picture? As a farmer winnows his wheat by throwing it up into the air, so is a wise man with knowledge. Ideas, concepts, data, relationships, history, personal experiences, failures, successes—all are being thrown every which way. Just being in the presence of such a person allows some of the wisdom to fall on the one standing by.

I can't describe how much I have learned by just standing around in the right places. In graduate school, these were the times I enjoyed the most. Just standing around with a prof after class or in the snack shack with a few other students firing questions right and left, and watching the prof handle even the most difficult of questions with ease. What is sad is that, when I get to campuses today, I don't see this happening. All of our campuses have become commuter diploma mills, where as soon as classes are over the students and faculty rush off to other jobs or classes.

When the wise man teaches, he brings refreshing, life-oriented knowledge:

The teaching of the wise is a fountain of life,
To turn aside from the snares of death. (13:14)

These are no abstract principles unrelated to what the student faces in life, but instruction that builds moral fabric into the soul of society. The wise man, by his understanding of life, becomes the refreshing source to a perishing and misguided world. Let he who is thirsty for moral relevance and skillful living find a wise man!

Not only is the wise man a man of knowledge, but he also makes his knowledge easy to learn! "The tongue of the wise makes knowledge acceptable" (15:2). A literal translation might be, "The tongue of the wise makes knowledge good." Because the wise is a learner first, he understands the nature of learning. From this he learns how to teach and make learning good to his listeners. As much as I believe in good teaching techniques, I believe we can be too focused on technique and miss the most important element in teaching: passion. My mentor, Professor Hendricks often etched in concrete this axiom: "If you want your students to bleed, you had better hemorrhage!" The passion of the heart is what makes any teaching acceptable and pleasure to the ears.

But the wise man does not live isolated in ivory towers or cloistered in quiet monasteries. His life is lived amidst the conflicts, pains, wars, and battles of men. But unlike so many others, he knows what to do after the conflicts are over. He knows it's time to pick up the pieces, bandage the wounds, and be a peacemaker and healer.

The Wise As Healer
I have a friend who happened to be stationed as a marine at Camp David when Jimmy Carter was president. What this means is he was there when the famous Camp David Accord was signed between the Egyptian president, Anwar Sadat, and Israeli

Prime Minister Menachem Begin. This event is even more significant today because the peace treaty signed in 1994 between Israel and Yasir Arafat had its beginning at Camp David.

The accord cost President Sadat his life for making peace with Israel. But who was the peacemaker? Despite the bad press Carter has gotten for not being able to get our hostages out of Iran, in my opinion he goes down as one of the best peace negotiators of all time (and one of the most vocal about his Christian faith).[10] Anyone who could bring Israel and the Arabs together deserves far more credit than a peace prize.

But what happened at Camp David? Much has been written about this event. But my friend provides an eyewitness account of one critical piece of the negotiation process. As a marine assigned to provide perimeter security for the three men (from a distance), he noticed how the three men once kneeled and prayed. Somehow, the president of the United States had so influenced these two world leaders by his own character that when asked to join him in prayer, they consented. What a picture of the kind of effect the wise man has on even the powerful of this world. A Jew, a Muslim, and a Christian on their knees! Jimmy Carter is a premier peacemaker, regardless of his politics. He was and is a wise man. A man who is not afraid of tackling the impossible messes of human conflict and trying to make sense out of them, and get two warring parties to reconcile.

Proverbs highlights this healing role of the wise man in several passages:

The wrath of a king is as messengers of death,
But a wise man appeases it. (16:14)

Scorners set a city aflame,
But wise men turn away anger. (29:8)

There is one who speaks rashly like the thrusts of a
    sword,
But the tongue of the wise brings healing. (12:18)

Did you notice the words here—"wrath," "death," "flames," "swords"? No easy stuff here. But the wise man is in the middle of it, trying to mend, heal, and appease. I must confess this is where I part company with the wise man. When conflict happens, I'm usually headed out the door. I don't consider myself the peacemaker, and in some instances have been more the peace-wrecker! But I do want God to cultivate more of this element in my character. I need it in all of my relationships—with my wife, with my children, in my employment. But my instincts are much more inclined to picking up the sword rather than the plowshare.

Perhaps I need to spend more time meditating on the implications of this proverb:

A wise man scales the city of the mighty,
And brings down the stronghold [strength] in which
    they trust. (21:22)

The point, perhaps, is that there is more than one way to take a city. Ross says, "It is more effective to use wisdom than to rely on strength. This proverb uses a military scene to describe the superiority of wisdom. It tells how the wise can scale the walls of the city of the mighty (gibborim) and pull down their trusted stronghold."[11]

Imagine a tactician looking at a heavily guarded city. Its walls are high and thick. Some ancient cities had double walls wide enough to accommodate chariots on the top, thus allowing quick reinforcement of troops wherever needed. The tactician realizes this is not a city to be taken by force of sheer power or battering rams, this one is going to take a little more craft. He has to think, do intelligence work, plant some spies over the wall at night.

In military strategic thinking, we talk about finding the enemy's "center of gravity," the one place that, if rendered inoperable, would bring the entire nation or city down. This is the point of the proverb. Strength does not necessarily conquer a city. The wise man uses his craft of persuasion, reconciliation, and negotiation rather than just sending in the troops!

In the final analysis, the wise man is even vindicated by the fool. In other proverbs the fool raged and laughed at the wise man when he attempted to correct him (29:9). At that time, the fool wrote off the wise man as irrelevant, high-minded, and a moral absolutist! But when push comes to shove, the bottom drops out of the economy, and the fool is broke, guess where he ends up? That's right, on the doorstep of the wise man:

> He who troubles his own house [apparently the fool]
>   will inherit wind,
> And the foolish will be servant to the wisehearted.
>   (11:29)

Apparently, the fool has no other option than to lower himself to becoming a household servant to the wise. It speaks highly of the wise to take him in! Such is his healing and peace-making heart. Although the wise man would probably not think of a fool who once raged and laughed at him finally coming to live in his house as a benefit of wisdom, Proverbs does declare that there are rich benefits accorded to wisdom.

The Benefits of Wisdom

Delighted to be but wise.
WILLIAM YEATS
MEN IMPROVE WITH THE YEARS

▼

*Four things are small on the earth
but they are exceedingly wise.*
PROVERBS 30:24

H aving been raised in the home of a minister, my kids are probably not expecting much of an inheritance when I die. I have already prepared them by telling them that my last will and testament reads, "Being of sound mind and body . . . I spent it all!"

Inheritance in the ancient world, and ours, is a big thing. Anyone who has been at the public reading of a will knows the aftershock and utter surprise that sometimes accompany these events. Just as the fool who disrupts his own household (Proverbs 11:29) ends up inheriting nothing (is this really a surprise—who would want to leave their estate to one who had caused them so much trouble?), so the wise person also has some benefits to being wise.

Honor Is a Benefit of Being Wise

Cinny and I have an old military friend who is now a retired air force general. During the end of the Vietnam War, Dick and Ann asked us to be their guests at a banquet honoring outstanding citizens of the state of Hawaii. Dick had been the public-affairs officer for the admiral of CINC PAC (Commander in Chief, Pacific), which meant he was sent to Hanoi to handle the press and public-relations issues for the release of American POWs. For his outstanding work, the state of Hawaii was honoring him as the "military person of the year." I can still remember Dick's acceptance remarks. Standing straight and tall in his formal air force whites, complete with sword and medals, he said, "I don't know why you are giving me this honor. I was just doing my job. Thank you."

Richard Abel, brigadier general, United States Air Force (retired), illustrates the essence of the wise man's honor. He does not seek it nor understand it when it comes to him, simply because the honor is not based on anything he did in particular, but on who he is. Proverbs states, "The wise will inherit honor" (3:35). What comes to the wise is something not sought but earned nevertheless. The word *honor, kobod*, has in mind "the weightiness of character" that demands the giving of such to those "deserving of respect, attention and obedience."[1] Given enough time, the wise man is honored by the recipients of his wisdom.

But another benefit of wisdom is the possession of wisdom itself.

Wisdom Is a Benefit of Being Wise

I often wonder why in the world I spent so much money on obtaining a master's and doctorate degree. They really haven't ensured that I make more money than someone else. In fact, I meet people all the time with less education who make much more money than I do. I'm sure almost everyone who enters my home to fix anything has more take-home than I do. Am I feeling sorry for myself? No, this is why I write books!

A change in attitude about the role of education has taken place in our country. Today, the liberal-arts curriculum in most schools is found wanting and fighting for survival. Why? Because both students and their parents are saying, "Get an education to do something." Be a CPA, a nurse, an aviation mechanic, study something that will prepare you to do something. Forget the history of ideas, philosophy, languages, or even Western civilization. What's so great about knowing all these things if you still can't find a job? Heard it before? In my weaker moments, I ask the same questions. But then I am reminded of the perspective of the wise man, which says, "If you are wise, you are wise for yourself" (9:12).

Even though the wise man's wisdom benefits the larger community, he doesn't think about his influence on others. Remember, he doesn't seek such things, he is just . . . being who he is. And by being who he is, he has a profound impact upon others. But what drives this wise man is not others but himself. For whose benefit is he wise? The literal Hebrew text might read, "If you are wise, you are wise to or for you." Kidner says this is the strongest expression of individualism in the Bible, and adds, "Your character is the one thing you cannot borrow, lend, or escape, for it is you."[2] In other words, wisdom has its own profit.[3]

This is very hard to explain to one who has never experienced it, but there is a deep satisfaction in knowing that you have an understanding of something, whether it will ever have a productive use or not. We are so driven by pragmatism today that it is hard for us to imagine that wisdom has its own built-in reward or benefit.

I have experienced this in my preaching, teaching, and writing. Sometimes while driving in my car or traveling cross-country in an airplane, I have a flash of insight and wonder. I see a new connection in my head, or I just wonder about something new. I can't wait to get home and get to a library to check out references and do some research. These are my most productive times, where I just get lost for hours on end, and have often gotten whole messages, books, or a new course outline out of the intense moment of wonder. Sometimes they come to nothing, but that's okay too, because I enjoyed the exploration.

What is always frustrating is trying to explain this phenomenon to "bean-counter" types who ask me to "justify" my time doing such things. My life doesn't fall into neat categories that are measurable moment by moment. Wisdom, as defined by the ancients, falls more in the category of art than science. It therefore defies managerial approaches and categories. When someone asks me how much time it takes me to write a book or prepare for a class or do sermon preparation, the only honest answer I can come up with is, "Till it's done." I never really know how much time that will take (future) or how much time it did take (past) because I don't even keep track of such things. An artist just knows when the painting is finished.

The wise man is wise for the benefit of himself. Wisdom and knowledge are his most beautiful and prized rewards. Wisdom is his pursuit, and the obtainment of such has its own rich benefit. But Proverbs mentions one other benefit that comes to the wise man.

The Wise Man Is Materially Rewarded

It stands to reason, if wisdom is the skill of living one's life properly before both God and man, then even in the financial area this skill should be observed. Proverbs confirms this view: "The crown of the wise is their riches" (14:24). What is placed upon the head of the wise man is some sort of material gain. The word for riches here, *'ashar*, originally meant "to abound with herbage or goods."[4] In agricultural societies, wealth was measured in terms of amount of grain harvested and number of livestock possessed (Genesis 13:2). When a man was wise enough to cooperate with the laws God laid down for raising crops and being a good steward of flocks, the benefit of his wisdom was very much material. In addition, Sister Wisdom makes a very conditional promise to her listeners. She says,

> I love those who love me;
> And those who diligently seek me will find me.
> Riches and honor are with me,
> Enduring wealth and righteousness.
> My fruit is better than gold, even pure gold,
> And my yield than choicest silver. (8:17-19)

Our sage promises to reward those who genuinely love and pursue wisdom. She will reward them with riches and wealth! And the wealth she will reward them with is enduring.

This material outlook bothers some people. It should bother us. When everyone is working so hard to just stay on top of things financially, here is a promise saying that a wise man will be rewarded materially for doing nothing but being wise! But I believe Wisdom knows our hearts. We probably wouldn't be interested in seriously seeking wisdom if there wasn't some promise of reward in it. The wise man does not seek the reward, but he is given the promise of material reward just the same. I can think of individuals like Aleksandr Solzhenitsyn and Mother Teresa of Calcutta who never sought the affirmation and wealth of the world but all the same were rewarded for their wisdom and achievement. I am also naive enough to believe that our God will not allow any of the unrewarded wise to go unrecognized. They will receive their reward as well at the judgment seat of Christ (Revelation 3:21, 4:10). I happen to believe that Heaven just might be complete with streets of gold and all kinds of material wealth. I'll just take Hawaii!

One thing I have always appreciated about the wisdom literature is how graphically the portraits are painted. Even such abstract concepts as wisdom are given a *National Geographic* twist. It is in this light that the collection of Proverbs is closed out with two colorful illustrations portraying what the essence of wisdom looks like. The first is from the realm of nature as found in four small creatures of God's creation. The second is from the domestic feminine realm as seen in the familiar passage on the woman of strength. These fitting conclusions give us a picture of what wisdom looks like when spelled out in both human and animal life.

WISDOM COMES IN SMALL PACKAGES

On the edge of the Sinai Desert, outside Beersheba, one can still see Bedouin traders passing through on their way to Arabia. One afternoon a week the Bedouin market is open for business as the ancient and modern cultures mix, barter, and

both go away thinking they got a deal! On one of these occasions, my guide and I sat down and watched some of the
ancient customs that filled this tent life. I asked my guide what
they were talking about during their afternoon tea breaks. He
replied, "A fascinating mix of politics, business, sex education,
women, and how to get the best mileage out of a camel." I
learned later that one of the main teaching devices during this
time was colorful proverbs that formed an analogy between
animal and human life.

We do the same thing today, but probably in less formal
ways. We say a person is "quick as a rabbit" or "slow as a snail,"
or speak of leaders as "soaring like eagles," or say someone got
"outfoxed" or "played possum." When we do this, we are using
a defining characteristic from the animal kingdom and apply-
ing it to human behavior. This is precisely what the proverbs
of Agar[5] do about life and, in particular, one element of wisdom. These proverbs give us a quick overview and summary
as to what wisdom looks like.

Agar places the punch line first:

> Four things are small on the earth,
> But they are exceedingly wise. (30:24)

In other words, wisdom comes in small packages. In a society
where greatness is equated to bigness, Proverbs pictures wisdom as something not related to size but sensibility. Each of
the four little creatures reflects a different aspect about the
nature of wisdom, but each confirms the conclusion: There is
significance in the most insignificant creatures. Likewise,
smarts has its own unique advantage over strengths. In fact,
smarts amounts to a greater strength!

A Little Preparation Is a Lot

As we have seen, the sluggard was not one to adequately prepare for the future. Therefore, he is told to go to the ant and
learn about the industry of the ant colony (6:6). Our writer
instructs,

The ants are not a strong folk,
But they prepare their food in the summer. (30:25)

One writer observes about these small insignificants:

Two of the most common species of the Holy Land,
the black ant (atta barbara) and the brown ant (atta
structor), are strictly seed feeders, and in summer lay
up large stores of grain for the winter use. Leave a
bushel of wheat in the vicinity of one of their subter-
ranean cities, and in a surprisingly short time the whole
commonwealth will be summoned to plunder. A broad
black column stretches from the wheat to their hole,
and you are startled by the result. As if by magic, every
grain seems to be accommodated with legs, and walks
off in a hurry along the moving column.[6]

From the ant we learn what wisdom looks like. It is wise
to prepare. The wise man thinks about the future and plans
for it accordingly. He also understands the times and knows
what to do at the right time. His sense of timing is also a
unique element of his skill. As the ant knows when to prepare (in the summer), so the wise knows when he needs to
do what he needs to do. His skill of living life smartly lies in
the little preparations he makes every day and on a timely
basis. The little he does, over time, amounts to a lot! Whatever a person wants to accomplish with his life, the key is not
in the big things but in little things. Whether it is exercise,
losing weight, investing, learning a new skill, writing a book,
or preparing for our own death, the smart way to do it is like
the ant. A little creature doing a little thing, every day.

Even our Lord told us that preparation is the key to faithfulness. We must be ready (prepared) awaiting his return (Luke
12:35-40), our lamps filled, our clothes ready, with the porch
light on! Preparation is important. It's what wise men do!

But we also need to know where to hide.

A Little Hole in a High Place

On one of my trips to Israel, our adventurous guide took us on a "wadi" walk. Wadis are dry riverbeds that in summer provide interesting material for making the Bible come alive. As we were walking along a riverbed that snaked its way through towering walls on each side, we noticed small rocks falling down into the canyon. We stopped and looked up. Our guide pointed to some little creatures scurrying for cover. In their quick exit, small loose rocks plummeted to the canyon floor. "Rock badgers," our guide said and kept on walking. Even though the badgers were gone and we continued on down the wadi, I kept looking up at the height of the walls on both sides of us and thinking of the craggy crevices into which they had crawled. I finally realized the meaning of the next verse,

> The badgers are not mighty folk,
> Yet they make their houses in the rocks. (30:26)

Scholarly opinion designates these creatures as the Syrian rock hyrax, who "never ventures very far from a safe crevice into which they can dash at the least alarm."[7] These creatures, about the size of rabbits, eat vegetable matter during the day outside their caves, but they are basically cave dwellers. Another writer says of them, "Their oval, brown furry bodies, with small ears and short tails, bounce along the crest of a ridge, as they nibble a blade of grass here and there and stop occasionally to take a sunbath. A seasoned male is always posted as look-out, and a warning shriek from him is enough to alert all these furry creatures and send them scurrying back to their caves."[8]

These experts agree, the rock badger or coney is anything but a strong folk. When God created this animal, He did not give it any offensive or defensive equipment. It doesn't run fast, its teeth are dull for munching grass not flesh, its feet are padded without claws, so it is very easy prey for both man and other larger animals. But God has gifted it with wisdom. This little creature makes its home in the inaccessible places of the earth—between rocks, in crevices, and in small holes in canyon walls—and then stays close. It has a wise instinct to find out where adequate protection lies and how to get there.

The badger is a symbol of wisdom because it knows where to flee. It knows where to build its home. Do we? The naive has no protection at all because he trusts everyone. The fool trusts only in himself, not a wise choice. The wise man must learn to trust and build his house in a place where he will be adequately protected.

The psalmist often alluded to (using the badger as an illustration [Psalm 104:18]) finding his secret place of security in the "rock" of his salvation.

The LORD is my rock and my fortress and my deliverer,
My God, my rock, in whom I take refuge. (Psalm 18:2)

Perhaps, in David's wilderness experience, as he was often fleeing for his life, he looked up at those same canyon walls I had and reflected on the artificial security of the palace he once enjoyed. At the same time, he noticed the rock badgers and where they built their homes. Perhaps David was reminded in those moments where his real security was. Not in the fortresses of men, or in the promises of his advisors, or even in his family, but in the only One who was truly adequate, the Lord God of Israel, his Rock. Jesus said the same thing when speaking of two foundations for our lives. One is sand, the other rock.

When we lived in Hawaii, our house was not far from the beach. On the windward side of Oahu, there was quite an erosion problem with the surf gradually eroding the beach. On one section of the beach where we loved to take evening strolls stood one of the stately, elegant Rothchild homes. It had about thirty feet of beach and a nice grassy yard that extended up another forty-fifty feet ending with the house. During the eight years we lived on the island we noticed the gradual loss of beach, then major sections of their lawn. I thought to myself, even as wealthy and famous as the Rothchilds are, there is not one thing they can do to stop the erosion of their land.[9]

Jesus was right, it is foolish to build a house on sand. It's even more foolish to build our lives on anything other than the Lord Himself. The badger, at least, knows where to build.

Wisdom Is No Lone Ranger

We have seen in the sluggard one who sees obstacles everywhere in his life. Most are invented, but some are probably legitimate. We all have obstacles or large tasks we avoid in our lives. What we learn from this next little creature is that wisdom is no lone ranger.

A big job needs to be broken down into smaller units so, with a sense of unified purpose, the larger task is made "bite-size." We are told,

> The locusts have no king,
> Yet all of them go out in ranks. (30:27)

The idea of "going out in ranks" comes from the verbal idea, *hatzatz*, of "dividing or cutting something in two."[10] The wisdom reflected in this idea is obvious. The little grasshoppers, or locusts, have no ability in their small strength to devastate an entire field. Yet, without strong leadership, they band together into divisions and progressively eat their way through a field. The prophet Joel speaks of their corporate ability en masse:

> What the gnawing locust has left, the swarming locust
>   has eaten;
> And what the swarming locust has left, the creeping
>   locust has eaten;
> And what the creeping locust has left, the stripping
>   locust has eaten. . . .
> Their appearance is like the appearance of horses;
> And like war horses, so they run. . . .
> They run like mighty men;
> They climb the wall like soldiers;
> And they each march in line,

Nor do they deviate from their paths.
They do not crowd each other;
They march everyone in his path,
When they burst through the defenses,
They do not break ranks. (Joel 1:4, 2:4-8)

Cohen says of them, "These insignificant creatures have an instinct which teaches them that unity and discipline in their ranks make them formidable."[11]

As an American male speaking for my gender, we have an almost insurmountable predisposition toward independence. As mentioned earlier in the book, I basically learned to do most of my problem solving alone.

Unfortunately, even the Church has not learned the wisdom of the locust. Every little church competes with the other churches down the street for the same people. Most church programing assumes that every church should have a youth ministry, or do pastoral counseling, or have evangelistic outreaches. Sometimes I wonder if we really think God has given every local church all the gifts. Ephesians 4:1-16 especially, the spiritual-gift passage, seems to apply to the universal Body of Christ and not every little local church.

Maybe God has given all the gifts any local community needs in the members of all the churches who name the name of Christ. Wisdom would then say we need to work more like locusts than eagles! Learn to cooperate, take big projects and ministries, and divide them up so that all the gifts in a community are utilized. Perhaps our harvest as locusts would be much larger than what any one of us could do on his own. The locust has the corporate sense of cooperation. It knows how to work together. That's wisdom. The next little creature builds on this concept of appropriate giftedness.

Wisdom Is a One-Trick Pony
I once worked with an individual, most of whose life was a mess. He was disorganized, his office arranged by "piling

systems" rather than filing systems. He could never find his cal-
endar to see where he ought to be next. It took a personal
assistant, a couple of secretaries, and his wife to get him
through most weeks. To those around him, he was a crisis-
management kind of person. He would push every deadline
down to the last minute. But when the deadline came, in spite
of all the running around and hair-pulling and panicking over
whether the project was going to be finished or not, Joe came
through. Not only would he come through, he would come
through big. He would present a project with such brilliance
and back it up with such outstanding visuals and documentation that everyone would just sit back and say, "That's it." What
I learned from this person is that even a one-talent man can
go a long way. Joe was what I call a one-trick pony. He had only
one trick or talent to perform, but what a gift. His gift allowed
him to gain access to very powerful boardrooms.

So it is with this next little character.

The lizard you may grasp with the hands,
Yet it is in kings' palaces. (30:28)

When we lived in Hawaii, we called these "geckos." They
are little lizards small enough to hold in one's hand. When we
first moved to the Islands, we thought they were rather both-
ersome. They went "yip, yip, yip, yip" in the night; they were
always on our walls, hiding behind pictures; and sometimes
they got mashed in the doorjambs accidentally. But locals told
us you can never get them out of your house—they are so
small they come in through the tiniest of cracks. Besides, they
reduce the fly and mosquito population in your home. So they
are your friends.

From these friends, we also learn something about what
wisdom looks like. If one would take the time to turn a gecko
over on its back and put its tiny feet under a microscope, one
would find thousands of microscopic hairs that allow the lizard
to cling to vertical surfaces, even ceilings.[12] Even the "foot,"
one scholar notes, "resembles a hand, with clearly defined and

articulated fingers."[13] I was somewhat amused, when taking a tour of the last Hawaiian queen's palace, to see geckos there. Their one skill—a unique capability to grasp vertical and upside-down structures—gives them access even to the palaces of kings and queens.

So what's the point? Simple. It is wise to develop one's skills. Though the lizard is small and vulnerable to capture by human hands, with its innate skills it can gain entrance into places of great significance. In other words, the lizard knows what it can do well, and does it. Do we have the same wisdom?

I believe doors can open for our gifts. I have seen it in my own life. During this time of living in Hawaii, I was a young, insignificant pastor in a fairly small church. But apparently, I had established a reputation as one able to minister in small groups and effectively teach the Bible. One day a total stranger called me and asked me if I would be willing to teach a small group of men who were meeting for prayer in the lieutenant governor's office of the state capitol. I consented and we began a Bible study at 6:30 a.m. every Friday. Three people showed up for the first meeting. But by the time I left, several years later, our little group had grown to sometimes as many as thirty, including sometimes the lieutenant governor. Again, I was reminded of my friend the gecko, or lizard—able to gain entry to kings' palaces. How? Because of a very specialized skill.

Wisdom says it is smart to develop one's skills. Our skills are what make us valuable both to our communities and to the cause of Christ. Knowing that you do something well and having something to do well are important elements in being a wise person.

I have known very few multi-talented people. I know they are around. But I believe most of us are just common little folk who, if we have one skill, are doing well. I am concerned today to see young people who have not cultivated any skills at all. But I also believe we have wasted a lot of emotional and physical energy trying to go on self-improvement programs to enhance our weaknesses. I may be overly pessimistic on this subject, but I believe we would better spend our time focused on building our strengths rather than trying to correct our weaknesses. It is our strengths, not our weaknesses, that will push us into places undreamed of.

> Do you see a man skilled in his work?
> He will stand before kings;
> He will not stand before obscure men. (22:29)

I still remember former Dallas Cowboy coach Tom Landry sharing his philosophy of coaching with a group of us. As I remember it, he said,

> In the NFL you really don't correct a player's weaknesses but only compensate for them. We will never make Tony Dorsett into a capable blocker; it's physically impossible for a one-hundred-eighty-pound halfback to successfully block a three-hundred-pound charging defensive end. When we want him blocked, we get someone else to block him. Tony is someone we must block for, and let him do what he does best, run!

Maybe it's not so bad being a one-trick pony. Maybe it's wise to let people find out what they do best and then let them do it. Isn't that really what the doctrine of spiritual gifts is all about (1 Corinthians 12, 14)? All the gifts need each other, and we need to let each member function appropriately in accordance with his talents.

So we can see what wisdom looks like by taking on the characteristics of these four little, wise creatures. Wisdom does come in small packages. But now we have come down to the final and most important reality. How does one appropriate or get wisdom? In other words, if I am a fool, sluggard, contentious wife, naive, scoffer, unwise friend, or into unjust gain, what should I do? How can I move toward becoming a wise person?

How to Become a Wise Person

There are not many wisdoms, but only one.
SAINT AUGUSTINE
CITY OF GOD

▼

If you seek her as silver.
PROVERBS 2:4

Personally, I dislike self-help books, even though I have been accused of writing some, and find most of them unenlightening. What I really react to is the premise inherent in the marketing category "self-help." To think that by reading a book—*one* book—I can bring about significant human developmental changes that have been in the making for twenty, thirty, forty, or fifty years, is to confirm the magic elixir of American snake oil. I think people gain significant new insights from such material, but whether or not real change is brought about is debated.[1]

Therefore, what I am *not* trying to do in this last section is give you five easy steps to becoming a wise person. I am giving you principles and processes that we must be aware of in order to see and live life differently. They are no guarantees to turn a fool into a wise man in five easy lessons or five short weeks. More clearly, these principles and processes focus on the three areas in which the skill of right living can begin to blossom. The first is in relation to God.

233

WISDOM TAKES GOD

It seems so basic and fundamental. But Proverbs begins and ends in the same place. There is no true wisdom without a relation to God (9:10). Since God is the designer of the human frame and the entire natural world (I believe He is), then it logically follows that the only way we can be wise in this world is to have a relationship with Him. But Proverbs underscores some specific elements of this required relation. To learn wisdom we first of all need revelation. Revelation is that divinely authored information about life that we all so desperately need. Proverbs 2:6 clarifies,

> For the LORD gives wisdom;
> From His mouth comes knowledge and understanding.

In the Bible we find the claim that what God reveals about Himself and about the world is to be considered as tested, pure, and a place of real refuge and protection (3:5-6). We are also told not to add anything to the words He has revealed to us (30:6) or delete anything (Revelation 22:19). To be smart about life, we need to be constant readers of the Scriptures God has given.

Today, there is much New Age thinking around, which is just the Old Age paganism with a new veneer. We can walk into any bookstore or hear talk-show experts or even listen to some of our own evangelical teachers who are "into" a confusing mix of pagan religion, Eastern mysticism, and evangelical terminology with good old American hype. Therefore, it is sometimes difficult to sort out what is truth and what is error. The Bible is the only way I know to do that.

To be wise we must have a relationship with God that is based on the truth of what God has revealed in the Scripture. The psalmist tells us it is the Law of the Lord that makes the simple wise (Psalm 19:7). The Apostle Paul says this to his younger colleague: "You have known the sacred writings which are able to give you the wisdom that leads to salvation through faith which is in Christ Jesus" (2 Timothy 3:15).

Wisdom comes through the knowledge of the Scriptures, the revelation of God.

We also need a particular response to it. We need to respond to this revelation with fear: "The fear of the Lord is the beginning of knowledge." A scary phrase indeed! What does it mean to fear the Lord? Does this mean to feel fearful, or to tremble in the our shoes all day long? No, this fear is different from other fears we feel. Dyrness calls the "fear of the Lord" the theological character of piety:

> Initial fear is not what the OT means by the "fear of the Lord." In fact, when Moses tells the people what God had revealed to him, he explicitly says, "do not fear" (Exo 20:20), and yet he goes on to say that God came so that the "fear of him" may be before their eyes (the root for fear is the same in both cases). Is this a contradiction? No, Moses wanted them to know that they need not fear as if they faced something unknown or unpredictable (the root cause of fear in pagan religions), but to live in the sober awareness of who God is.
>
> The Hebrew fear of the Lord was to be unique. In pagan religions people live in constant fear of the spirits which they must seek to appease . . . Israel's fear of God was rather an awesome realization that the holy God had turned to them and had chosen them to be his people. . . . So fear was not primarily an emotion, but a way of life based on a sober estimate of God's presence and care. Such an attitude includes emotion, but so far from being a disintegrative force, this fear leads to life and satisfaction (Prov 19:23).[2]

My own definition, based on the understanding detailed above, would be the recognition and reception of who God really is without compromise. Of course, we are always finding out more about how God works in our lives, but fundamentally to fear Him is to grant the proper recognition of who He really is, and submit to His authority over our life.

When this is done, we can "get a life," as my teenager some-times says, and sleep soundly at night.

> The fear of the LORD leads to life,
> So that one may sleep satisfied, untouched by evil.
>   (19:23)

A proper recognition, however, is still not enough upon which to build this solid foundation for wisdom. Repentance is also required. The fear of the Lord must lead to "turn[ing] away from evil" (3:7). Sister Wisdom cries,

> Come, eat of my food,
> And drink of the wine I have mixed.
> Forsake your folly and live. (9:6)

It is clear from the study of this entire book that wisdom does not just happen. Many of the characters studied desired wisdom but could not obtain it. The reason is simple. They did not want to forsake their folly. We like our toys, our excuses, our behaviors, the attention that comes to our quirks. Wisdom says plainly, "That's fine, it's your choice, but you won't learn from me without giving up the folly." A bumper sticker said it all: "He who has the most toys when he dies, still dies." No matter what we have or don't have when we die, the wise has the last laugh. We still die. Some will die in their folly, others won't!

In order to be wise, we must identify where in our lives the foolishness is. Once identified, if it is something that needs to be thrown out, put away, or burned, then that's what we need to do. Even though I realize such things as addictions, obsessions, and compulsions are very difficult to walk away from, there is a growing abundance of research literature (not even claiming any spiritual resources) that claims that more and more persons simply quit "cold turkey" when they finally reach a serious point in their lives. In one writer's words, "They finally grow up."[3] In my words, they repented! We can't be wise without turning away from those things that cause us to be stupid, foolish, unjust, or evil.

These three elements—revelation, recognition, repentance—make up what it means to be wise before God. But what does it mean to be wise before men?

WISDOM TAKES OTHERS

Life teaches some hard lessons. Sometimes they come through events that are beyond our control, sometimes through things we thought we wanted and were thus under our control, at other times, through the people we engage daily. Everyday messages, events, voices, circumstances, meetings, telephone calls, and such all compete for our time and attention. In the midst of messes we face every day, sometimes we don't take the time to ask what is really going on here, or what God wants us to learn through this situation. As a friend of mine once said, "Life is nothing but one situation after another." Or my phrase, "I'm so busy living my life, I don't have the time to think about my life."

What Proverbs encourages us to do in order to learn wisdom is to listen to life. We need to first of all listen to the reproofs that come through life's hassles and hustles. Proverbs says,

> He whose ear listens to the life-giving reproof
> Will dwell among the wise. (15:31)

The verse can be taken two ways. First, the one having listened to the reproof in a situation then goes to the house of the wise in order to gain insight into it. Or, the one having listened to the reproof that comes from life will end up being a wise person, living among those considered wise. But realities are true. Either way, it is wise to listen to life's circumstances, and to listen to the reproof that often comes through other people.

Going a little further, if one wants to be wise, then he must walk with wise men. Proverbs says, "He who walks with wise men will be wise" (13:20). The role other people play in our lives is critical to who we are and who we will become. Our associations determine many of our perceptions, attitudes, and behavior.

Today, these associations are not only the people we spend time with daily, but the associations we form in the artificial world of television and literature. What we read and watch have become far more powerful socializers than the real people we deal with. The power of MTV, the popular sitcom or the latest drama, even CNN or the Weather Channel all compete for our time and our brains. (I'm a C-Span junkie myself.) These *via media* associations are critical to attitude and perception formation. The question we need to ask ourselves is, "Do we consider this use of time wise, or is this program a wise program?" I accept that we all need the little diversions from reality now and again, and need some time to unwind with a brainless novel. But still, am I doing this consciously knowing this is brainless, or at some point are the values of the brainless entertainment causing me to be less wise? As one of my professors once said, "The greatest evil of television is not what it imparts but what it inhibits."

The reality is this: We need other people in our life to help us be wise. Wisdom is not a do-it-yourself thing. It is interpersonal, relational, and mutual. I don't think we can really be wise about God and life without having some other people to be mirrors and goads for us. I need the sharp, pointed stick in my rear occasionally in order for me to "get the point." The reproof builds some wisdom in my life. I also need the wise friend who not only sticks it to me but also sticks in there with me closer than my own brother. If I really want to be wise, I need to look around and find some wise men. Find the places they congregate, if they do, identify them one by one, and then start picking their brains. I hope the profiles in this book will help you identify what they look like.

But in the final analysis, wisdom has to do not only with God and others, it has to do with *you*. Yes, Proverbs is very clear on this subject. No one else can want you wise. One of my more self-inflicted punishments is leafing through various Christian magazines and looking at the college and seminary ads. Some of the claims are as outrageously untrue as secular advertising promises. If a certain toothpaste can give sex appeal, then the right Christian school can make you a man or woman of God. Now, I must say I teach at a school that has to put marketing language in its literature, so my own school is not immune. We all promise some things in order to attract students. But my concern here is not *that* we market or project an image, but what we in fact do promise in our advertising. If we are promising to prepare every student for "successful ministry," or to be a "man of God," or even to be a biblical scholar, are we in fact able to pull that off with every student? Of course, the claim can't match the reality. But beneath all these ads runs the same premise: The institution is responsible to make the student into something. I ask, *Where is the responsibility of the student?*

Proverbs doesn't play a game here. Wisdom says the key factor in learning wisdom is *you*—the learner, the student, the disciple—and what you do with what wisdom gives you. Solomon says,

> Now therefore, O sons, listen to me,
> For blessed are they who keep my ways.
> Heed instruction and be wise,
> And do not neglect it.
> Blessed is the man who listens to me,
> Watching daily at my gates,
> Waiting at my doorposts.
> For he who finds me finds life,
> And obtains favor from the LORD.
> But he who sins against me injures himself;
> All those who hate me love death. (8:32-36)

It is obvious who bears the ultimate responsibility for being wise here. The learner. The final choice we all have to make is to answer the question, How badly do we want to be wise? Are we willing to station ourselves daily at wisdom's doorpost?

I know I'm not. I, like the naive and the sluggard, don't get the point until I feel some pain. To be wise it is up to me to do something about it. I am going on thirty years of being a follower of Christ. I think when I first got started on this journey, I had received either too heavy a dose of the sovereignty of God, or I had a rather magical view of life. At any rate, wherever I got it, the life application was the same. I just expected God to drop everything out of the sky miraculously. I even thought at times that it was wrong to really go after something. It might just be my own desire. In this naive confusion, I would sort of spiritualize the confusion and insecurity and say, "I won't do anything until God makes it very clear to me." I finally saw this for what it was—irresponsibility! I didn't want to take responsibility for my life. Proverbs was the book that jarred my thinking and revealed my irresponsibility. Wisdom called me as her son,

> My son, if you will receive my sayings,
> And treasure my commandments within you,
> Make your ear attentive to wisdom,
> Incline your heart to understanding;
> For if you cry for discernment,
> Lift your voice for understanding;
> If you seek her as silver,
> And search for her as for hidden treasures;
> Then you will discern the fear of the LORD,
> And discover the knowledge of God. (2:1-5)

In this extended metaphor, wisdom stands before the foolish sons and daughters of the world saying, "Won't you come and listen to me? It's your responsibility." She says in effect, "My job is to educate you. Your job is to want the education so much you will make it your life's ambition." But this is not an easy task. Wisdom is likened to gold and silver. What gold and silver represents in the world of men, so wisdom represents to the world God has made.

As I look out at my front yard, I see trees, leaves, the house across the street, a little stream that runs beside our property, but no gold or silver. In fact, I have never seen gold or silver merely lying on the ground for anyone to take. Apparently, God put the precious metals of the earth in deeply hidden places where only the diligent, hardworking, and creative can get at them.

So it must be with wisdom. We are told to seek after wisdom as for silver and gold. I have never done such, but I am told by both panners and miners that finding gold or silver is not easy. When our family went to Australia for the summer, while in Broken Hill, New South Wales, we had the opportunity to go down into the deepest zinc mine in the world. Upon entering an elevator shaft with other miners, we descended for about twenty minutes. It took that long. Finally, as we emerged from the elevator one-mile deep in the earth, we saw the miners blasting and chipping away in the bowels of the earth in order to find, not gold and silver, but zinc ore.

Our search for wisdom both ends and begins here. If we want to live our lives rightly before God and men, we must dig deeply into God and His Word. The precious knowledge about life does not lie on the surface. What is on the surface are the cheap things, the things that will burn—wood, hay, stubble. Our world today generates such things faster than we can buy them. Superficiality, artificiality, and rank dishonesty are being sold on the surface as precious truth and knowledge. To those who want quick knowledge, or even a quick spirituality, there is plenty on the market. Those who seriously want wisdom and life skills that will withstand the fickle fashions and trendy truths of the world must be willing to dig deep and descend into the vast caverns of the knowledge of God. To want this kind of wisdom is the beginning of the search, but the search only makes us hunger for more! Dig deep, and in all your acquiring, get wisdom!

· NOTES ·

CHAPTER ONE: THE SEARCH FOR WISDOM
1. The author's paraphrase of Proverbs 3:13. The word usually translated "blessed" is *'ashere*, which has the idea of right direction. Therefore, the favor that comes to this person (*'adam*) is based upon being rightly directed in life.
2. The INTJ stands for: I = introversion, N = intuition, T = thinking, J = judging. What this means, according to the scale, is that I am an "intuitive introvert." Intuitive introverts "usually have original minds and great drive for their own ideas and purposes. In fields that appeal to them, they have fine power to organize a job and carry it through with or without help. Skeptical, critical, independent, determined, sometimes stubborn. Must learn to yield less important points to win the most important." Taken from materials available from Consulting Psychologists Press, Inc., Palo Alto, CA. Copyright Isabel Briggs Myers, 1976, and Consulting Psychologists Press, 1988.
3. I watched a television news-magazine program recently (I don't remember which) where one community was so convinced that they needed to do moral education in their public-school system that they got all the teachers, parents, and administrators together and agreed upon a core set of values that should be taught. There was plenty of disagreement on many values, but they were able to come to a certain consensus on values like cooperation, honesty, industry, and responsibility. When asked how such a diverse group of people could come together on some important issues, the common refrain was that they "had to do something because the situation was so bad."
4. For an excellent overview of American twentieth-century education, see Gerald L. Gutek, *A History of the Western Educational Experience* (New York: Random House, 1972), chapter 23, pages 382-408.

CHAPTER TWO: THE WISDOM OF THE PROVERBS
1. Thomas Fuller, *Gnomologia,* quoted by G. L. Apperson, *Dictionary of Proverbs* (Herfordshire, England: Wordsworth Editions Ltd., 1993), page 695.
2. Term used by Kathleen A. Farmer, in *Proverbs and Ecclesiastes: Who Knows What Is Good?* International Theological Commentary series (Grand Rapids, MI: Eerdmans, 1991), page 3.
3. Farmer notes, "The casual reader might assume that Solomon is speaking here to one of his children. However, in the Hebrew Bible the terms 'father' and

'son' are often used metaphorically to refer to a teacher-student relationship (e.g. 2 Kings 2:3-5, 12)." Farmer, page 26.

4. Hans Walter Wolfe, *Anthropology of the Old Testament* (Philadelphia: Fortress, 1974), pages 206-207.

5. For all the bad press about being a "Machiavellian," Machiavelli was concerned that the Italian princes knew very little about wise administration of people. Therefore, as his most valued of treasures he offers his "knowledge of the deeds of great men," which he had acquired "through a long experience of modern events and a constant study of the past." Some of the topics covered are how to handle conspiracy, how to reward merit, how to be good to the right people and not good to the right people, how to handle first impressions, flattery, and fortunes. In my opinion, all these subjects would be crucial for anyone in power or authority today! Niccolo Machiavelli, *The Prince* (New York: Oxford, 1952), page 31.

6. Kenneth T. Aiken, *Proverbs*, Daily Study Bible series (Philadelphia: Westminster, 1986), page 4.

7. See Allen Ross's excellent and concise treatment of the authorship problems in Proverbs in *The Expositor's Bible Commentary* (Grand Rapids, MI: Zondervan, 1991), vol. 5, pages 886-888. Most recent evangelical scholars recognize that Solomon was the author of some of the sections, while other sections were common collections written by other authors (Hezekiah, Amenemope, Lemuel, and Agur).

8. Ross, pages 904-907.

9. R. Laird Harris, Gleason L. Archer, Jr., and Bruce K. Waltke, eds., *Theological Wordbook of the Old Testament* (Chicago: Moody, 1980), vol. 1, page 283.

10. Aiken, page 10.

11. William Dyrness, *Themes in Old Testament Theology* (Downers Grove, IL: InterVarsity, 1979), page 197.

12. C. Stephen Evans, *Wisdom and Humanness in Psychology* (Grand Rapids, MI: Baker, 1989), pages 68-70.

13. Dyrness, page 189.

14. Aiken, page 10.

15. Dyrness, page 192.

16. See this story written up and quoting David Maybury-Lewis in David Roth, *Sacred Honor* (Grand Rapids, MI: HarperCollins/Zondervan, 1993), page 35.

17. Peter's "cowardice" on the night of betrayal and arrest is sometimes used to argue for Peter's personality change after the Holy Spirit had come upon him (Luke 22:57, Acts 2:14). I see this more as empowerment of his already existent outgoing, bold temperament. His "cowardice," I think, was very logical based upon his continuing lack of understanding about the Crucifixion (Matthew 16:13-23). After Jesus appeared to Peter in Galilee and restored him, apparently that was the cure for his "cowardice" (John 21:12-17).

18. Bonnidell Clouse, *Moral Development: Perspectives in Psychology and Christian Belief* (Grand Rapids, MI: Baker, 1985), page 101. Theologians like Norman Geisler in *Ethics: Alternatives and Issues* (Grand Rapids, MI: Zondervan, 1971) argue that Christ had to come and through His Holy Spirit produce in humans the moral change that the law was unable to do (see Romans 8:1-7). And Old Testament scholars like Walter Kaiser in *Toward Old Testament Ethics* (Grand Rapids, MI: Zondervan, 1983) argue that even under the Old Covenant, moral decisions were internal (see pages 7-9).

19. William Gesenius, Edward Robinson, and Francis Brown, *A Hebrew and English Lexicon of the Old Testament* (London: Oxford Press, 1907), page 912.

20. I am indebted to Dr. Bruce Waltke, now professor of Old Testament at Regent

College, Vancouver, for his insights on the covenantal name, Yahweh. This material was given to the writer while a student at Dallas Theological Seminary in a course on the Psalms in 1975. Material is taken from course notes from lectures.

21. Noah Webster, *The History of the United States* (New Haven, CT: Durrie and Peck, 1832), page 336-337.

CHAPTER THREE: THE NAIVE

1. A. Cohen, ed., *Proverbs*, Soncino Books of the Bible (London: Soncino Press, 1946), page 2.
2. Francis Brown, S.R. Driver, and Charles A. Briggs, *Lexicon* (London: Oxford University Press, 1972), page 834.
3. Kenneth T. Aiken, *Proverbs*, Daily Study Bible series (Philadelphia: Westminster, 1986), page 94.
4. F. Delitzsch, *Commentary on the Old Testament* (Grand Rapids, MI: Eerdmans, 1872), vol. 6, page 161.
5. M. Scott Peck, *People of the Lie: The Hope for Healing Human Evil* (New York: Simon & Schuster, 1983), page 47.
6. The word *waywardness, meshubah*, has the idea of apostasy toward God. See Jeremiah 8:5.
7. William McKane, *Proverbs*, Old Testament Library (Philadelphia: Westminster, 1970), page 276.
8. The word *crown, yacetir*, has the idea of having the head surrounded with a wreath or crown. See William Holladay, *A Concise Hebrew and Aramaic Lexicon of the Old Testament* (Grand Rapids, MI: Eerdmans, 1971), page 167.
9. Literal translation shows it is the law of Yahweh that "turns" the soul around (*meshiyamah*), the soul being the complete, animated personality of the person made in God's image.

CHAPTER FOUR: THE SLUGGARD

1. Translation by A. Cohen, ed., *Proverbs*, Soncino Books of the Bible (London: Soncino Press, 1946), page 127.
2. Francis Brown, S.R. Driver, and Charles A. Briggs, *Lexicon* (London: Oxford University Press, 1972), page 782.
3. Derek Kidner, *Proverbs*, Tyndale Old Testament Commentaries, D.J. Wiseman, ed. (London: Tyndale, 1972 reprint), page 42.
4. I realize fully that some individuals suffer from energy deficiencies that are purely physical or biochemical in nature. I don't believe this is the individual that Proverbs envisions as the sluggard. The biblical sluggard reflects more of an interplay between behavioral choices and personal temperament.
5. Brown, Driver, and Briggs, page 16.
6. Cathy Grossman, "Whine of the Times," *USA Today*, 26 April 1994, page 1.
7. To balance this statement, I must make it clear that we are also seeing an increasing number of young adults in the X Generation who are willing to work and want to find meaningful work but, because of cutbacks and economic downturns, cannot find the kind of work for which they were educated. Therefore, just because a college student is working as a waiter does not mean that this person could be identified as a sluggard.
8. Someone asked me recently whether I thought Philadelphia was a safe city. I answered, "Oh, sure, as long as you stay away from North Philly, South Philly, and West Philly." The person replied, "Oh, then East Philly is okay?" I said, "Yes, that's the Delaware River!"
9. The Hebrew "hedge of thorns," *kimsukat hadeq*, implies the road of the sluggard being blocked with thorns, or fenced about with thorns. Allen P. Ross, *The*

Expositor's Bible Commentary (Grand Rapids, MI: Zondervan, 1991), vol. 5, page 997.

10. The word for highway, *salal*, has the idea of "throwing up earth over obstacles." Brown, Driver, and Briggs, pages 699, 700.

11. F. Delitzsch, *Commentary on the Old Testament* (Grand Rapids, MI: Eerdmans, 1872), vol. 6, page 226.

CHAPTER FIVE: THE WICKED

1. Sam is the diabolic Satan character in the play who "masquerades" as a just saint and emissary of God during a Purim play within a play in a Shamgorod inn, circa 1649. Elie Wiesel, *The Trial of God* (New York: Schocken Books, 1979), page 158.

2. Wiesel, pages 157-161.

3. R. Laird Harris, Gleason L. Archer, Jr., and Bruce K. Waltke, eds., *Theological Wordbook of the Old Testament*, vol. 2, pages 854-855.

4. Harris, Archer, and Waltke, page 863, on *rasha'*.

5. Marguerite Shuster, *Power, Pathology, Paradox: The Dynamics of Evil and Good* (Grand Rapids, MI: Zondervan, 1987), page 133.

6. C. H. Toy, *Proverbs*, International Critical Commentary series (reprint, Edinburgh: T & T Clark, 1970), page 411.

7. William McKane, *Proverbs*, Old Testament Library (Philadelphia: Westminster, 1970), page 422.

8. Anthony Storr, *Human Destructiveness* (New York: Ballantine, 1991), pages 92-93.

9. M. Scott Peck, *People of the Lie: The Hope for Healing Human Evil* (New York: Simon and Schuster, 1983), page 136.

10. Translation by Allen P. Ross, *The Expositor's Bible Commentary* (Grand Rapids, MI: Zondervan, 1991), vol. 5, page 973.

11. Peck, page 67.

12. A. Cohen, ed., *Proverbs*, Soncino Books of the Bible (London: Soncino Press, 1946), page 29.

13. Translation by Ross, page 960.

14. "Data Shows Condoms Only Sixty-Nine Percent Effective Against HIV," *UTMB News*, News and Information Office, University of Texas Medical Branch at Galveston, 10 June 1993, page 1; Susan Weller, "A Meta-Analysis of Condom Effectiveness in Reducing Sexually Transmitted HIV," *Social Science Medical Journal* (Great Britain: Pergamun Press Ltd., 1993), vol. 36, no. 12, pages 1636-1644.

15. M. L. Weems, *The Life of George Washington* (Philadelphia: Joseph Allen Press, 1800), page 6.

16. I am thankful to David Barton for highlighting this episode in American history in his work *Keys to Good Government* (Aledo, TX: Wallbuilder Press, 1994), page 9.

17. The word *transgression* is *pesha'*, a word denoting the rebellion against rulers and the social order that God has ordained. See Harris, Archer, and Waltke, page 741.

18. Toy, page 510.

19. The Hebrew text here might be translated, "In the multiplying or crowding of the righteous, the people throw a party or celebrate." Free translation of the Hebrew by the author.

20. There is also a subtle Hebrew play on words here. The Hebrew word for rejoice is *yesammach*, while the Hebrew word for groan is *ye'anach*, a simple Hebrew rhyme that makes the two words parallel in thought. The idea might be, which do you want to do, *ye'anach* or *yesammach?*

21. Noah Webster, *The History of the United States* (New Haven, CT: Durrie and Peck, 1832), pages 336-337.

22. I use the 1920s as the artificial beginning point after the infamous "Scopes Monkey Trial," which drove the church underground with reference to science and

the larger cultural world. The date 1976 is the election of Jimmy Carter, the first outwardly "born-again" Christian president who demonstrated that a Christian could both get elected and be a Christian while in the "ungodly" environment of American politics.

CHAPTER SIX: THE WEALTHY

1. Kenneth T. Aiken, *Proverbs* (Philadelphia: Westminster, 1986), page 180.
2. Francis Brown, S.R. Driver, and Charles A. Briggs, *Lexicon* (London: Oxford University Press, 1972), page 799.
3. See R. Laird Harris, Gleason L. Archer, Jr., and Bruce K. Waltke, eds., *Theological Wordbook of the Old Testament* (Chicago: Moody, 1980), vol. 1, page 213.
4. A. Cohen, ed., *Proverbs*, Soncino Books of the Bible (London: Soncino Press, 1946), page 57.
5. Translation given by Allen P. Ross, *The Expositor's Bible Commentary* (Grand Rapids, MI: Zondervan, 1991), vol. 5, page 1064.
6. Cohen, page 149.
7. Brown, Driver, and Briggs, page 793.
8. Grant Wardlaw, *Political Terrorism* (Cambridge, England: Cambridge University Press, 1982), pages 29, 31.
9. Ross, page 1060.

CHAPTER SEVEN: THE WEALTHY AND THE POOR

1. John Clark, *Paraemiologia,* Anglo-Latina, quoted by Apperson, *Dictionary of Proverbs,* page 671.
2. Ross, page 1026.
3. Quoted in Cohen, page 90.
4. Ross, page 977.
5. The Hebrew verb *natzal*, in the niphal stem, means "to take away, or be snatched away." Francis Brown, S.R. Driver, and Charles A. Briggs, *Lexicon* (London: Oxford University Press, 1972), page 664.
6. See the verb *chaqar*, "examine," which means to examine something carefully and expose its weaknesses. Brown, Driver, and Briggs, page 350.
7. Verbal form, *tamam*. Brown, Driver, and Briggs, page 1070.
8. R. Laird Harris, Gleason L. Archer, Jr., and Bruce K. Waltke, eds., *Theological Wordbook of the Old Testament*, vol. 2, page 974.
9. Ross, page 991.
10. See P. J. O'Rourke's excellent and humorous treatment of the United States government, *Parliament of Whores* (New York: Atlantic Monthly Press, 1991). Especially his chapter "Poverty Policy: How to Endow Privation," pages 123-141.
11. Aiken, page 192.
12. Aiken, page 193.

CHAPTER EIGHT: THE CHILD

1. Kenneth T. Aiken, *Proverbs* (Philadelphia: Westminster, 1986), page 54.
2. R. Laird Harris, Gleason L. Archer, Jr., and Bruce K. Waltke, eds., *Theological Wordbook of the Old Testament*, vol. 2, page 586.
3. Francis Brown, S.R. Driver, and Charles A. Briggs, *Lexicon* (London: Oxford University Press, 1972), pages 120-121.
4. Wendy Kaminer, *I'm Dysfunctional, You're Dysfunctional* (Reading, MA: Addison-Wesley, 1992), page 18.
5. Aiken, page 146.
6. Kaminer, page 18.
7. Horace Bushnell, *Christian Nurture* (reprint, Grand Rapids, MI: Baker, 1961),

page 23.

8. Judy Dunn and Robert Plomin, *Separate Lives: Why Siblings Are So Different* (New York: Harper and Row, 1990), page 151.

9. Dunn and Plomin, page 153.

10. Quoted in Dunn and Plomin, page 172.

11. Aiken, pages 146-147.

12. R. Laird Harris, Gleason L. Archer, Jr., and Bruce K. Waltke, eds., *Theological Wordbook of the Old Testament* (Chicago: Moody, 1980), vol. 1, page 387.

13. See Derek Kidner, *Proverbs*, page 147.

14. William McKane, *Proverbs*, Old Testament Library (Philadelphia: Westminster, 1970), page 364.

15. Brown, Driver, and Briggs, page 335.

16. A. Cohen, ed., *Proverbs*, Soncino Books of the Bible (London: Soncino Press, 1946), page 154.

17. Allen P. Ross, *The Expositor's Bible Commentary* (Grand Rapids, MI: Zondervan, 1991), vol. 5, page 982.

18. Brown, Driver, and Briggs, page 1007.

19. Brown, Driver, and Briggs, page 30.

20. Harris, Archer, and Waltke, vol. 2, page 562.

21. Brown, Driver, and Briggs, page 726.

22. Brown, Driver, and Briggs, page 904.

23. Taken from the autobiography of Mark Twain, quoted in Dunn and Plomin, page 1.

CHAPTER NINE: THE PARENT

1. Harold B. Smith, "Superkids and Superparents," *Christianity Today*, September 18, 1987, page 14.

2. *Family Therapy Letter*, vol. 2, no. 3, March 1990, published by Brown University.

3. Rodney Clapp, *Families at the Crossroads* (Downers Grove, IL: InterVarsity, 1993), pages 142-143.

4. See the following works for thought-provoking and serious critiques of the modern counseling and self-help movements: Stan J. Katz and Aimee E. Liu, *The Codependency Conspiracy* (New York: Warner Books, 1991); Stanton Peele, *Diseasing of America: Addiction Treatment out of Control* (Boston: Houghton Mifflin, 1989); Thomas Szasz, *The Myth of Psychotherapy* (Syracuse, NY: Syracuse University Press, 1978); Gerald G. May, *Addiction and Grace* (San Francisco: Harper, 1991); and Bernie Zilbergeld, *The Shrinking of America: Myths of Psychological Change* (Boston: Little, Brown, and Co., 1983).

5. Zilbergeld, page 277.

6. Stanton Peele's term for kids who quit heroin and other drugs when they finally get serious about their lives. Peele, pages 175-176.

7. Zilbergeld notes, "People change all the time, but most change is not planned. Different ages, environments, and situations cause alterations of mood, thought and behavior." Zilbergeld, page 220.

8. Clapp, page 142.

9. A. Cohen, ed., *Proverbs*, Soncino Books of the Bible (London: Soncino Press, 1946), page 3.

10. Brown, Driver, and Briggs, page 889.

11. Ann Blackman, Priscilla Painton, and James Willwerth, "Bringing Up Father," *TIME*, June 28, 1993, page 54.

12. Blackman, Painton, and Willwerth, page 55.

13. Henry B. Miller, "The Father and Sex Role Development," in *The Role of the Father in Child Development*, ed. Michael E. Lamb (New York: John Wiley and Sons, 1981), page 348.

14. Miller, pages 349-350.
15. Cohen, page 10.
16. Henry Cloud and John Townsend, *Boundaries* (Grand Rapids, MI: Zondervan, 1992), page 29.
17. Cohen, page 3.
18. Miller, pages 332-333.
19. Miller, page 331.
20. Miller, page 342.
21. See John Martin Rich and Joseph L. DeVitis, *Theories of Moral Development* (Springfield, IL: Charles C. Thomas, 1985), page 88, for overview of Kohlberg's theory.
22. John Bradshaw, *Healing the Shame That Binds You* (Deerfield Beach, FL: Health Communications, 1988), page vii.
23. Francis Brown, S.R. Driver, and Charles A. Briggs, *Lexicon* (London: Oxford University Press, 1972), page 387, Hebrew word *yagon*.
24. Brown, Driver, and Briggs, pages 494-495.
25. Cohen, page 126.
26. The Hebrew verb *zalal*, "to be light, or worthless or to make light of something." It is the opposite of what it means to honor parents, which is granting them significance and worth. Brown, Driver, and Briggs, page 272.
27. Peele, page 181.
28. Quoted in Margie M. Lewis with Gregg Lewis, *The Hurting Parent* (Grand Rapids, MI: Zondervan, 1988), page 152.
29. Lewis, page 154.
30. John Charles Ryle, *The Upper Room* (1888; reprint, Edinburgh: Banner of Truth, 1977), pages 257-258.

CHAPTER TEN: THE WIFE
1. George Barna, *The Future of the American Family* (Chicago, IL: Moody, 1993), page 68.
2. Stephen Grunlan, *Marriage and the Family* (Grand Rapids, MI: Zondervan, 1984), page 81.
3. Grunlan, page 82.
4. Barna, page 72.
5. Rodney Clapp, *Families at the Crossroads* (Downers Grove, IL: InterVarsity, 1993), page 131.
6. Barna, page 70.
7. George Gilder, *Men and Marriage* (Gretna, LA: Pelican, 1986), page 58.
8. Francis Brown, S.R. Driver, and Charles A. Briggs, *Lexicon* (London: Oxford University Press, 1972), page 248.
9. Anne Moir and David Jessel, *Brain Sex* (New York: Bantam, Doubleday, Dell, 1989), page 147.
10. Lance Morrow, "Are Men Really That Bad?" *TIME*, 14 February 1994, pages 53-59.
11. Gloria Steinem, *The Revolution from Within* (Boston, MA: Little, Brown, and Co., 1991); Naomi Wolf, *Fire with Fire* (New York: Random House, 1993); Wendy Kaminer, *I'm Dysfunctional, You're Dysfunctional* (Reading, MA: Addison-Wesley, 1992); Camille Paglia, *Sex, Art and American Culture* (New York: Random House, 1992) and *Sexual Personae* (New York: Random House, 1991).
12. Robert and Cynthia Hicks, *The Feminine Journey* (Colorado Springs, CO: NavPress, 1994), page 115.
13. C. H. Toy, *Proverbs*, International Critical Commentary series (reprint, Edinburgh: T & T Clark, 1970), page 280.
14. Brown, Driver, and Briggs, page 192.

15. Quoted by A. Cohen, ed., *Proverbs*, Soncino Books of the Bible (London: Soncino Press, 1946), page 126.
16. Brown, Driver, and Briggs, page 860.
17. Rabbi Metsudath David as quoted by Cohen, page 182.
18. See Toy, page 488, and Cohen, page 182.
19. See Carol Gilligan's work on male-female differences in perception of the world and relationships, *In a Different Voice: Psychological Theory and Woman's Development* (Cambridge, MA: Harvard University Press, 1982); and Deborah Tannen's work on linguistic differences, *You Just Don't Understand: Men and Women in Conversation* (New York: Ballantine Books, 1990).
20. Anthony Storr, *Human Destructiveness* (New York: Ballantine, 1991), pages 92-93.
21. Warren Farrell, *Why Men Are the Way They Are* (New York: Berkeley Books, 1986), page 161.
22. Brown, Driver, and Briggs, page 49.
23. See William McKane, *Proverbs*, Old Testament Library (Philadelphia: Westminster, 1970), page 366.
24. Harry Schaumburg, *False Intimacy* (Colorado Springs, CO: NavPress, 1992), for more information on the nature of sexual addictions.
25. Allen P. Ross, *The Expositor's Bible Commentary* (Grand Rapids, MI: Zondervan, 1991), vol. 5, page 951.
26. Dr. Bernie Zildergeld, *Shrinking of America* (Boston, MA: Little, Brown & Co., 1983), page 251.
27. Ross, page 1129.
28. For full development of this metaphor, see *The Feminine Journey*, pages 163-180.
29. Ross, page 1029.
30. Brown, Driver, and Briggs, page 747.
31. Ross, page 968.
32. Brown, Driver, and Briggs, page 381.
33. The Hebrew *magor* is used of a spring of water or any flow from the body. Leviticus 20:18. Brown, Driver, and Briggs, page 880.
34. Azaria Alon, *The Natural History of the Land of the Bible* (Jerusalem, Israel: Paul Jerusalem Publishing House, 1969), page 238.

CHAPTER ELEVEN: THE FOOL

1. Quoted in David Barton, *Keys to Good Government* (Aledo, TX: Wallbuilder Press, 1994), page 4.
2. P. J. O'Rourke's best-selling humorous but unfortunately true look at the United States government. *Parliament of Whores* (New York: Atlantic Monthly Press, 1991).
3. Statement from the preamble to the United States Constitution.
4. Francis Brown, S.R. Driver, and Charles A. Briggs, *Lexicon* (London: Oxford University Press, 1972), page 17.
5. R. Laird Harris, Gleason L. Archer, Jr., and Bruce K. Waltke, ed., *Theological Wordbook of the Old Testament* (Chicago: Moody, 1980), vol. 1, page 19.
6. Harris, Archer, and Waltke, page 449.
7. Kathleen A. Farmer, *Proverbs and Ecclesiastes: Who Knows What Is Good?* International Theological Commentary series (Grand Rapids, MI: Eerdmans, 1991), page 78.
8. Quoted in Shannon Brownlee and Steven V. Roberts, "Should Cigarettes Be Outlawed," *U.S. News & World Report*, April 18, 1994.
9. Stanton Peele, *Diseasing of America: Addiction Treatment out of Control* (Boston: Houghton Mifflin, 1989), pages 174-175.

10. F. Delitzsch, *Commentary on the Old Testament* (Grand Rapids, MI: Eerdmans, 1872), vol. 6, page 259.

11. Richard Cole (Associated Press), "Father Awarded $500,000 in Suit Against Two Therapists," *Philadelphia Inquirer*, May 15, 1994.

12. A. Cohen, ed., *Proverbs*, Soncino Books of the Bible (London: Soncino Press, 1946), page 116.

13. Translation by Cohen, page 86.

14. Brown, Driver, and Briggs, page 144.

15. Kenneth T. Aiken, *Proverbs* (Philadelphia: Westminster, 1986), page 102.

16. A thought strikes me when I hear this word *validate* used in psychotherapy. I understand in psychotherapy it means to grant genuine validity to a person's feelings and that originally the word *validus* (Latin) meant "to have power, or to be strong," taking on the meaning of having legal force. Today, in the counseling office, to validate means to agree emotionally with someone that his feelings are justified. In other words, a person does not feel the power to say his own feelings are valid, they must be validated, like our parking tickets, by someone else before the person sees the power as being given to him.

17. A literal translation of 29:11 might be, "All his spirit goes out of the fool, but the wise man soothes (his spirit) in the afterwards." It may imply the wise is angered the same as the fool, but the wise doesn't let the anger out, but deals with it afterwards. He has the ability to quell his own spirit without letting all his mind, or anger, be known to men. Today some psychotherapists would not call this wisdom but denial!

18. Brown, Driver, and Briggs, page 166.

19. Stanton L. Jones and Richard E. Butman, critique of Carl Rogers's "Person-Centered Therapy," in *Modern Psychotherapies* (Downers Grove, IL: Inter-Varsity, 1991), page 267.

20. Cohen, page 60.

21. Brown, Driver, and Briggs, page 860.

22. *Adjustment reaction* is a broad, common, clinical term found in the DSM IIIR (*Diagnostic Statistical Manual*, third edition, revised). As a Christian counselor I use this category probably most often to describe those having difficulty adjusting to some new issue in their life (usually bad).

23. Brown, Driver, and Briggs, page 610.

24. Brown, Driver, and Briggs, page 772.

CHAPTER TWELVE: THE FOOL'S REWARD

1. A. B. Cheales, *Proverbs & Folklore*, quoted by Apperson, *Dictionary of Proverbs*, page 223.

2. The word for controversy here is the word for judgment, *shaphat*, which in the niphal stem carries the idea of "going to court, or seek a claim." See William Holladay, *A Concise Hebrew and Aramaic Lexicon of the Old Testament* (Grand Rapids: Eerdmans, 1971), page 380.

3. Allen Ross, "Proverbs," in *The Expositor's Bible Commentary* (Grand Rapids, MI: Zondervan, 1991), vol. 5, page 1113.

4. Translation given by Ross, vol. 5, page 985.

5. Francis Brown, S.R. Driver, and Charles A. Briggs, *Lexicon* (London: Oxford University Press, 1972), page 79.

6. Ross, page 985.

7. See the article on the word "zmm" by S. Steingrimsson, in *Theological Dictionary of the Old Testament*, Johannes Botterweck, et al., ed. (Grand Rapids, MI: Eerdmans, 1980), vol. 4, pages 87-90.

8. C. H. Toy, *Proverbs*, International Critical Commentary series (reprint, Edin-

burgh: T & T Clark, 1970), page 213.
  9. Quoted in Kathleen M. Gow, *Yes, Virginia, There Is a Right and Wrong* (Wheaton, IL: Tyndale, 1985), page 28.
 10. Ross, page 1088.
 11. Cohen, page 174.
 12. Allan Bloom, *The Closing of the American Mind* (New York: Simon & Schuster, 1987).
 13. Ross, page 1089.
 14. Ross, page 1089.
 15. Toy, page 477.
 16. Aiken, page 105.
 17. Quoted in Cohen, page 85.
 18. Harris, Archer, and Waltke, pages 376-377, on the word *yakah*.
 19. William McKane, *Proverbs*, Old Testament Library (Philadelphia: Westminster, 1970), page 274.

CHAPTER THIRTEEN: THE WISE

  1. Hans Walter Wolff, *Anthropology of the Old Testament* (Philadelphia: Fortress, 1974), page 206.
  2. Quoted in Philip Yancey, ed., *The Classics We've Read, The Difference They've Made* (New York: McCracken Press, 1993), page 127, in response to the question, "What do you do?"
  3. Kenneth T. Aiken, *Proverbs* (Philadelphia: Westminster, 1986), page 10.
  4. Story told and then changed by the author, in Yancey, page 127.
  5. Allen P. Ross, *The Expositor's Bible Commentary* (Grand Rapids, MI: Zondervan, 1991), vol. 5, page 1027.
  6. I actually quoted the writer as a negative illustration, but this was too close for those who view themselves as the ultimate determiners of what constitutes truth. Since my complainant quoted me in print, I guess he is just as guilty of the same error. Since I quoted a New Age author, I am New Age; since he quoted me, that makes him New Age as well. Great logic!
  7. One passage does show an active intentionality on the part of the wise: "He who is wise wins souls" (11:30). However, the commentators as well as the Greek Septuagint are very confusing on this verse. If the verse is to parallel "The fruit of the righteous is a tree of life," then the image is that of life-giving properties that are inherent in the person. The verb *laqach*, "take," is far more active and reflects the wise actively taking "souls." What is really meant here is hard to determine.
  8. See the following material for further documentation and discussion on the subject of mentoring: Paul D. Stanley and J. Robert Clinton, *Connecting* (Colorado Springs, CO: NavPress, 1992), page 38; Samuel Osherson, *Finding Our Fathers: The Unfinished Business of Manhood* (New York: Free Press, 1986); Joan Jeruchin, *Women and Mentors* (Radnor, PA: Uncommon Individual Foundation).
  9. Francis Brown, S.R. Driver, and Charles A. Briggs, *Lexicon* (London: Oxford University Press, 1972), page 279.
 10. For President Carter's personal view of what happened at Camp David read his own works, *The Blood of Abraham: Insights into the Middle East* (Boston: Houghton Mifflin, 1985) and *Negotiation: An Alternative to Hostility* (Mercer University Press, 1984). In the first work, President Carter openly talks about how he and President Sadat discussed their respective faiths. Rumors circulated prior to Sadat's death that he was a "closet" Christian! See pages 8-9 for President Carter's personal conversations.
 11. Ross, page 1056.

CHAPTER FOURTEEN: THE BENEFITS OF WISDOM

1. R. Laird Harris, Gleason L. Archer, Jr., and Bruce K. Waltke, eds., *Theological Wordbook of the Old Testament* (Chicago: Moody, 1980), vol. 1, page 427.
2. Derek Kidner, *Proverbs*, page 83.
3. F. Delitzsch, *Commentary on the Old Testament* (Grand Rapids, MI: Eerdmans, 1872), vol. 6, page 204.
4. Francis Brown, S.R. Driver, and Charles A. Briggs, *Lexicon* (London: Oxford University Press, 1972), page 799.
5. There is some confusion as to who this person was. I prefer the argument by Aiken, which places him as a non-Israelite sage who hailed from the same region in North Arabia as King Lemuel (31:1). This puts the person very much in the Semitic-Arabian context of proverbs of this sort. See Kenneth T. Aiken, *Proverbs* (Philadelphia: Westminster, 1986), pages 253, 218-219.
6. Quoted in A. Cohen, ed., *Proverbs*, Soncino Books of the Bible (London: Soncino Press, 1946), page 32.
7. Article on "Coney" by G. S. Cansdale, in *The Zondervan Pictorial Encyclopedia of the Bible*, ed. Merril Tenny (Grand Rapids, MI: Zondervan, 1975), vol. 1, page 937.
8. Azaria Alon, *The Natural History of the Land of the Bible* (Jerusalem, Israel: Paul Jerusalem Publishing House, 1969), page 247.
9. This home, like many of the other Rothchild homes around the world, is staffed by servants who keep it ready for any Rothchild family member or guest who might drop in. We were never invited in! Even the Army Corps of Engineers tried building a retainer wall on this side of the island to stop the erosion. It slowed it down for a couple of years, and then finally the surf won!
10. Brown, Driver, Briggs, page 346.
11. Cohen, page 207.
12. Article entitled "Lizard" by G. S. Cansdale, in *The Zondervan Pictorial Encyclopedia of the Bible*, Merril C. Tenny, ed. (Grand Rapids, MI: Zondervan, 1975), vol. 3, page 947.
13. Alon, page 199.

CHAPTER FIFTEEN: HOW TO BECOME A WISE PERSON

1. See Stanton Peele, *Diseasing of America: Addiction Treatment out of Control* (Boston: Houghton Mifflin, 1989); Stan J. Katz and Aimee E. Liu, *The Codependency Conspiracy* (New York: Warner Books, 1991); Bernie Zilbergeld, *The Shrinking of America: Myths of Psychological Change* (Boston: Little, Brown, and Co., 1983). All challenge the current beliefs of human transformability under the guise of therapy and self-help.
2. William Dyrness, *Themes in Old Testament Theology* (Downers Grove, IL: InterVarsity, 1979), page 162.
3. Stanton Peele says, "Apparently, as people mature they find they can achieve more meaningful rewards than those offered by drugs and overdrinking," page 66; and "My view explicitly refutes the theory that (1) the addiction exists independently of the rest of a person's life and drives all of his or her choices; (2) it is progressive and irreversible, so that the addiction inevitably worsens unless the person seeks treatment; (3) addiction means the person is incapable of controlling his or her behavior," page 3.

· AUTHOR ·

Robert Hicks's masculine journey has taken him down many roads. As an educator, Dr. Hicks is professor of Pastoral Theology at the Seminary of the East in Philadelphia. As a counselor, he was cofounder of Life Counseling Services, located in the Philadelphia area. As a chaplain in the Air National Guard, he serves an A-10 fighter group. As a communicator, he has authored *The Masculine Journey* (NavPress, 1993) and *Uneasy Manhood* (Nelson, 1991), which deal with men's issues, *Returning Home* (Revell, 1991), in response to the Gulf War, and *Failure to Scream* (Nelson, 1993), a well-researched look at post-traumatic stress disorder. He and his wife, Cinny, have coauthored *The Feminine Journey*. He holds degrees in psychology, theology, and family studies and has pursued post-doctoral work in religious studies (Villanova University).

In 1985, Dr. Hicks was honored with the American Legion nomination for "Chaplain of the Year," an award presented by President Reagan for Dr. Hick's work with the families and survivors of the Delta 191 crash at Dallas–Ft. Worth Airport.

Dr. Hicks resides in Berwyn, Pennsylvania, a Philadelphia suburb, with Cinny, two children, and one dog. He also has one married daughter.